W9-CVY-354

★ DALE PATTERSON ★

CLOSE, BUT NO CIGAR

*Runner-ups,
Nearly-Weres
and Also-Rans*

Red Deer Press

Copyright © 2019 Dale Patterson

All rights reserved. No part of this publication may be reproduced, stored in a retrieval system or transmitted, in any form or by any means, without the prior written permission of Red Deer Press except in the case of brief excerpts in critical reviews and articles.

Published in Canada by Red Deer Press
195 Allstate Parkway, Markham, ON   L3R 4T8

Published in the United States by Red Deer Press,
311 Washington Street, Brighton, Massachusetts, 02135

2 4 6 8 10 9 7 5 3 1

Red Deer Press acknowledges with thanks the Canada Council for the Arts and the Ontario Arts Council for their support of our publishing program. We acknowledge the financial support of the Government of Canada through the Canada Book Fund (CBF) for our publishing activities.

Library and Archives Canada Cataloguing in Publication
Title: Close but no cigar : runnerups, nearly-weres and also-rans / Dale Patterson.
Names: Patterson, Dale R., 1952- author.
Identifiers: Canadiana 20190152133 | ISBN 9780889955516 (softcover)
Subjects: LCSH: Biography.
Classification: LCC CT105 .P38 2019 | DDC 920.02—dc23

Publisher Cataloging-in-Publication Data (U.S.)
Names: Patterson, Dale, author.
Title: Close But No Cigar / Dale Patterson.
Description: Markham, Ontario : Fitzhenry & Whiteside, 2019. | Summary: "History, humor, trivia, reference, and short stories on runner-ups/second place finishers in performing arts, music, science, politics, sports, explorers, space, and culture in the United States, Canada and the world" – Provided by publisher.
 Identifiers: ISBN 978-0-88995-551-6 (pbk.)
 Subjects: LCSH: Biography -- Miscellanea. | BISAC: HISTORY / General.
Classification: LCC CT105.P388 |DDC 920.02 – dc23

Cover and interior design by Tanya Montini
Printed in Canada by Houghton Boston

Red Deer Press

To Sherree, a great wife and a wonderful mother.

TO
CLAIRE
ENJOY!!!

CONTENTS

"In glorifying those who are first,
the second is often forgotten."

–New York Times

INTRODUCTION

History is all about the winners, the heroes, the top dogs, isn't it? But what about those who almost made it, the "mighta, coulda, shoulda, wouldas" of history?

That's what *Close, But No Cigar* is all about—a celebration of those who fell just short of the mark, the second-place finishers and nearly-weres of history.

Consider Elisha Gray, who filed a caveat for the telephone on February 14, 1876 just two hours after Alexander Graham Bell filed his patent application. Or Harold Stassen, who ran for president 10 times between 1944 and 1992 but never won the key to the White House. Then there's Lord Halifax who in 1940 was the frontrunner to become Prime Minister of England. One unfortunate day he went to the dentist, missed a key meeting with an influential supporter, and the job went to Winston Churchill.

How about Jug McSpaden, who set a PGA Tour record with 13 runner-up finishes in 1945, the same year his good friend Byron Nelson set a tour record with 18 wins? Then there's the fascinating story of Sham, who in 1973 arguably ran the second-fastest time in Kentucky Derby history, only to finish second to Secretariat, who clocked the fastest time ever.

We'll also turn the beacon to Peter O'Toole, who was nominated for Best Actor an incredible eight times—the most nominated person never to win a competitive acting Oscar. You'll also read about sound recording mixer

Kevin O'Connell, the "unluckiest nominee in the history of the Academy Awards," who received a record 20 nominations with nothing to show until finally winning on his 21st attempt.

And who can forget–I mean, remember–the story of William Dawes, whose daring gallop that spring night in 1775 outshone the exploits of Paul Revere, but whose name has somehow been consigned to the dustbin of history?

How about the folks who came first but have since come second in our collective memories? Bob Horn, the first host of American Bandstand who was later replaced by Dick Clark. Or Masanori Murakami, the first Japanese-born player in the major leagues now forgotten to Hideo Nomo who came three decades later.

And we'd be remiss not to include some of the biggest losers of all-time, big busts like the Cleveland Spiders–"the sorriest shell of a team ever seen"– that posted a 20-134 record in 1899. And the race horse Zippy Chippy, who ran 100 races between 1991 and 2004 without a win, but nevertheless received piles of fan mail and thousands of visitors. Yes, we all love a loser.

So delve in and discover the fascinating flip-side of fame, the *mighta, coulda, shoulda,* and *wouldas* that gave it everything they had to make it *Close, But No Cigar.*

BEHIND THE QUOTE

Some things never change.

As many of us have found out the hard way, it's pretty tough to win a carnival game without knowing the trick to it. The games are rigged to look easy, but are in fact very difficult and you can spend a lot of money trying to win a prize. It's good for the vendor, but not for the player.

Nowadays carnival prizes are selected to attract kids—stuffed animals, toys, inflatable cartoon characters—but it wasn't always that way. In the late 19th and early 20th centuries, prizes were aimed at adults, with cigars a popular reward for the lucky (and few) winners. If you didn't win, then no cigar, and carnival barkers got into the habit of belting out "close, but no cigar!" to encourage fairgoers to play again. An early description of this practice is found in Robert Machray's 1902 book, *The Night Side of London*.

Should you score twenty you will win a cigar. But you do no more than score nine. Undiscouraged, or perhaps encouraged by this fact, you spend another penny, and another, and another—but you don't get the cigar, and it is well for you that you don't! For there are cigars and cigars. On you go, and next you try your hand at the cocoa-nuts, or the skittles, or the clay-pipes, or in the shooting-alleys. And so on and on—until your stock of pennies and patience is exhausted.

As the fairs moved around, so did the phrase, and eventually "close, but no cigar" spread into everyday vernacular.

The expression made it to print by the late 1920s. The first use of it in a newspaper was in the May 18, 1929 edition of *The Long Island Daily Press,* which uses "Close; But No Cigar" (note use of semi-colon instead of a comma) as the headline for an article about one Hugo Straub, who "finished second in no less than two presidential races within one week."

The expression flourished in print afterward, even popping up in the eminent *New York Times* on August 2, 1938.* It had already appeared in film three years earlier, where Barbara Stanwyck exclaims in *Annie Oakley,* "Close, colonel, but no cigar."

This was the early start of an expression which continues to be used to this very day—even if most people didn't know about its origins.

---

* The line for the *Times* reads, "From Montauk comes another interesting story, described by Walt Willis as 'close, but no cigar.'"

CHAPTER 1

ENTER STAGE RIGHT

"Close only counts in horseshoes and hand grenades."
– Frank Robinson

OVERLOOKED BY OSCAR

"The lovely bugger ..."

He was one of the leading film stars of the 20th century, yet it was *Close, But No Cigar* for Peter O'Toole when it came to his profession's highest honor. In fact, the Irish-born actor came home empty handed from the Academy Awards a record *eight times* without winning for Best Actor in a Leading Role.

O'Toole's bridesmaid run began when he was nominated for his portrayal of T.E. Lawrence in the 1962 epic *Lawrence of Arabia*. After starting out in theater taking on Shakespearean roles, Lawrence of Arabia was O'Toole's first major film role. Any other year than this, O'Toole's magnificent work would have surely snagged him an Academy Award but this time, he had the misfortune of going up against Cary Grant's memorable portrayal of Atticus Finch in *To Kill A Mockingbird*.

After that, the Oscar losses mounted for O'Toole. He was a Best Actor nominee for *Becket* (1964), *The Lion in Winter* (1968), *Goodbye Mr. Chips* (1969), *The Ruling Class* (1972), *The Stunt Man* (1980), *My Favorite Year* (1982) and *Venus* (2006). Along the way he broke his good friend Richard Burton's record of seven Best Actor nominations without a win.

O'Toole did finally win an Oscar—albeit an honorary one—in 2003 after initially asking the Academy to defer it until he was 80. "I am still in the game and might win the lovely bugger outright," he exclaimed.

He would accept it anyway and after receiving the statuette from Meryl Streep, he turned to the crowd and said, "Always a bridesmaid, never a bride my foot! I have my very own Oscar now to be with me 'til death do us part."

 TRIVIA: Peter O'Toole got the role in *Lawrence of Arabia* only after Marlon Brando and Albert Finney turned it down.

OSCAR OSTRACIZED

"The whole concept of awards is silly."

In the early '70s, it seemed to be less about who won the Oscar than who rejected it.

George C. Scott, who called the Academy Award ceremony a "two-hour meat parade" (it's about twice as long now!), pointedly refused to attend the ceremony that brought him his first Best Actor Oscar for *Patton* in 1971. He said he turned down the Oscar as he did not want to compete with other actors. "I don't want any part of it," said Scott, so *Patton* producer Frank McCarthy accepted on his behalf. Nine years earlier, Scott turned down the Best Supporting Actor nomination for *The Hustler*, though he won anyway.

In 1973, Marlon Brando created quite a row when he sent Native American activist Sacheen Littlefeather to the podium to read a 15-page letter explaining why he didn't want the Oscar for *The Godfather*. Brando wanted to draw attention to the treatment of Native Americans in the film industry. Citing time limitations, Littlefeather spoke for just over a minute to polite applause, and scattered boos. Despite the relatively mild nature of the speech, the Academy thereafter permanently banned proxies from accepting Oscars.

But Scott and Brando aren't the only ones who spurned Oscar. Hardly. Katharine Hepburn had little use for the award. In 1933, she wasn't on hand to pick up her Best Actress nomination for *Morning Glory* and was also a no-show when she won in 1967 for *Guess Who's Coming to Dinner*; in 1968 for *The Lion in Winter*; and in 1981 for *On Golden Pond*. In fact, Woody Allen has been nominated for 24 Academy Awards (winning four), dating back to his first in 1977 for *Annie Hall,* and he's never shown up.

The very first person to outright refuse Oscar was screenwriter Dudley Nichols in 1936 for *The Informer*. His refusal stemmed from a boycott of the Academy Awards by actor, writer and director guilds who were attempting to form independent unions. When Academy Award president Frank Capra sent the statuette to Nichols, he stood his ground, saying that to keep it "would be to turn my back on nearly a thousand members who ventured everything in the long-drawn-out fight for a genuine writers' organization." Nichols finally accepted his Oscar in 1938 after the National Labor Relations Board OK'd the Screen Writers Guild as the bargaining group for film writers.

 TRIVIA: Harold Russell (Best Supporting Actor, 1946) is the only known Academy Award winning actor to sell his Oscar, doing so in 1992 to offset his wife's medical expenses.

THE WRONG MIX

"I don't get discouraged."

He's Oscar's biggest loser. Sound recording mixer Kevin O'Connell was nominated a record 20 times for an Academy Award before finally winning on his 21st try.

O'Connell's losing streak began in 1983 when *Terms of Endearment* lost to *The Right Stuff* in the sound mixing category. The Long Island native set the record for futility in 2006 when *Memoirs of a Geisha* was beaten out by *King Kong*–his 18th Oscar nomination without a win. But the streak ended in 2017 for his work on *Hacksaw Ridge*.

O'Connell told Bill Whitaker of *CBS News* in 2009 that he had enough Oscar nominations to cover a wall, and unused acceptance speeches to fill a drawer. But as the man called "the unluckiest nominee in the history of the Academy Awards" notes, "Golly, how many people win an Oscar? How many people get nominated for an Oscar in their life? It's insane, just to be part of that is an incredible feeling, so I don't get discouraged."

 TRIVIA: There were no sound citations until the third Academy Awards.

OSCAR TRAILBLAZERS

"It has been a long journey."

Nearly a quarter century separates the first African-American Academy Award winner from the second.

In 1940 Hattie McDaniel, born in Kansas to former slaves, became the first black person to win an Academy Award, getting the Best Supporting Actress nod for her role as Mammy in *Gone with the Wind*. But it was a bittersweet win–McDaniel couldn't attend the movie's premiere in Atlanta because of Jim Crow laws while movie ads portraying McDaniel (and other black people) were banned in the South. Her winner's speech at the Oscars on February 29, 1940 was said to have been written for her by the film studio and, to make matters worse, she and her escort had to sit at a segregated table at the back of the Cocoanut Grove in Los Angeles where the event was held that year.

It took 24 more years for a second African-American to win a competitive Academy Award. In 1964, Sidney Poitier took home the Best Actor Oscar for his role in *Lilies of the Field*. Raised in the Bahamas but born in Miami, Poitier had to change his strong island accent before he could make it in America.

Onstage at the 1964 Academy Awards, actress Anne Bancroft gave Poitier a peck on the cheek as he accepted the prize. Needless to say, it was one of the most controversial kisses in Oscar history. "It has been a long journey to this moment," he would say, reflecting on a life born in poverty to a Bahamas tomato farmer.

Poitier continued to blaze a trail for African-Americans with three ground-breaking roles in 1967, all dealing with race: *Guess Who's Coming to Dinner?, In the Heat of the Night* and *To Sir with Love*. Poitier later turned his attentions to directing where his credits include *A Piece of the Action, Uptown Saturday Night, Stir Crazy* and *Ghost Dad*. He was knighted in 1974, received an Honorary Oscar in 2002, and was awarded the Presidential

Medal of Freedom from President Obama in 2009. Sir Sidney Poitier served as Bahamas Ambassador to Japan for a decade beginning in 1997.

As for Hattie McDaniel, she would later be criticized for taking on roles considered race-based stereotypes. In response she would say, "Why should I complain about making $7,000 a week playing a maid. If I didn't, I'd be making $7 a week being one." Eventually her film roles dried up and she returned to her roots in radio, playing a maid on CBS Radio's *The Beulah Show*. She started filming a TV version of it but was soon diagnosed with breast cancer and died in 1952 at age 57.

 TRIVIA: James Baskett was the first black person to win an Honorary Oscar, for his performance as Uncle Remus in the 1948 Walt Disney movie *Song of the South*.

ALSO-RAN ACTRESSES

"An artist of impeccable grace and beauty ..."

She was one of Hollywood's most versatile actresses of the '40s, '50s and '60s–a star who played everything from a nun to an adulteress–but Deborah Kerr never got a date with Oscar.

Kerr holds the record for most Academy Award nominations for Best Actress without a win, with six. The English-born Kerr was first spurned by Oscar for her role as an alcoholic wife in the 1949 drama *Edward, My Son*. She missed again in her role as an adulteress in *From Here to Eternity* in 1953 (remember the famous beach scene with Burt Lancaster?). Loss #3 came in 1956 for her work as a widowed schoolteacher in *The King and I*.

Kerr's losing streak continued in 1957 with *Heaven Knows, Mr. Allison,* in which she played a nun. In 1958 she lost for her role as a spinster in *Separate Tables*. She made it a perfect 0-for-6 in 1960 when she was defeated for her part as a sheep-herder's wife in *The Sundowners*.

Appalled by the explicit sex and violence in movies, Kerr retired from the screen in the late '60s but continued in theater and TV. However, the film world didn't forget her—in 1994 the Academy gave Kerr an honorary Oscar, recognizing her as "an artist of impeccable grace and beauty, a dedicated actress whose motion picture career has always stood for perfection, discipline and elegance."

Kerr has company in misery. Thelma Ritter used to hold "Come Over and Watch Me Lose Again" parties on Oscar night during her run of six loses on the Best Supporting Actress card (1950 to 1962). Glenn Close was also in the mix, losing three times each for Best Actress and Best Supporting Actress from 1982 to 2011. Close, however, put it all in perspective. When asked about the fact she's never won an Oscar despite six nominations, she pointed out that given the number of people working in acting or hoping to get work, and the number of movies produced each year, "How can you possibly think of yourself as a loser?"

 TRIVIA: Deborah Kerr accepted her role in *From Here to Eternity* after Joan Crawford was rejected because she wanted her own cameraman.

LUCCI'S LAMENT

"The streak is over!"

It was one of the most remarkable losing streaks in entertainment history, a streak that had a life of its own, inspired jokes and even a song.

Eighteen times, Susan Lucci was nominated for Outstanding Lead Actress in a Daytime Drama Series. Eighteen times, she lost.

Finally, in 1999, at the Daytime Emmy Awards in New York, presenter Shemar Moore screamed to the expectant crowd: "The streak is over!"

Lucci had finally won an Emmy.

Lucci joined the cast of *All My Children* in 1970. She initially auditioned for the part of sweet, innocent Tara Martin, but the show's producers thought she was a perfect fit for a new character: the sexually charged, status-conscious Erica Kane. Lucci played the part for 41 years until the show's cancellation in 2011. Called by *TV Guide* "unequivocally the most famous soap-opera character in the history of daytime TV," Erica Kane was married nine times to six men, kidnapped, survived both a plane and car accident, engineered a prison break, battled drug addiction and had U.S. TV's first legal abortion in 1973.

Lucci, who was rumored to have lost her temper at early losses, began to accept the slights with aplomb as time went by. In 1990, for instance, when she was guest host on *Saturday Night Live*, the cast and crew carried Emmy statuettes past her as she delivered her opening monologue. She also lampooned her own hunger for an Emmy in a commercial for a sugar substitute called *The Sweet One*.

"Sure I was disappointed," Lucci told *People* following her 1999 win. "But winning the Emmy was never the focal point of my life. The work—acting—really is the point, and that's not just rhetoric. I don't begrudge anyone for having won."

But sometimes losing can have an upside, as Lucci's friend Joan Rivers told *People*. "The luckiest thing that ever happened to her is not winning. Everyone knows who she is because of it."

 TRIVIA: Susan Lucci was nominated twice more for Outstanding Lead Actress after her 1999 win, losing both times.

BIG THREE SECONDS

The second Academy Awards had a lot of firsts.

Staged April 3, 1930 at the Ambassador Hotel in Los Angeles, the second Academy Awards marked the first time the winners weren't announced in advance. Believe it or not the previous years' winners were revealed three months before the original Academy Awards ceremony (so much for suspense). Also, the second Academy Awards was broadcast on radio for the first time (KNX Los Angeles devoted an hour to it). William C. DeMille, brother of pioneering film icon Cecil B. DeMille, was the host. It was also the first and only time there were no official nominees (though research years later has uncovered a list of unofficial nominees). And for the first time no silent films won an award (and wouldn't again until *The Artist* won Best Picture in 2011). Not bad for a sophomore showing.

The second Grammys held on November 29, 1959 were the first to be televised, sort of. It was presented on TV as a taped "Sunday Showcase" on NBC (they weren't televised live until 1971). But not everyone was all that too enthused about it. Critic Harriet Von Horne, for instance, opined in the *New York World Telegram* that the Grammys were "pandering to the primitive, uninformed taste that mars so much of TV fare. Here was a costly show, brilliantly produced ... and it had the whole range of music to choose from. So we had a reading by Shelley Berman instead of Carl Sandburg. We had the clanging, twanging Kingston Trio when we might have had Ethel Merman."

If you've never heard of the Antoinette Perry Award, you're not alone. That's the formal, rarely used name of the Tony Award for excellence in Broadway theater. The Tony Awards honor Antoinette "Tony" Perry, an actress and director who co-founded the American Theater Wing during the Second World War. Perry died in 1946 and the first Tony Awards were held April 6, 1947 at the Waldorf-Astoria Hotel in New York. This second name came about by accident when host Brock Pemberton referred to the award as a "Tony" at this, the first award ceremony.

 TRIVIA: Oscar Hammerstein is the only person named Oscar to have won an Oscar (twice for Best Original Song).

CHAPTER 2

FLAT NOTES

"Second place, tied with last."
– Ted Chaough, *Mad Men*

SECOND BEST

"The golden apple was within my grasp."

He's the Beatle who almost was.

On August 16, 1962–with the Beatles on the brink of stardom– Pete Best got stunning news from manager Brian Epstein. The Beatles drummer of the past two years had been fired and replaced by Ringo Starr. Two months later, the Beatles exploded onto the scene with their first chart record–"Love Me Do"–and would go on to become one of history's most successful recording acts. But Best could only watch and wonder, "what if."

Born Randolph Peter Best on November 21, 1941, in Madras, India, the future Beatle migrated to Liverpool with his family on Christmas Day 1945. His mother had a coffee club in the basement of her house and as luck would have it, the first group to play her Casbah Coffee Club was the Quarrymen, who later became the Beatles. Best was recruited by the then-named Silver Beatles in 1960 and travelled with them on a tour to Hamburg.

The group shortened its name to the Beatles, honed their sound and, at the directive of new manager Brian Epstein, cleaned up their image by switching from leather jackets to suits. In the spring of 1962, the Beatles got their first recording contract from EMI, and the future seemed bright for John, Paul, George and Pete. But 10 weeks and one day after their first recording session, Best was gone and The Beatles became John, Paul, George and Ringo. The greatest party in rock 'n' roll history was about to begin, and Pete Best wasn't invited.

Devastated by his dismissal, Best went home, cried and didn't leave his house for two weeks. He fell into depression and attempted suicide in the mid-'60s. Best knocked around the music industry for a few years with little success (though he did have one cleverly titled album–*Best of the Beatles*). He left the music business in 1968 and began a long career in the civil service. At the urging of his mother, Best ended a 20-year hiatus from music in 1988. He and his group, The Pete Best Band, have been touring ever since.

Best says Epstein told him he was fired because "he wasn't a good enough drummer," but speculation has centered on Best's supposed lack of compatibility with his bandmates, his moodiness, his hairstyle and maybe because he was just a little too popular with the ladies for the other Beatles' liking. We may never know. According to Best, only McCartney knows the real reason and he's not talking.

"The golden apple was within my grasp and it was taken away from me," Best told the *AARP Bulletin* in 2010. "The severity of the situation once I got back home again brought me to tears."

 TRIVIA: Paul McCartney played drums for the Beatles for a short time before Pete Best; before that the drummer was Norman Chapman.

A MIDSOMMER NIGHT'S NIGHTMARE

"The lost bard of Woodstock."

Performing at Woodstock should have been a sure ticket to fame and fortune, right?

Not for Bert Sommer.

Sommer, a folk singer and former member of the baroque-rock group The Left Banke, played a 55-minute set on the first night of Woodstock. The highlight of Sommer's 10-song set was his rendition of Paul Simon's "America." It earned the frizzy-haired, blue-eyed native of Albany, New York, a standing ovation. But perhaps fitting considering Sommer's life-long obscurity, the announcer acknowledged his set by calling him Bert "Sommers" (not Sommer) just as he had when he introduced him.

Despite appearing on rock music's biggest stage, Sommer was quickly forgotten. Not one second of his performance was included in the Woodstock film, and none of his songs appeared on the Woodstock album. Capitol Records vice-president Artie Kornfeld said the omission was due to Sommer having recorded for Capitol, and not Atlantic, who held the Woodstock recording rights. Sommer's friend Victor Kahn said the spurned musician was devastated. "Here was the most famous event in the world and he's not getting any credit for it."

Sommer released his second album, *Inside Bert Sommer*, after the Woodstock film and album. It contained a song he wrote about Woodstock, "We're All Playing in The Same Band." Nevertheless, his music career never took off, despite two more albums and opening gigs with the likes of Poco, Delaney & Bonnie and Friends, and the Allman Brothers. He pursued an acting career and played in local bands before dying of respiratory failure in July of 1990–just 12 days after his final concert. He was 41.

Like other forgotten Woodstock acts such as Quill, Sweetwater and the Keef Hartley Band, Sommer has become a rock music footnote. Even his name was omitted from the original plaque commemorating the August 15-18, 1969 Woodstock festival at Bethel, New York.

"Bert Sommer was the lost bard of Woodstock" says *Wall Street Journal* pop and rock critic Jim Fusilli. "For me, Sommer did a wonderful set on the first day ... then he completely disappeared from the mythology of Woodstock."

 TRIVIA: Bert Sommer was in the original Broadway cast of *Hair,* and his large shock of frizzy hair appears on the original playbill for the production.

KASEY AT THE MIC

"You can't listen to her without crying."

S he was one of the most listened to voices of her time, the original singer on one of the biggest hits of the 1970s–but have you ever heard of Kasey Cisyk?

Born in the Ukraine in 1953, Cisyk was one of the most popular commercial singing voices of the '70s and '80s. She is best known for the long-running *Have You Driven a Ford Lately* advertising campaign. By 1989–about halfway through its 17-year run–Ford estimated that some 20 billion people had heard her sing that iconic jingle. No corporate soloist has enjoyed a longer run with a commercial.

Cisyk originally wanted to be an opera singer. She studied at the Mannes College of Music in Manhattan but gravitated toward jingles as a way to make ends meet. She sent out tapes while singing in clubs. There was a trickle of interest at first, then an avalanche as more and more companies discovered her voice. Suddenly, Cisyk went from no work to almost too much. In fact, the woman they called "The Jingle Diva" recalled one typical day where she sang for *Trans World Airlines* and *Coca-Cola* in the morning, then *Hartz Mountain, Eastern Airlines, Datsun, L'Eggs* and *McDonald's* in the afternoon, followed by a six-and-a-half-hour late-night session ending at 3 a.m.

Jingle singers by definition are anonymous, but Cisyk managed to stay under the radar even though she originally recorded one of the biggest hits of the '70s. In 1977, Cisyk sang the soundtrack version of "You Light Up My Life" for the movie of the same name. Joe Brooks, the film's director, wanted to release it as a single, but Cisyk didn't. So he re-recorded "You Light Up My Life" with Debby Boone. It went on to spend 10 weeks at #1. By the time Cisyk finally agreed to release her nearly identical version, it was too late: it sputtered at #80. Not only that, the record didn't include her name but instead listed the singer as "Original Cast."

It seemed Cisyk was destined to remain anonymous–at least publicly–

except for a couple of Ukrainian love-song CDs she recorded in 1988 which proved to be extremely popular. Finally, people could put a name to the voice.

The woman who eventually became known as "the heavenly voice of Ukraine" died in 1998 of breast cancer a few days before her 45th birthday. As one fan commented, "You can't listen to her without crying."

 TRIVIA: Debby Boone's father, Pat Boone, had six #1 songs on the Billboard chart in the '50s and '60s.

TWIST OF FATE

"If you're looking for youth ... just take a dose of rock 'n' roll."

Hank Ballard is famous—he's in the Rock & Roll Hall of Fame—but he could have been a lot more famous.

You see, Ballard was the guy who originally wrote and recorded "The Twist."

As lead vocalist of Hank Ballard and the Midnighters, Ballard had several big mid-1950s R&B hits like "Work with Me, Annie," and the answer songs "Annie Had a Baby" and "Annie's Aunt Fannie."

In November 1959, the Detroit-born Ballard released "Teardrops on Your Letter." "The Twist" was placed on the B side (Ballard himself liked "The Twist" better but his producer, Henry Glover, wanted the A side to be "Teardrops," a song he'd written himself).

Despite being relegated to the B side, "The Twist" did attract attention and was played at dances around the country. Baltimore DJ Buddy Dean—who hosted a dance show on TV—noticed how much the teenagers liked it and alerted *American Bandstand* host Dick Clark. After initial reluctance—Ballard had been associated with sexually "dirty" songs—Clark finally played it on his show to rave reviews. Clark then attempted to get Ballard to play live on *American Bandstand*, but that fell through. So Clark looked for someone else to cover the song, and settled on Chubby Checker, whose stage name had been given to him by Clark's wife (it was a play on Fats Domino). Checker recorded the cover in just 35 minutes. It took three takes, with the Dreamlovers providing backing vocals.

Checker's version, which sounded a lot like Ballard's, rocketed to the #1 spot on the Billboard charts for one week in September 1960. It eventually died down as a teenage craze, but then, after Checker made an appearance on *The Ed Sullivan Show* in 1961, it started to become popular with adults. It was re-released and shot to the top spot on Billboard for two weeks in January 1962. "The Twist" is the only non-Christmas song to reach #1 on Billboard in two separate chart runs.

Ballard wasn't unhappy at Checker's success with the song–he says without Chubby Checker and Dick Clark the song would never have been a hit, something that sparked Ballard's career. Plus, he enjoyed the royalties, which were substantial over the years.

Ballard fared not too badly after "The Twist"–he and his group had top-10 hits with "Finger Poppin' Time" and "Let's Go, Let's Go, Let's Go." He was also named to the Rock & Roll Hall of Fame in 1990–though the original Midnighters were not. Ballard died of cancer in 2003 at the age of 75–a man who proved that sometimes you have to take a back seat to get ahead.

 TRIVIA: Hank Ballard's cousin Florence Ballard was a founding member of The Supremes.

SECOND BILLING

"We expected something special."

What would come to be known as the "Greatest Jazz Concert Ever" played second-fiddle to a boxing match.

On the night of May 15, 1953, jazz giants Charlie Parker

(alto sax), Dizzie Gillespie (trumpet), Charles Mingus (bass), Bud Powell (piano) and Max Roach (drums) played jointly for the first and only time ever–to mostly empty seats at Toronto's renowned Massey Hall.

Only 600 turned out to view this avant-garde quartet, with attendance not helped by the fact the show was not advertised (the promoter was hoping "word of mouth" would do the trick–it didn't). There was also a major distraction: the well-hyped Rocky Marciano-Jersey Joe Walcott fight, which was staged that same night at Chicago Stadium and broadcast to eager fans across North America on radio.

At least one of the musicians seemed more interested in the fight. Don Brown, then 20 and a spectator at the concert, said Gillespie "kept running backstage to check on the fight. I don't think it even lasted 60 seconds (Marciano won) ... It was really chaos."

Globe and Mail reviewer Robert Fulford trashed the concert, pointing out the lack of decorum. But that lack of decorum was worse than Fulford realized. Parker spent an extended intermission at a local bar and had to practically be dragged back onstage. Because ticket sales were so low, the musicians couldn't get paid, either. The concert might have been forgotten had Mingus not grabbed the tapes which had been made in a booth above the stage. Those tapes would later become the gold-standard record, *Jazz at Massey Hall.*

"We expected something special and in retrospect it was," said Brown years later. "But I sort of laugh at the 'greatest jazz concert ever' thing. I don't think it was that. But boy it certainly was an experience."

 TRIVIA: For contractual reasons, Charlie Parker is identified on the album as Charlie Chan, after the fictional detective. After forgetting his horn, he was also forced to source a local plastic sax for the event.

SOMETIMES #2
DOES WIN OUT—ON THE FLIPSIDE

"We never thought it was a single."

Remember "B" sides? They were the forgettable, often unlistenable tunes hidden on the flipsides of 45 RPM records, you know, the ones you bought for the hit tune on the "A" side.

But sometimes the "B" side became the hit.

Case in point: "Tequila" by the Champs. On December 23, 1957, a singer named Dave Burgess went into the Hollywood recording studio of Challenge Records to lay down a few tracks. Burgess had yet to have a hit with Challenge but was hoping to score with his new single "Train to Nowhere." Accompanied by the Flores Trio, led by Danny Flores, Burgess cut the song but as the session was coming to an end, realized he needed a "B" side. So the group recorded "Tequila," which Flores wrote on a visit to Tijuana but had forgotten until that day. The group also needed a name so they called themselves the Champs, after label owner Gene Autry's horse Champion. "Train to Nowhere" didn't go anywhere, but DJ's dug the flipside and "Tequila" went to #1 on the Billboard singles chart on March 17, 1958. The Champs had only that one hit and disbanded in 1965.

When Capitol Records released "Biding My Time" by Anne Murray in the spring of 1970, everyone thought it would be a big hit. It wasn't, barely making the charts in Canada, her home country. But then a DJ in Cleveland flipped it over, liked what he heard—and so did his listeners. The song was "Snowbird," Murray's breakthrough hit, and it reached #8 on the Billboard Hot 100 and #1 on the Billboard Adult Contemporary chart. Murray earned two Grammy nominations for the tune and was named Best New Artist of 1970. "What are the chances of someone flipping a single by a new artist," Murray marvelled years later. "It's amazing." Murray went on to become a Canadian singing legend with more than two dozen Hot 100 hits including four Top 10s and the 1978 #1, "You Needed Me." And it all started with a "B" side.

"Black Water," from the Doobies album *What Were Once Vices Are Now Habits,* was thrown in as the flipside to, "Another Park, Another Sunday." But DJs liked the "B" side better and so did the public, as "Black Water" shot to the top of the Billboard Hot 100 on March 15, 1975. It was the first #1 song for the Doobie Brothers and incredibly, one of 27 Hot 100 hits they would produce between 1972 and 1989.

"Maggie May" wasn't destined for success. In fact, it barely made it to Rod Stewart's *Reason to Believe* album, so there was no way it would be released as an "A" sider. The record company simply slapped it on the back of the Tim Hardin-written ballad "Reason to Believe" and released the 45 in the summer of 1971. But surprise! Radio programmers and the public liked "Maggie May" better. Much better. Recorded in just two takes, the song about a relationship Stewart had 10 years earlier became the London-born singer's first #1 song on the Billboard Hot 100. The album also went to the top of the Billboard album chart and Stewart went on to become one of the leading rock stars of all-time. As for "Reason to Believe," it stalled at #62.

Hard to believe, but the surf instrumental classic "Wipe Out" was originally a "B" side. The Surfaris didn't consider themselves an instrumental band so the original "A" side of the 1963 release was a vocal tune called "Surfer Joe." "Wipe Out" was only recorded after the engineer told the group they needed something to put on the flipside of the disc. Recorded in just three takes, manager Dale Smallin originally wanted to call the song "Stiletto" (that's Smallin doing "The Witch Laugh" at the beginning of the song). "Wipe Out" was passed between several record labels until Dot Records decided to finally release it on the "A" side with "Surfer Joe" on the flip. "Wipe Out" went all the way to #2 on the Billboard Hot 100 while "Surfer Joe" languished at #61. In 1966 "Wipe Out" was re-released and made it to #16. It was the band's only Top 40 single.

The first rock and roll song to go to #1 on the Billboard singles chart was actually a "B" side. On April 12, 1954, Bill Haley & His Comets stepped into the Decca Records studio in New York to record their first single, "Thirteen Women (And Only One Woman in Town)." They had three-and-a-half hours to record this and another song, but it took them three hours to finish "Thirteen Women." That left 30 minutes to record the "B" side, so they quickly laid down "(We're Gonna) Rock Around the Clock" in just two takes. Bill Haley loved the song, but his record company said it would never sell. "Thirteen Women" with "Rock Around the Clock" on the flipside only reached #23 on Billboard in 1954. "Rock Around the Clock" probably would have been forgotten had it not been discovered by film director Richard Brooks who played it under the credits of the 1955 movie, *Blackboard Jungle*. Teenagers went crazy for the song so it was re-released in June 1955. "Rock Around the Clock" shot to #1 on July 9, 1955 and it stayed there for eight weeks. The rock era had begun–straight from the "B" side.

 TRIVIA: The first commercially produced 45 RPM record was *Texarkana Baby* by Eddy Arnold in 1949.

SUPREMELY FORGOTTEN

"She regrets (leaving the group) sometimes."

They are the lost Supremes.

Diana Ross, Mary Wilson and Florence Ballard *were* the Supremes during their glory years in the 1960s, a decade that saw them produce an astounding twelve #1 singles, including "I Hear a Symphony," "Baby Love" and "You Can't Hurry Love." However, the names of two women who sang with the group before their hit-making days have been largely forgotten.

Betty McGlown helped found the Primettes, forerunner of the Supremes, in 1959. At the time, McGlown was dating Paul Williams, then singing with the Primes which later became the Temptations. The group's manager and booking agent, Milton Jenkins, was putting together a sister act for the Primes which would be called the Primettes. He discovered Florence Ballard, who led him to Diane (later Diana) Ross and Mary Wilson. McGlown—who had an "in" because of her connection with Williams—also joined the group, making it a quartet.

During her brief time with the Supremes, McGlown sang back-up vocals on only two songs, Wilson's "Pretty Baby" and Ross's "Tears of Sorrow." They are her only known recordings. McGlown left the group in 1960 to get married and became Mrs. Betty Travis. According to *The Supremes* author Mark Ribowsky, McGlown never regretted the decision. She died in 2008 in Royal Oak, Michigan, at age 66.

Barbara Martin replaced McGlown and spent some two years in the group before leaving in 1962 with a baby on the way. "Barbara was on that first album *Meet the Supremes*," says Mary Wilson of her former group-mate. "She had met the love of her life and when we signed, she left. And she's still with the same guy all these years later, the only one who's had the (same) man the entire time." Wilson adds though, "She regrets (leaving the group) sometimes."

 TRIVIA: Mary Wilson, a native of Greenville, Mississippi, is the only member of the original Supremes not born in Detroit.

#2 WITHOUT A BULLET

"Number two tries harder and all that."

They were one of the leading groups of the late '60s and early '70s, but incredibly, Creedence Clearwater Revival never quite reached the top.

The San Francisco-area band holds a rather undesirable record—the most #2 songs on the Billboard Hot 100 *without* posting a #1 song.

CCR began its *Close But No Cigar* run in March 1969 when "Proud

Mary" reached the runner-up spot for two weeks then slipped. Their follow-up, "Bad Moon Rising," also peaked at #2 for a single week in June of the same year, followed by their next release, "Green River," which made it to #2 for a week in September of the same year.

CCR revisited the #2 spot for a fourth time in March 1970 with "Travelin' Band." Members Tom Fogerty, John Fogerty, Doug Clifford and Stu Cook were bridesmaids for a fifth and final time when "Lookin' Out My Back Door" had a two-week run at #2 in September 1970.

Bandleader John Fogerty was philosophical about not making it to the top of the pops, saying, "Number two tries harder and all that." The group did get a measure of revenge in 1993 when they were inducted into the Rock and Roll Hall of Fame.

 TRIVIA: Madonna has the most Billboard Hot 100 #2 songs with six, but she also has a dozen #1 singles.

ROCK TAKES SECOND PLACE

"All he wanted to do was put a smile on your face."

In the middle of psychedelia, Canada's musical spotlight was held by a middle-aged guy with a trumpet.

Bobby Gimby was an unlikely candidate to top the charts in 1967. The 48-year-old trumpeter had led bands since the 1940s and was a noted song and jingle writer, but this was a year that had seen the emergence of artists such as The Doors, Jefferson Airplane and the Grateful Dead. But patriotism trumped it all and for rock groups attempting to reach the top of the charts in Canada in April 1967, it was *Close, But No Cigar.*

Canada's centennial year was 1967, and the country whose motto is "From Sea to Sea" was celebrating in style. Special coins were issued, a Centennial Train traversed the country, and Canadians were encouraged to begin Centennial projects to mark the 100th anniversary. The Centennial Flame was lit on Parliament Hill, and a series of shows called *The Canada Festival* promoted the arts. Towering over it all was Expo 67, a world-class exposition set in Montreal.

Canadian pride was never higher, and the Saskatchewan-born Gimby tapped right into it. He wrote the song "Canada" (pronounced *Ca-na-da*) for a 30-minute Centennial documentary. The song became so popular it was soon released as a single. "Canada" was a huge success, reaching #1 on the Canadian charts and selling 75,000 copies of sheet music. Gimby would become even more ubiquitous as "The Pied Piper of Canada," seen on TV or at Expo 67 wearing a cape and playing his jewel-encrusted trumpet with hordes of school children in tow. Ah, patriotism.

Gimby was named an officer of the Order of Canada in 1967, and "Canada" was named Middle-of-the-Road record of the year. He went on to record Centennial songs for the provinces of Manitoba and Saskatchewan, hosted the CTV show *Sing a Song* in 1975, and led the Bobby Gimby Orchestra during the 1980s.

Gimby died June 20, 1998 at a nursing home in North Bay, Ontario. At his funeral, his coffin was draped with a Canadian flag with his trumpet placed on top of it. His grand-daughter Elizabeth Bougerol said of Gimby, "whether you were the Queen or the milkman, all he wanted to do was put a smile on your face."

As for major U.K. and U.S. hit tunes like the Stones' "Ruby Tuesday" and the Monkees' "I'm a Believer," well they just had to wait 'til the Canadian hoopla died down.

 TRIVIA: In the 1960s, Gimby composed "Malaysia Forever," which has become the unofficial anthem of that south-east Asian country.

BANDSTAND BEGINNINGS

"I knew it was a hit immediately."

*A*merican Bandstand made Dick Clark a household name and a very rich man, but he was actually the program's second host. The original host of what became U.S.-network TV's longest-running music show was a Pennsylvania-born disc jockey named Bob Horn. Born Donald Loyd Horn in 1916, the son of a surveyor and First World War veteran, Horn took the on-air name Bob Horn at WRAW Reading in the 1930s. By the late '40s he had one of the top radio shows in the Philadelphia market, the late night *C'mon and Dance* at WIP. Horn then moved to rival station WFIL where he hosted *Bob Horn's Bandstand*. So popular was his radio show that WFIL management needed little convincing when Horn approached them about taking the show to television.

Bob Horn's Bandstand debuted in September 1952. And it initially bombed as the show consisted mostly of poor-quality videos. So they decided to have Horn play records and let kids from local high schools dance to them. Bingo! The show re-launched the next month and by the third day 1,000 kids were trying to cram into a studio designed to hold 250. "I knew it was a hit immediately," said Charlie O'Donnell, WIBG-AM news director at the time and later the announcer on *American Bandstand*. "You felt it. You had to rush home to watch Bob Horn if you wanted to know what was happening in music."

One of the stipulations Horn had to deal with was having Lee Stewart of the Mad Man Muntz electronics store as his co-host. That guaranteed their first sponsor but as the show gained in popularity the Stewart account wasn't. Stewart was then dumped as co-host in 1955 and Horn continued as the solo host.

Then it all fell apart for Horn. In 1956, he was arrested for drunk driving and quickly placed "on vacation" from *Bandstand*. The timing was especially bad as his station was in the middle of an anti-drunk driving campaign. But it got worse. Horn was later slapped with four statutory rape charges and four charges of corrupting the morals of a minor. His first trial on those charges ended with a hung jury. The second trial ended with a not guilty verdict.

Horn's career was toast at that point, but he didn't help his cause any by getting into an accident on the day of his indictment. Five people were injured, including two children. The cops also nailed him for drunk driving and driving the wrong way down a one-way street. Finished in Philadelphia, Horn moved to KILT Houston where he did a show as Bob Adams. He soon left the air and became a salesman for the station, later starting a successful ad agency.

Meanwhile, Dick Clark was "horning in" on his act, so to speak, taking over hosting duties at *Bandstand* on July 9, 1956. Clark was a hit, becoming one of North America's most recognized TV stars when ABC took the show national in 1957 where it was rebranded *American Bandstand*. Incredibly, Clark continued to host the series until 1988.

Clark died of a heart attack in 2012; at age 82 he was hailed as an American icon. Bob Horn was mowing his lawn in July 1966 when he was felled by a heart attack. He was 50 and forgotten. His epitaph at Forest Park Cemetery in Houston simply reads "Bandstand."

"Just as Martin Block was the first disc jockey, Bob Horn was unequivocally the first person to put kids dancing on TV," early *Bandstander* Harvey Sheldon said in 1997. "It would be like forgetting George Washington to forget Bob Horn."

 TRIVIA: Buffalo TV sportscaster Rick Azar once filled in for Clark on *Bandstand.*

NO STRANGER TO SUCCESS

"It was just a thing that came out of my head."

The British Invasion began with a guy wearing a bowler hat, a goatee and tooting a clarinet.

Two years before the Beatles owned the charts and ushered in a tsunami of other English artists, this eccentric Briton became the first British artist to reach #1 on the Billboard Hot 100.

Born Bernard Stanley Bilk in Somerset, England in 1929, the artist who became known as Mr. Acker Bilk got his musical start behind bars. Sent to prison for three months in 1947 for falling asleep on guard duty, Bilk whiled away the time learning how to play the clarinet. He formed his own band and appeared on such shows as the *BBC Beat Show*. While riding in a taxi one day, Bilk wrote a melody he called "Jenny," and later renamed it "Stranger on the Shore." "I didn't think it was much different from any of the rest of it," Bilk said. "It was just a thing that came out of my head, that's all. I didn't sort of work on it or do much at all with it."

"Stranger on the Shore" shot to #1 on the Billboard Hot 100 in May 1962. It peaked at #2 on the British chart, stayed on the chart for an eye-popping 55 weeks, and was the top-selling U.K. single of that year. Two years later, the dam burst wide open when the Beatles ushered in the full-blown British Invasion.

 TRIVIA: The first British artist to top the U.S. charts was Vera Lynn with "Auf Wiederseh'n Sweetheart" in 1952.

MARKED MAN

"I wanted to have fun."

D avid Marks can be excused for wondering "what if?"

It was 1962. Brian, Dennis and Carl Wilson had just formed a new surf band and asked Marks to join. Marks lived across the street from the Wilsons in Hawthorne, California. Marks jammed with the Wilsons for years and got to know them well. By the time he joined, the Beach Boys had already released their first single, "Surfin'" in 1961, but wanted Marks' rhythm guitar to upgrade the band's sound.

The Beach Boys soon landed a deal with Capitol Records and had seven Top 40 hits with Marks in the lineup, including top ten smashes "Surfin' USA" and "Surfer Girl." He toured with the Beach Boys, doing over 100 concerts with the band in addition to several national TV appearances. However, Marks left the group in the summer of 1963 after an argument with Beach Boys manager (and father) Murry Wilson. "I quit because Murry was on my case, and I wanted out," Marks told *People* in 1993. "He wanted me to regard it as a business. I wanted to have fun."

"When I quit the band, Carl Wilson told me to laugh all the way to the bank," Marks says. "The only thing is, I never got to the bank." After leaving the Beach Boys, Marks focused on his fledgling band, the Marksmen, but despite packing them in for concerts the group didn't sell many records. Marks played with several other bands before leaving the music business in the late '60s to study jazz and classical guitar. He reunited with the Beach Boys onstage in 1971 but declined an offer to return to the group.

Marks, who battled drug and alcohol addiction, checked into a rehab clinic in 1989. He did odd jobs, including ushering at Dodger Stadium.

Asked in 2012 if he regretted leaving the Beach Boys, Marks responded, "Oh, not really. I would say that overall, the experience was probably equal to what I would've gotten if I had stayed in the Beach Boys. It was a very rounded experience through the years."

TRIVIA: The Beach Boys have more charted Billboard Hot 100 singles than any other American group.

CHAPTER 3

POLITICAL ANIMALS

"Finishing second in the Olympics gets you silver.
Finishing second in politics gets you oblivion."

– Richard Nixon

BORN TO LOSE

"I know I've had an impact ..."

I f at first you don't succeed, try, try again.

And in the case of Harold Stassen, keep right on trying.

Stassen was born into politics. His father was a multi-term mayor of West St. Paul, Minnesota. A man seemingly on the fast-track to success, Stassen graduated from high school at 15, got his bachelor and law degrees from the University of Minnesota at 22 and was elected district attorney for Minnesota's Dakota Country at age 23. In 1938, he was elected Governor of Minnesota, at 31 the youngest governor in the state's history. Among his accomplishments during his three terms: bringing the first African-American officer into the state's National Guard.

But the "Boy Wonder" wasn't finished yet. In 1940, he delivered the keynote address at the Republican National Convention and helped Wendell Willkie win the GOP nomination.

It was then, in 1944, that he made the first of his many failed bids for the presidency. After serving in the Second World War, he made a strong bid for the Republican nomination in 1948, scoring a number of early primary wins before losing to Thomas Dewey in the last Republican convention to go more than one ballot (this one went three).

Undaunted, Stassen ran again for president in 1952. He lost, badly. He also ran—and lost—in 1964, 1968, 1976, 1980, 1984, 1988 and 1992. But that's not all—he ran for the Pennsylvania Republican nomination in 1958 and 1966, losing both times. He was runner-up in the Philadelphia mayoral race in 1959 and finished a distant second in a bid for the Minnesota Republican Senate nomination in 1978. He also failed in bids for Minnesota governor and a Minnesota congressional seat in 1986. He made his final bid for public office in 1994, a (you guessed it) losing bid for the Republican Senate nomination.

Stassen died in 2001 at age 93. He had been the oldest living governor.

CLOSE, BUT NO CIGAR

"I sometimes wish people would ask not how many times I've run a political campaign, but how many times I've been right on the issues."

TRIVIA: Harold Stassen and his wife Esther were married 71 years.

TOOTH IN POLITICS

"If Halifax had better teeth, we might have lost the war."

A dental appointment changed the course of history.

In the early days of the Second World War, the frontrunner to replace Neville Chamberlain as England's prime minister was Edward Wood, better known as Lord Halifax. On May 10, 1940, influential British politician R.A.B. Butler went to Halifax's office to offer him the Labour Party's support for a contingency government under the foreign secretary. However, Halifax wasn't there—he had left to go to the dentist.

The timing proved fateful. That same day Germany invaded Holland and Belgium. Having missed his meeting with Butler, Halifax didn't get the support he needed and the momentum swung to Winston Churchill. That night, Chamberlain resigned, Churchill became prime minister and Halifax got the key to the *Close, But No Cigar* executive washroom.

Churchill's leadership and steely resolve during the Battle of Britain proved a turning point in the war. By contrast, Lord Halifax was one of the architects of Britain's appeasement policy toward Nazi Germany prior to the war.

Halifax was appointed British ambassador to the U.S. shortly after his brush with the prime minister's office. He retired in 1946 and died 13 years later, aged 78.

A line in the 2004 Alex Bennett play, *The History Boys,* puts the Halifax near-miss into perspective. In an effort to illustrate the randomness of events, a character in the play says, "If Halifax had better teeth, we might have lost the war."

TRIVIA: Lord Halifax was born without a left hand.

GLASS CEILING

"False votes."

It was *Close, But No Cigarillo* for Hillary Clinton.

The first woman nominee for president of a major U.S. party, Democrat Hillary Clinton, came within an eyelash of the presidency in 2016. She won the popular vote by three million only to lose 304-227 to Republican candidate Donald Trump in the electoral college.

But while Clinton came the closest of any women who strived for the presidency, she was hardly the first to strive for the White House.

Victoria Woodhull was the first of her gender to run for America's highest office, and she did so at a time when women weren't allowed to vote. A pioneer in seeking a woman's right to vote, Woodhull argued that women already had the right to vote under the Constitution, but the Supreme Court ruled against her. Therefore, any woman who showed up at the polls to vote for her in the 1872 election was arrested. Woodhull ran three more times for president, but with women still not allowed to vote, the end result was the same.

Belva Anne Lockwood did a little better in 1884. She actually got on the ballot, but was ridiculed in newspapers that warned men that her election would usher in a "dangerous" form of "petticoat rule." Lockwood reportedly received 4,000 votes, but believed she actually received more, fruitlessly petitioning Congress that many of her votes were either not counted or thrown in waste baskets as "false votes." Lockwood ran again in 1888 but had even less success.

In 1964, Margaret Chase Smith became the first woman to get more than one vote at a major party's nominating convention. She received 27 votes at the convention that crowned Barry Goldwater the Republican nominee. Smith lost every primary leading up to the election, but did have a best showing of 25% of the votes in the Illinois primary.

Shirley Chisholm, the first African-American elected to Congress, received 152 votes at the 1972 Democratic convention. It was far short of the number she needed to receive the nomination, but did ensure her the right to address the convention that elected George McGovern as its nominee.

Also running for president in 1972 was Linda Jenness, despite her not being of the legal age of 35 to run for the big chair. Nonetheless, her Socialist Workers Party ticket appeared on the ballot in half the states and received 80,000 votes.

Elizabeth Dole was showing up strongly in the polls when she began her run for the Republican nomination in 2000. But the North Carolina senator dropped out of the race early due to insufficient campaign funding and the nomination went to Texas Governor George W. Bush.

 TRIVIA: Hillary Clinton has run for office five times–New York Senator (twice), Democratic Party leadership (twice), and president (once), and won the popular vote each time.

ONE VOTE AWAY FROM THE WHITE HOUSE

"I Still Trust in The People."

If misery loves company, then Al Gore has a soulmate in Samuel Tilden. The U.S. presidential election of 1876 was one of the closest in history, literally decided by one vote.

And just like Gore more than a century later, Tilden would get more popular votes than his opponent, but still lose.

Born in 1814 in New Lebanon, New York, Tilden overcame ill health to become a successful corporate lawyer with powerful clients in business and the railroads. He got involved with Democratic Party politics in the 1840s. His prosecution of the notorious Tweed Ring and the reforms stemming from it led to his election as governor of New York in 1874. He added to his reputation as a reformer when he unmasked the Canal Ring, a cabal of politicians and contractors who had defrauded the state of money earmarked for canal construction.

Tilden's accomplishments did not go unnoticed. The Democrats nominated him for president in 1876. His Republican opponent was Ohio governor Rutherford B. Hayes. After a campaign marked by mud-slinging on both sides, Tilden appeared to have won the election by nearly three million in the popular vote and a 184-165 count in the all-important electoral college. But as that 20th-century philosopher Yogi Berra would say decades later, "It ain't over till it's over."

Twenty electoral votes in South Carolina and Louisiana remained in dispute. For Hayes to become president, he had to win all 20 of those votes. Tilden just needed one. The Constitution was unclear on what to do, so Congress created an electoral commission to settle it. The 15-member commission was made up of 10 Congressional representatives–five from each party–and five Supreme Court justices, two Republican and two Democrat.

The tie-breaking ballot on all 20 electoral votes would be cast by Justice Joseph Bradley, considered the most impartial of the remaining judges. So much for that theory. Justice Bradley, a long-standing Republican, voted along party lines 20 out of 20 times and Hayes became the 19th president of the United States by that single vote. Democrats unhappy with the result started calling Hayes "Rutherfraud" or "His Fraudulency."

Democrat party leaders refused at first to accept the result, but a deal was reached that Tilden would concede if federal troops were removed from Southern states. The arrangement allowed Southern whites to resume pre-Civil War political supremacy (not good for African-Americans, many of whom lost the right to vote). Tilden, who didn't seem to have much fight in him, surrendered and was never a factor in presidential politics again. He spent his remaining years living as a recluse, dying in 1886 in Yonkers, New York. His tombstone–in direct reference to the 1876 election–reads, "I Still Trust in The People."

Even in death, Tilden continued his public service. A lifelong bachelor, Tilden left the bulk of his $6 million estate in trust to help establish a free public library in New York City. The New York Public Library opened its doors May 24, 1911. One of the very first requested items was N.I. Grot's *Ethical Ideas of Our Time.* Fitting, as Tilden was regarded as one of the most ethical politicians of his day.

 TRIVIA: John Quincy Adams (1824), Benjamin Harrison (1888) and Hillary Clinton (2016) also won the popular vote but lost the election. Adams and Harrison became presidents later.

HEADLINE NEWS

"Dewey Defeats Truman."

They say the only poll that counts is the one on election day.

Thomas Dewey found that out the hard way.

In 1948, the New York governor and relentless former crime-fighting special prosecutor appeared a lock to defeat President Truman and become the 34th president of the United States.

All the polls said so. Both the Gallup and Crossley polling organizations gave Dewey a five-point lead on the eve of the election; Roper had stopped polling two months before the election, believing Dewey's victory to be a foregone conclusion. "My whole inclination is to predict the election of Thomas E. Dewey by a heavy margin and devote my time and efforts to other things," declared pollster Elmo Roper. The final *New York Times* survey predicted Dewey would drub Truman by more than 3-1 in the electoral college. "Never argue with the Gallup Poll. It has never been wrong and I very much doubt it ever will be," Dewey huffed years earlier and that, as far as the governor was concerned, was that.

But that wasn't that. The first sign of trouble for Dewey came in the early returns from New Hampshire–he wasn't doing as well as expected in that Republican stronghold. Yet he was ahead, but just barely, in returns from some of the big upstate cities in New York. He narrowly took New York while the returns only worsened for Dewey throughout the night.

By late morning Truman–the same man who had a 36% approval rating just a few months earlier–had taken Ohio, Illinois and California. Truman won the election. At a train stop in St. Louis, Truman gleefully waved a copy of the *Chicago Tribune*. The headline read "Dewey Defeats Truman." Seems the pro-Republican Trib had to get a paper out, so they went with the expectations of their Washington correspondent. Truman's reply: "That ain't the way I heard it."

The result was a disaster for the polling firms. George Gallup's son said his father was forced "to visit many newspaper clients after the election to lure them back after 30 cancelled their poll service." Elmo Roper's son, who was actually a Democrat, said that he and his father "saw our man winning, but our company going down the tubes." The *New York Times'* James Reston further noted that, "we overestimated the tangibles and underestimated the intangibles."

What went wrong? One theory is that the polls showing a likely Dewey win energized Democrat voters to get out and vote, and had just the opposite effect on Republican voters, who stayed away from the polls out of overconfidence. Radio comedian Fred Allen joked that Truman was "the first president to lose in a Gallup and win in a walk."

Neither Truman nor Dewey ever ran on a presidential ticket again. Facing low approval ratings, Truman announced in March 1952 that he was not running for re-election. Truman published his memoirs (he needed the money), helped build his presidential library and died in 1972 at 88. Dewey retired as New York governor in 1954, continued as a Republican power broker and made millions from his law practice. He turned down several appointments, including a seat on the U.S. Supreme Court, before dying of a heart attack in 1971, eight days before his 69th birthday.

Some say Dewey's finest hour may have come in his concession speech, when the weary but gracious defeated candidate told reporters, "I was just as surprised as you were, and I gather that is shared by everybody in the room, as I read your stories before the election." Dewey added, "I have no regrets whatever. It has been grand fun, boys and girls. I enjoyed it immensely."

 TRIVIA: Thomas Dewey briefly considered a career as a professional singer.

DONALD TRUMPS THE ODDS

"I'm in business and proud of it."

Until Donald Trump came along, businessmen running for U.S. president had an automatic one-way ticket to runner-up status and oblivion.

The first businessman with no previous political experience to be nominated on a major ticket was Horace Greeley. The New Hampshire-born Republican got into the newspaper business as editor of a new literary paper, the *New-New Yorker*, in 1834. It led to him publishing campaign literature on behalf of the Whig Party, and to his founding of the *New York Tribune* in 1841. A foe of slavery, capital punishment, liquor, tobacco, gambling, prostitution, but against a women's right to vote (?!), Greeley joined the fledgling Republican Party in 1854. His star in the party fell in the mid-1860s when he opposed Lincoln's re-nomination and bailed Confederate president Jefferson Davis out of prison.

By the early 1870s, Greeley was a fan of neither the Republicans or their president, General Ulysses S. Grant. So he ran for president on the

Liberal Republican ticket in 1872 against the Civil War hero. He also got the Democratic nomination as they didn't want to split the vote. Despite taking the conciliatory approach that both sides were "eager to clasp hands across the bloody chasm," Greeley lost badly to Grant. Adding to Greeley's miseries was the death of his wife five days before the vote. Three weeks after the election Greeley himself passed, the rigours of the campaign having taken their toll. He was 61.

You thought Trump was an unlikely presidential candidate? How about Wendell Willkie? The Indiana-born lawyer was a Democrat until 1939, but quietly switched parties to run for the 1940 Republican presidential nomination. Despite having no political experience—"I'm in business and proud of it" said the prospective candidate—Willkie swept past party stalwarts Robert Taft and Thomas Dewey to win the nomination. Looking for an edge in mid-campaign, Willkie adopted an anti-war stance, saying if elected he would not send troops to Europe. But Roosevelt swept to an easy victory becoming the first president elected to a third term. Four years later, Willkie was dead at 52–a victim of coronary thrombosis.

Then there was Ross Perot. The billionaire founder of Electronic Data Systems announced his independent candidacy in February 1992 on CNN's *Larry King Live*, with the caveat that his supporters get him on the ballot in all 50 states. They accomplished that by September, but by then Perot had stunned his supporters by dropping out of the race. He re-entered in October, just in time for the debates, which he dominated with his folksy straight-talk. Perot got 19% of the vote in the November election–best in terms of popular vote by a third-party candidate since Theodore Roosevelt in 1912. Perot ran again in 1996 with considerably less success. He pretty much dropped out of the public eye for good after a poor debate performance with vice-president Al Gore on CNN. Asked what he would like to have as his epitaph, Perot responded, "Made more money faster. Lost more money in one day. Led the biggest jailbreak in history. He died."

Donald Trump broke the jinx. After suggestions he might run for governor of New York, the billionaire businessman decided to go for the

White House in June 2015. The Ladbrokes betting firm set the odds of him winning at 150-to-1, but Trump defied the pollsters, the pundits, his own party and just about everyone else in defeating Hillary Clinton in the general election of 2016. Trump became the first person with no previous political or military experience to win the American presidency.

TRIVIA: Trump's wife Melania is the first naturalized U.S. citizen to become First Lady of the United States.

BRYAN THE BRIDESMAID

"You shall not crucify mankind upon a cross of gold."

For someone who fought so hard against the gold standard, it's fitting that William Jennings Bryan settled for silver in his presidential ambitions.

Bryan ran three times on the Democratic presidential ticket, losing each time. But "The Great Commoner" as he was called became one of the most popular politicians of his time due to his spellbinding oratory and unwavering commitment to liberal causes. He helped bring about income tax, Prohibition, the right of women to vote and the creation of the Department of Labor.

Bryan burst onto the national scene in 1896 when, at age 36, the former Nebraska congressman won the Democratic nomination for president (to this day he's still the youngest person to have run for president on a major party ticket). Bryan was national leader of the Free Silver Movement, which favored silver over the gold standard preferred by rich Eastern bankers and industrialists. At the Democratic Convention of 1896 the "Boy Orator of the Platte" stirred his party with this, from his "Cross of Gold" speech:

> *Having behind us the producing masses of this nation and the*
> *world, supported by the commercial interests, the laboring*

interests, and the toilers everywhere, we will answer their
demand for a gold standard by saying to them: "You shall
not press down upon the brow of labor this crown of thorns;
you shall not crucify mankind upon a cross of gold."

Bryan traveled 18,000 miles in 27 states to deliver 500 speeches to promote his bid for the White House. He addressed more than five million people in what was the birth of the modern American presidential campaign. On the other hand, his opponent, the well-financed Republican candidate William McKinley, stayed at home and conducted a traditional "front porch" campaign. McKinley won the electoral vote 271-176.

Bryan lost the rematch to McKinley in 1900, despite typically speaking six hours a day over a gruelling election campaign. Silver was a dead issue by then so the talk in 1900—in the wake of the Spanish-American War—was imperialism, and Bryan was an avowed anti-imperialist. The McKinley Republicans outspent the Democrats 10-1 and easily captured the electoral college 292-155.

Undaunted, Bryan made one more presidential run, in 1908, against Theodore Roosevelt's hand-picked successor, William Taft. Trust-busting and corporate dominance were the dragons of the day and Bryan's slogan was "Shall the People Rule?" The answer was no. Taft easily won the electoral college 321-162 giving Bryan his worst defeat yet. He never ran for president again.

Bryan retired from politics in 1915 but got one more shot at the spotlight in 1925 when he prosecuted John Scopes in Dayton, Tennessee, for teaching evolution over divine creation. Known as the "Scopes Monkey Trial," Bryan railed against Darwinian science and won the case. Scopes was found guilty and fined $100, but in keeping with past defeats, the verdict would be later overturned on a technicality.

Five days after the trial, Bryan ate a large meal, took a nap and never woke up. He was 65.

 TRIVIA: The 493 electoral votes William Jennings Bryan amassed in his three runs for the presidency are a record for any candidate who never won the White House.

BALLOT BOX BLUES

"For me, dreaming is simply being pragmatic."

General William Tecumseh Sherman is remembered for saying, "If nominated I will not run; if elected, I will not serve."

Long-time Israeli politician Shimon Peres was just the opposite. He served, but wasn't elected.

The Polish-born Peres guided Israel through three terms as prime minister without once being fully elected to his country's highest office. The first was in 1977 when he became acting prime minister, succeeding Yitzhak Rabin who had stepped down but could not legally resign at the time. Peres held the job for two months before losing the election to Menachem Begin and his Lukid Party coalition government.

Peres lost the election to Menachem Begin in 1981 and in 1984, again coming close as his party won more seats than any other. However, since his Alignment Party was unable to find enough coalition seats to form a majority, an unusual power-sharing agreement was reached with Lukid. Under the deal, Peres served as prime minister for two years while Begin took the job of foreign minister. Two years later their roles would reverse.

It was *Close, But No Cigar* for Peres again in 1988 as his Alignment Party lost by one seat to Lukid, now led by Yitzhak Shamir. Peres and the Alignment Party renewed the coalition with Lukid but this time Peres did not share the prime minister's role. Peres would later lose the party leadership to his old rival Yitzhak Rabin but old Israeli politicians never seem to completely fade away. After Rabin was assassinated in 1995, Peres— who had been serving as foreign minister—took over the prime minister's job for the third time without having ever been fully elected to the position.

Peres made a bid to run Israel in 1996 but for the fourth time lost to Lukid's Benjamin Netanyahu. In Israel's first direct election for prime minister, Peres was defeated by 50.5% to 49.5%. But the Israeli politician wasn't done losing—in 2001 he was narrowly beaten by Moshe Katsav in the race for the mostly ceremonial position of Israeli president.

But you can't lose them all. In 2007, the nearly-man of Israeli politics was finally elected, this time becoming the nation's ninth *president.* It capped a long political career that began in 1959 and concluded with Peres having held every major Israeli cabinet position over a 54-year career. When he retired in 2014, Peres was—at 90—the world's oldest head of state. He died two years later at age 93.

 TRIVIA: Golda Meir, Israel's fourth prime minister, grew up in Milwaukee where she helped her mother run a grocery store.

SECONDARY SECRETARY

"Being a woman has only bothered me in climbing trees."

It was a major step toward gender balance when in 1933, Frances Perkins became the first female cabinet minister in U.S. history.

The second step took a while.

Perkins was inspired by a tragedy. On March 25, 1911; she witnessed first-hand the deaths of 146 garment workers, mostly women, in the Triangle Shirtwaist Fire in Manhattan. As a result, Perkins began fighting for worker rights. She became New York State's labor commissioner in 1929 and four years later, President Roosevelt named her Secretary of Labor. "Being a woman has only bothered me in climbing trees," Perkins said to critics of her appointment. She went on to support Roosevelt's New Deal, fought for minimum wage and helped boost the Social Security System. She was one of only two cabinet ministers to serve throughout Roosevelt's 12 years in office.

But change doesn't come quickly, and in this case it was glacial.

Twenty more years passed before a second woman was named to the

U.S. cabinet. Roosevelt himself didn't name any more women, and his successor, Harry Truman, had all-male cabinets. But one of Dwight D. Eisenhower's earliest acts upon becoming president in 1953 was to name Oveta Culp Hobby first secretary of the Department of Health, Education and Welfare. The Texas-born Hobby gained prominence during the Second World War when she headed the first Women's Auxiliary Army Air Corps. Hobby served three years as HEW secretary, her major accomplishments besides founding the agency, include approving Jonas Salk's polio vaccine in 1955. After leaving HEW, she became publisher of the *Houston Post*, a position she held until 1983. She died in 1995.

You'd think Hobby's appointment would have opened the door to more women. It didn't. In fact, it took another 22 years before Patricia Roberts Harris became the third woman to serve as a U.S. cabinet secretary. She followed in Hobby's footsteps becoming HEW secretary in 1977 (the agency was renamed the Department of Health and Human Resources during her time in office). Since then, another 29 women have served as secretaries in the U.S. cabinet, including Madeline Albright, Condoleezza Rice, and Hillary Rodham Clinton in the highest-ranking post, Secretary of State.

We'll leave the last word to Hobby. "Regard each man, each woman, as an individual, not as a Catholic, a Protestant, or a Jew, not as an Indian, American or European. Like or dislike a person for his own intrinsic qualities—not because he belongs to a different race or subscribes to a different religion. Dignify man with individuality."

TRIVIA: The first U.S. cabinet under George Washington had just five secretaries: State, War, Treasury, Postmaster General and Attorney General.

PRESIDENTIAL SECOND

"The most insignificant office."

The second U.S. president was also the first to hold the country's second-highest office.

John Adams succeeded George Washington as president of the U.S., serving from 1797 to 1801. Before that he had served as Washington's vice-president for eight years. A key figure in America's fight to gain independence from Britain, Adams was a strong critic of the oppressive taxes and tariffs Britain imposed on colonial America.

Born in 1735 in Braintree (now Quincy), Massachusetts, the future president was a direct descendant of Puritan colonists. He graduated from Harvard in 1755 and began a career in law three years later. Despite his opposition to British rule, he made a name for himself defending British soldiers accused of murder in the Boston Massacre. While this action didn't aid his popularity, it did cement his reputation as a fair and principled man.

Adams got involved in the patriot cause and was elected to the Massachusetts assembly in 1774. It was he who nominated George Washington as commander-in-chief of the Continental Army, and it was Adams who nominated Thomas Jefferson to draft the Declaration of Independence. Adams helped negotiate the Treaty of Paris, which ended the Revolutionary War, and during a decade-long stay in Europe, arranged several treaties of commerce with several European nations. After returning from Europe where he served as America's first ambassador to Britain, he was elected in 1789 as vice-president for the first of two terms under Washington.

Adams took a dim view of the vice-presidency. "My country has in its wisdom contrived for me the most insignificant office that ever the invention of man contrived or his imagination conceived," he said. Washington kept his vice-president in the dark on important matters during his eight years as president which frustrated Adams. When Washington retired in 1796, Adams ran for the big chair and won, edging out Thomas Jefferson. Much of

Adams' one term as president was focussed on peace between the U.S. and France. It was an unpopular stance, but not as unpopular as his Alien and Sedition Acts, giving government broad powers to deport "enemy" aliens and arrest opponents of government. Not surprisingly, Adams was defeated by Jefferson in his 1800 re-election bid.

After the defeat, Adams retired to his farm in Massachusetts. He wrote extensively and had a long correspondence with his rival, Thomas Jefferson. He lived long enough to see his son John Quincy Adams become the sixth president in 1825. In one of the great coincidences of history, he and Jefferson died on the same day—July 4, 1826—on the 50th anniversary of the signing of the Declaration of Independence. Adams's last reported words were "Thomas Jefferson still survives," though he had no way of knowing that Jefferson had died first.

 TRIVIA: Adams became the first president to live in the White House, which in those days was variously referred to as the "President's Palace," "Presidential Mansion" or the "President's House."

THE OTHER WHITE HOUSE

"It's a home, not an institution."

As the home and office of one of the most powerful persons on Earth, the White House is one of the world's most recognizable buildings. But what about the home of his second-in-command, the vice-president?

Built in 1893, nearly a century after completion of the White House, the vice-president's residence is located at Number One Observatory Circle on the grounds of the United States Naval Observatory in Washington, D.C. Originally, the Queen Anne style house was home to the superintendent of the Naval Observatory, but in 1923 the chief of naval operations liked it so much he evicted the superintendent and moved in himself. That changed in 1974 when Congress agreed to refurbish the house to accommodate the vice-president. Previously, vice-presidents lived in their own homes, but cost of ever-changing security measures proved too much and a permanent residence was needed.

The first vice-president to actually live at Number One Observatory Circle was Walter Mondale. Gerald Ford was eligible but he took over from Nixon before he could move in. His vice-president, Nelson Rockefeller, chose not to live in the three-story, 9,150-square-foot brick mansion, and used it instead for entertaining. However, every vice-president since Mondale has lived in the house.

The presence of the vice-president hasn't interrupted work at the Naval Observatory. Scientists there still make observations of the sun, moon, planets and stars. They also determine and distribute precise time, and publish astronomical data needed for accurate navigation.

 TRIVIA: The vice-president also has a ceremonial office, located next to the West Wing on the White House premises.

MILLER TIME

"Who the hell is William Miller?"

As obscure losing vice-presidential candidates go, William Miller might be the most obscure.

Miller, a seven-term representative from New York, was Barry Goldwater's surprise pick for vice-president when the Arizona senator ran for president in 1964. Goldwater said he choose the little-known Miller "because he drives (Lyndon) Johnson nuts," referring to the presidential Democratic candidate in 1964. So obscure was Miller that it led to a Democrat campaign slogan, "Here's a riddle, it's a killer / Who the hell is William Miller?"

Born in Lockport, New York, in 1914, Miller was an outstanding debater in high school—one contemporary remembers him as a "scrappy little son-of-a-gun." He got an early taste of politics when he was elected head of the student government at Notre Dame. Admitted to the bar in 1938, Miller served as an assistant prosecutor at the Nazi war criminal trials at Nuremburg. He was named assistant district attorney for Niagara County, appointed to district attorney by New York Governor Thomas Dewey and then elected to the post in 1948. Though initially reluctant to get into politics, Miller served 14 years in Congress after winning an election for New York representative in 1950. Still, he was a virtual unknown when picked by Goldwater.

A supporter of civil rights legislation, statehood for Alaska and Hawaii, and an increase in minimum wage, Miller was nonetheless more interested in politics than policy, a "partisan hell-raiser more than a lawmaker" is how one biographer describes him. Miller won the chairmanship of the Republican Congressional Committee in 1960, and helped lead his party to a remarkable 22-seat increase that November. Despite a less-than-stellar showing by his party in the 1962 elections, Goldwater offered the vice-presidential spot to him in 1964 with the words, "Bill, I'm going to be walking down a long, lonely road. I wondered if you'd like to come along."

Despite Miller's relentless attacks on Johnson, the Goldwater-Miller ticket went down to one of the worst defeats in history. While Goldwater would serve as U.S. Senator for Arizona until 1987, Miller left politics forever. "I worked so hard as a candidate for vice-president, and it turned out so badly, that I decided I'd never work again," he quipped. Not one to take himself seriously, Miller appeared in a 1975 American Express TV commercial during which he asked, "Do you know me?" The fact is, few did, even though he had run for vice-president just a decade earlier.

 TRIVIA: William Miller was the first Catholic to run for vice-president on a Republican ticket.

A MAN OF THE PEOPLE

"How inestimable is an honest man?"

S ir John A. Macdonald is such a towering figure in Canadian history that the man who followed him as the second prime minister has been completely overshadowed. Nevertheless, Alexander Mackenzie had more than his share of accomplishments. You just have to dig for them.

Mackenzie literally helped build Canada. A stonemason by trade, he helped construct the Welland Canal, the Martello Towers at Fort Henry and many other structures that stand to this day. But his biggest accomplishment is something Canadians look upon with pride every day: the Parliament Buildings. Mackenzie oversaw drafting and completion of the iconic structures. In fact, the Mackenzie Building in the West Block is named after him.

Born in Scotland in 1822, Mackenzie arrived in Canada when he was 20 and quickly plunged into politics. He helped Reform politician George Brown—founder of the *Toronto Globe*—win a seat in the Legislative Assembly of the Province of Canada in 1851. Mackenzie launched his own paper, the *Lambton Shield*, and followed Brown into the legislative assembly in 1861. He was elected to parliament in the first Canadian elections in 1867 and became the first official Liberal Party leader in 1873. It was good timing for Mackenzie, who became prime minister later that year when the Conservative government of Sir John A. Macdonald fell.

Honest and hard-working, Mackenzie made the best of his only term as prime minister. He created the Supreme Court of Canada, established the offices of the Auditor General and the Attorney General and streamlined the way government worked. He initiated use of the secret ballot, and the requirement that all ridings vote on the same day. He founded the Royal Military College, and the North West Mounted Police, today's RCMP.

Mackenzie's downfall was the economy—the country was in such severe financial depression during his term that he was unable to alleviate it. A free trade agreement with the U.S. that eliminated high protective tariffs on Canadian goods did not help matters either. In addition, Mackenzie's meddling in the transcontinental railway slowed CPR construction to a crawl. The Liberals were swept out of power by the Macdonald Conservatives in 1878 and Mackenzie resigned as Liberal leader two years later.

Mackenzie refused a knighthood three times because it didn't jibe with his working-class upbringing (he is the only prime minister of the first eight who was never knighted). On a tour of Fort Henry, for instance, Mackenzie asked his soldier escort if he knew the thickness of the wall beside them. When the soldier said no, the former stonemason replied—no doubt with a twinkle in his eye—"I do. It is five feet, ten inches. I know, because I built it myself."

Mackenzie stayed on as MP until his death in 1892 caused by stroke suffered in a fall where he struck his head. His last words were "Oh, take me home."

> **TRIVIA:** The last Canadian prime minister to be knighted was Sir Robert Borden in 1914.

THE PERENNIAL CANDIDATE

"Champion of hookers, gamblers and dope smokers."

He's the biggest political loser on the planet, yet John "The Engineer" Turmel keeps coming back for more.

Turmel is in the *Guinness World Records* for the most elections contested and the most elections lost. Since 1979, the self-described professional gambler from Brantford, Ontario, has lost 94 out of 95 contested elections. He'd have a perfect record except for the fact that a scheduled 2008 by-election was cancelled (he considers that a tie).

Turmel's quixotic journey through the Canadian electoral process began with the federal election of May 1979. Running as the "champion of hookers, gamblers and dope smokers," Turmel won 193 votes as an independent in Ottawa West. Regrettably, his campaign to abolish interest rates didn't quite catch on. But no problem, there are plenty of elections, and multiple levels of government.

Since that first loss, Turmel has run federally, provincially and municipally. He's run every year except 1989 and 1992. He's run for Social Credit, Social Credit Party of Ontario, Independent Social Credit, Christian Credit, Abolitionist Party, Independent Abolitionist, Pauper Party, Independent creditiste and as an Independent. He's run in Ontario, Quebec and Nova Scotia. He's run for Member of Parliament (MP), Member of Provincial Parliament (MPP), Member of the National Assembly (MNA), Member of the Legislative Assembly (MLA), mayor, regional chair and alderman. He lost every time ... badly.

"I want no cops in gambling, sex or drugs or rock and roll, I want no usury on loans, pay cash or time, no dole," Turmel told the *Toronto Star* before another losing campaign.

While he's never come close to winning, Turmel did garner 3,123 votes and a personal high of 3.8% of the vote when he ran for mayor of Ottawa in 1988. It placed him a distant third—nearly 67,000 votes behind incumbent Jim Durrell. But over the years, wearing his trademark white engineering hard hat and royal flush tie, Turmel—who calls himself a "Libertarian Socred"—has remained a crowd favorite. And he doesn't lack for optimism. "You never know, someone's going to pick it up."

 TRIVIA: John Turmel's busiest political year was 1980, when he ran in five elections.

NEARLY PRESIDENT

"I never wanted to be vice-president of anything."

What if?

That's a question political junkies love to ask. And the speculation can be fascinating.

"I never wanted to be vice-president of anything." That famous quote belongs to Nelson Rockefeller, the four-term New York governor who nonetheless served as vice-president of the U.S. from 1974 to 1977. Rockefeller, a moderate who failed in three attempts at the Republican presidential nomination, was thrust into the national spotlight when Gerald Ford chose him to be his vice-president after the resignation of President Nixon. But Rockefeller was nearly elevated into the top job when two assassination attempts against Ford failed in September 1975. If either one of those attempts had succeeded, Rockefeller would have become president. Had Rockefeller defeated Jimmy Carter in 1976, he would have been the ninth president to die in office (fatal heart attack in 1979). Whoever was serving as Rockefeller's vice-president would have become president. All of this would have completely changed the course of history (no President Carter, probably no President Reagan) and the world today would be a different place indeed.

Richard Nixon's loss to John F. Kennedy in the 1960 election was one of the narrowest in history. So many things could have changed the outcome. Had Nixon been healthier for the TV debates–he had not completely recovered from a knee injury–he might have looked less sickly and therefore more attractive to voters. Had Nixon not pledged to campaign in all 50 states–an unheard-of concept today–he could have concentrated more on the "swing states" and the outcome might have been different. Had Nixon won in Illinois and Texas–both of which he lost narrowly amid suspicions of voter fraud–he would have had just enough votes to prevail in the electoral college. If Nixon had become president there would have been no Camelot, no Peace Corps, no Bay of Pigs and no JFK assassination theories.

After Nixon lost in 1960, he came back to win a similarly tight one eight years later. This time his opponent was Hubert Humphrey, vice-president under a very unpopular President Lyndon Johnson. Humphrey won his party's nomination after Johnson declined to run again, while Nixon continued a remarkable political comeback by capturing the Republican nomination. Nixon edged Humphrey in the November 1968 election, and the Democratic nominee could only wonder what if? What if Humphrey had known of and publicized Nixon's behind-the-scenes manoeuvres where he advised South Vietnam's president to hold off on peace talks with a promise of a better deal under a Nixon administration? What if the closely-contested states of California, Ohio and Illinois had gone for Humphrey instead of Nixon, giving the Democrat a clear victory in the electoral college? What if the campaign had lasted just a few days longer, by which time Humphrey's late surge of support might have pushed him ahead? A Humphrey victory would have meant no Watergate, no Spiro Agnew in the vice-presidency and no endless parade of comedians impersonating Richard Nixon. But it never happened and "The Hump" went to his grave in 1978 having never made it to the White House for anything other than a visit.

 TRIVIA: The first presidential election lasted nearly a month, from December 15, 1788 to January 10, 1789. Presidential elections didn't become single-day affairs until 1848.

ALMOST PRIME MINISTER

"The greatest prime minister Canada never had."

They had the keys to 24 Sussex practically in their hands, but never got to open the lock.

The list of folks who almost lived at the official Ottawa residence of the Canadian prime minister makes for some interesting "what if" scenarios.

Prime Minister Duff Roblin? The Manitoba premier almost won the Progressive Conservative leadership in 1967, losing to Nova Scotia premier Robert Stanfield by fewer than 100 out of 2,100 votes cast on the fifth and final ballot. We'll never know if Roblin would have gone on to become prime minister, but he almost got his chance.

Robert Stanfield came agonizingly close to the PM's job. In his first bid in 1968, he lost to newly minted Liberal leader Pierre Trudeau. In 1972, his Conservative party lost again, narrowly beaten by the Trudeau-led Liberals. Stanfield fell to Trudeau again in 1974, resigned his party's leadership in 1976, and the man some call "the greatest prime minister Canada never had" never did get the big job after three consecutive general election losses.

It's hard to imagine Canada in the late 20th century without Pierre Trudeau, but his election to the Liberal leadership in 1968 was not a slam-dunk. Trudeau led comfortably after the second ballot and went on to win on the fourth over runner-up Robert Winters. But who knows what would have happened if Winters and Paul Hellyer, second and third respectively, had combined forces? We'll never know. Winters died of a heart attack the next year after a game of tennis. He was 59.

After Trudeau resigned as Liberal leader in 1979, former cabinet minister Donald Macdonald was considered a strong contender to replace him (as was future PM John Turner). But before a Liberal leadership convention could be held, the minority Progressive Conservative government fell in a confidence vote and the country was plunged into an election campaign. Trudeau resumed the Liberal leadership, won the election, and Macdonald never did become PM.

 TRIVIA: The first prime minister to live at 24 Sussex—now almost uninhabitable due to poor maintenance—was Louis St. Laurent.

CHAPTER 4

HISTORIC TIMES

"In war there is no prize for runner-up."
– Lucius Annaeus Seneca

WRONG ADDRESS

"The world will little note, nor long remember what we say here ..."

I t was supposed to be the main event.

It turned out to be a non-event.

On November 19, 1863, 15,000 spectators gathered at the site of the Battle of Gettysburg–the Civil War's bloodiest clash. They were there to hear former Secretary of State Edward Everett speak at the consecration of the National Cemetery at Gettysburg. The event had been delayed several weeks to accommodate Everett, a highly regarded public speaker and former governor and senator from Massachusetts. Almost as an afterthought, organizers invited President Abraham Lincoln.

Everett's 13,607-word speech was given entirely from memory. It took him two hours. He spoke about the tragedy of war, and compared the battle at Gettysburg to the Greek's struggle for freedom several millennia earlier. He concluded by saying "wheresoever throughout the civilized world the accounts of this great warfare are read, and down to the latest period of recorded time, in the glorious annals of our common country there will be no brighter page than that which relates the battles of Gettysburg."

Everett's marathon over, Lincoln got up and addressed the crowd for two minutes. His 272-word speech, now known as the Gettysburg Address, has come to be regarded as one of the greatest speeches in American history. He began: "Four score and seven years ago our fathers brought forth on this continent, a new nation, conceived in Liberty, and dedicated to the proposition that all men are created equal." And finished: "that we here highly resolve that these dead shall not have died in vain—that this nation, under God, shall have a new birth of freedom—and that government of the people, by the people, for the people, shall not perish from the Earth." In his eulogy to the slain president two years later, Senator Charles Sumner called the Gettysburg Address "a monumental act," adding "the battle itself was less important than the speech."

Everett wrote to Lincoln the very next day. "I should be glad," he said, "if I could flatter myself that I came as near to the central idea of the occasion, in two hours, as you did in two minutes." Neither men had much longer to reflect on the significance of the speeches, however. Everett died January 15, 1865 after catching a cold, and Lincoln was assassinated three months to the day after that.

In his address, Lincoln also said, "the world will little note, nor long remember what we say here..." Lincoln was half right, but only with regards to Everett's "Gettysburg Oration" which is long forgotten today.

 TRIVIA: Abraham Lincoln was an accomplished wrestler who reportedly only lost one out of 300 matches.

RIDING INTO OBLIVION

I am a wandering, bitter shade,
Never of me was a hero made;
Poets have never sung my praise,
Nobody crowned my brow with bays;
And if you ask me the fatal cause,
I answer only, "My name was Dawes."

−*The Midnight Ride of William Dawes*, Helen F. Moore

Everyone knows the story of Paul Revere, the American patriot whose midnight ride made him a national hero.

However, there was another man who rode that night on the same mission. He took a longer, more dangerous route and—unlike Revere—managed to avoid capture.

But while Revere has become an American hero, William "Billy" Dawes has disappeared into the ashbin of history.

On April 18, 1775, American revolutionary leader Dr. Joseph Warren got wind of a British plan to cross the Charles River and march to Lexington to arrest John Hancock and Samuel Adams (the same Samuel Adams they named a beer after two centuries later). So Warren chose two men to go warn them: Revere–a wealthy Boston silversmith and colonial militia officer–and Dawes–a tanner who was active in Boston's militia.

Dawes was first to leave, at about 9:30 p.m., taking a land route to Lexington. He was a frequent traveller who was already friendly with the British guards so Dawes was able to move around freely (in fact Dawes barely made it out of Boston before the British halted all outgoing travel). He arrived at Lexington about 12:30 a.m., about half an hour after Revere, who had left at 10:00 p.m. and travelled the first part of his route by boat.

Dawes vanished into obscurity afterward. He went into the grocery business and was a supplier of provisions to the Continental Army. Some reports say he fought at the Battle of Bunker Hill. He died February 25, 1799 at age 54.

Why did Revere find such a lofty place in the history books while Dawes doesn't even get a sidebar? Better PR, mostly. In 1861, Henry Wadsworth Longfellow penned "Paul Revere's Ride," which glorified the achievement and ignited the American imagination. Dawes, on the other hand, did not draw any artistic attention, except for Helen F. Moore's 1896 parody of Longfellow's poem, excerpted above. Another reason may also have been that Revere kept a detailed account of his mission, while Dawes's role is mostly undocumented.

Fittingly for one so obscure, even Dawes's final resting place is in doubt– in 2007 it was discovered that he was probably, buried in his wife's family plot in Forest Hills Cemetery, not Boston's Kings Chapel Burial Ground as originally believed.

 TRIVIA: Paul Revere did not yell "The British are coming!" on his midnight ride because most colonists still considered themselves British and that, of course, would have been confusing. Instead, his accounts and those of eyewitnesses tell us he yelled, "The Regulars are coming out!"

LITTLE-KNOWN PIONEER

"I didn't get up."

One became a hero, the other slipped into oblivion.

On December 1, 1955, Rosa Parks made history when she refused to give up her seat on a city bus in Montgomery, Alabama. It was a major volley in the early years of the U.S. civil rights movement and led to many reforms. Parks–"The First Lady of Civil Rights"–would go on to become a national icon, winning a flood of honors before her death in 2005 at age 92.

But Parks wasn't the first black woman to refuse to give up her seat on an Alabama bus. Nine months before Park's brave stand, another American woman in Montgomery did exactly the same thing, but her efforts were barely acknowledged.

Her name was Claudette Colvin, and if you haven't heard of her, you're not alone.

On March 2, 1955, Colvin–a 15-year-old student–was coming home from school on a bus in Capital Heights, Montgomery. She was sitting near an emergency exit when four whites boarded. The driver then ordered her and three other black passengers to give up their seats. While the others complied, Colvin refused. "I'd moved for white people before," Colvin recalled, but she had recently been reading about the great abolitionists during Black History Month and said, "The spirit of Harriet Tubman and Sojourner Truth was in me. I didn't get up."

Colvin's actions violated local law, and police were called. The 15-year-old was charged with disorderly conduct, violating the segregation ordinance, and assault and battery. She was then thrown into a cell by herself but her family bailed her out. Her family and community were scared of retribution by the white community and on her release guarded the house while her father sat inside with a shotgun should the KKK arrive.

Colvin was sentenced to probation for violating the segregation ordinance, but was one of four woman plaintiffs in the *Browder v. Gayle* case that successfully overturned bus segregation in Montgomery and Alabama in 1956. Colvin later had a child and, experiencing difficulty in finding a job in the wake of her case, moved to New York in 1958. She spent the next three-and-a-half decades working as an aide at a Manhattan nursing home, had a second son and retired to the Bronx in 2004 where she now lives.

 TRIVIA: Montgomery was the first capital of the Confederate States of America.

FORGOTTEN FLIGHT

"It was like she never existed."

H arriot Quimby was one of the greatest flyers of her time.

But her timing was awful.

On April 16, 1912, Quimby made history by becoming the first woman to fly solo across the English Channel. Flying from Dover, England to Calais, France, Quimby covered the 25 miles in 59 minutes. It was quite an accomplishment for the 37-year-old, especially considering she had been flying for less than a year.

Quimby came to aviation quite by chance. Born in Michigan in 1875 and raised in California, Quimby moved to New York City in 1903 where she started writing for *Leslie's Illustrated Weekly*. For the next nine years, she did theater reviews, wrote about everything from political scandal to household tips, and travelled to Europe, Mexico, Cuba and Egypt as a photojournalist. But Quimby's life changed in October 1910 when she covered an aviation event and got the flying bug.

Quimby began taking flying lessons the next spring and proved to be a natural. In August 1911 she became the first American woman to receive a pilot's license from Aero Club of America. She then immediately started flying in exhibitions in the U.S. and Mexico. Flying was a dangerous business in those early days, but Quimby–described by one columnist as "a glamorous, green-eyed beauty"–brought style to it. She often wore a plum-colored satin flying suit and elaborate jewellery. Her spirit attracted attention and the *London Daily Mirror* agreed to fund her Channel flight in exchange for exclusive coverage. Quimby didn't disappoint, earning the nickname "America's First Lady of the Air."

Unfortunately for Quimby, her achievement was completely over-shadowed by one of the 20th century's biggest stories. Just one day earlier, the *Titanic* hit an iceberg and sank, killing more than 1,500 and relegating Quimby to the back pages. Some papers didn't even mention her flight.

What little fame Quimby had didn't last long. Her vibrant life and blossoming career were tragically cut short less than three months later. On July 1, 1912, she and a passenger were killed when her plane unexpectedly fell 500 feet during an aviation meet in Boston Harbor. And with that, Quimby slid off history's tarmac. "No one remembers Harriot Quimby. It was like she never existed," wrote one pundit about this brave flyer, despite the fact that she paved the way for Amelia Earhart and so many others.

 TRIVIA: Pilot licences weren't mandatory in the early days of U.S. aviation–the federal government didn't start licensing pilots until 1927.

PAGE TWO

The assassination of John F. Kennedy overshadowed a few other significant events.

Two well-known authors died November 22, 1963, the day JFK was killed. British-born Aldous Huxley, whose best-known work was *Brave New World,* died. He was 69. So too did Irish-born author C.S. Lewis, whose children's classic, *The Chronicles of Narnia,* sold 100 million copies in 41 languages. He was 64.

JFK's assassination also overshadowed the debut of BBC's *Dr. Who,* which would go on to become the longest-running science fiction television program of all time. The JFK assassination also put a pall over the first U.S. TV appearance of the Beatles on *The CBS Morning News with Mike Wallace.*

 TRIVIA: There have been at least 20 known attempts on the lives of sitting and former American presidents, including presidents-elect.

FORGOTTEN FIRE

"Wind, people, horses, screamin'."

It was the worst fire in U.S. history, killing at least 1,500 and possibly as many as 2,500.

But the Peshtigo Fire of 1871 has been largely forgotten, mainly because the Great Chicago Fire raged the very same night.

It was one of history's fieriest nights. Just after 9 p.m. on Sunday, October 8, 1871, a fire broke out at 137 DeKoven Street in Chicago when—as legend has it—a cow kicked over a lantern at Mrs. O'Leary's barn (in fact, the cause of the fire has never been determined). The blaze spread quickly, thanks to Chicago's abundant wood structures and the fact there had been a severe drought that summer. Chicago firefighters got a late start on the conflagration as a watchman initially sent them to the wrong address. By the time it was all over, up to 300 people lay dead, 3.3 square miles of Chicago had burned to the ground, and more than 100,000 were left homeless. It was called the Great Chicago Fire, and it was one of the 19th century's greatest disasters.

That same night, another major fire was brewing some 350 miles to the north. Several small fires set to clear forestland were accidentally fanned by strong winds. The result was a major firestorm. It led to the so-called "forgotten fire" of Peshtigo, Wisconsin, which remains the deadliest fire in U.S. history. Not helping matters was the fact that Peshtigo was centered around a woodenware factory, the largest in the country. An area twice the size of Rhode Island was burned and 12 communities were destroyed, none worse than the nearby settlement of Brussels. As the *State Gazette Extra* of October 10, 1871 said of that town:

> *Raged with terrific violence, destroying about one hundred and eighty houses, and leaving nothing of a large and flourishing settlement but five houses. On Monday morning, two hundred people breakfasted on four loaves of bread. Hopeless and homeless, they camp out on their land, and seemed struck dumb by their great losses. As the flames spread, people ran for their lives. Survivor Jane Phillips wrote this riveting account:*
>
> *Horses manes and tails blowin' to the right, on fire. Rigs coming out on the road everywhere. Some was wrecked and the people started to run on foot ... Little crick, wood bridge burnin' ... People digging themselves into the mud of a crick bed. Wind about to tip our wagon over. Passed a buggy, upset, women and children runnin' ... open well by the road. ... Man shovin' women and children down it. Teams, cows, people runnin' for the river. Goin' down hill. Rose, hold onto the babies! Hogs in the road! Hogs in the road! Wagon bounced right through a blazin' herd of hogs. Horses and oxen jammed into trees by the riverbank. Bridge on fire. Wind, people, horses, screamin' ... My shirt was on fire, ripped it off. I jumped out to get Rose and the little ones down to the water. Nothin' in the box ... empty.*

Despite the horrors and enormity of the tragedy, the press focused almost entirely on the Great Chicago Fire. The Peshtigo Fire, however, was much more widespread, covering by some estimates 1.5 million acres. And the official Peshtigo death toll of 1,500 could actually have been as high as 2,500. Who knows how many itinerant workers vanished, and how to count those who died and were found in piles of ashes never to be identified?

 TRIVIA: The Camp Fire in northern California in 2018 killed about 90 people.

KING'S NEAR-MISS

"I'm so happy that I didn't sneeze."

It's hard to imagine the 20th century without Martin Luther King. His work in the civil rights movement–highlighted by the Freedom Rides of the early '60s and his "I Have a Dream" speech in 1963–made him an American hero.

But history hangs on a hairsbreadth–a turn of fate–and a long-forgotten would-be assassin came perilously close to preventing King's soaring accomplishments.

On September 20, 1958, King was autographing copies of his first book, *Stride Toward Freedom*, at a department store in Harlem. A stylishly dressed African-American woman came up to the table where he sat and asked, "Are you Martin Luther King?" When King answered in the affirmative, the woman reached into her handbag and pulled out a letter opener. "The next minute I felt something beating on my chest," King later said. He had been stabbed. The civil rights leader was rushed to hospital where doctors saved his life in an operation that lasted several hours. The tip of the blade touched his aorta; he would have died had he as much as sneezed.

The woman's name was Izola Ware Curry. Born in 1916 in Georgia, Curry received little education and suffered from paranoid delusions that completely controlled her adult life. She bounced around from job to job, town to town, and by 1958 was renting a room in Harlem. Curry believed that King and the National Association for the Advancement of Colored People were persecuting her. Her delusions began to focus more and more on King which sparked her assassination attempt.

A grand jury indicted Curry on charges of attempted first-degree murder. She faced a 25-year prison sentence but was diagnosed with severe "insanity" and spent the rest of her life in institutions. She died in 2015 at a nursing home in Queens, New York. She was 98 and outlived King by 47 years.

King eerily referenced the assassination attempt in his "Promised Land" speech the night before he died in April 1968. In a speech at the Mason Temple in Memphis, King told of a letter he received from a ninth-grade girl who said how happy she was that he hadn't sneezed after he was stabbed. King told his audience that he was also happy he didn't, because if he had, he would not have seen the Freedom Rides of the early '60s, or given his "I Have a Dream" speech, or seen the passage of the Civil Rights Act of 1964, or have led the Selma-to-Montgomery marches of 1965. King concluded, "I'm so happy that I didn't sneeze."

Less than 24 hours later, King was shot to death as he stood on the balcony of the Lorraine Hotel in Memphis. The civil rights pioneer was 39.

 TRIVIA: Martin Luther King's legal name at birth was Michael King.

SAVED FROM A WATERY GRAVE

"It is that frightful death."

The list of notables who perished on the *Titanic* reads like a Who's Who of early 20th-century society.

Real estate magnate John Jacob Astor IV, mining heir Benjamin Guggenheim, Macy's co-owner Isidor Strauss and presidential aide Major Archibald Butt–these were among the most famous of the 1,500 who died

April 15, 1912 in America's worst peacetime maritime disaster.

But there were a number of other very well-known people who almost made the journey from Southampton, England to New York and survived only by a twist of fate.

Italian wireless pioneer Guglielmo Marconi passed up a free ticket on the ill-fated ship, opting to cross the Atlantic on the *Lusitania* three days earlier. Seems he had paperwork to do and preferred the stenographer on the *Lusitania*. Marconi, whose wireless invention was used to save some 700 lives on the *Titanic*, got lucky again in 1915 when he sailed on *Lusitania* just before the Germans sunk it. Marconi went on to see the Golden Age of Radio in the '20s and '30s before dying in 1937 at 63.

Chocolate magnate Milton Hershey had planned to sail home to America after spending the winter in France. But Hershey, who had paid a 10% deposit of $300 upfront, cancelled his *Titanic* reservations due to business matters and sailed on the German liner *Amerika* instead. Ironically, *Amerika* was one of several ships that sent ice warnings to the *Titanic*, which blithely sailed full-steam ahead toward disaster. Hershey lived four more decades– dying in 1945 at age 88, having built the largest chocolate manufacturing company in the U.S.

Financier J. Pierpont Morgan, who had his own private suite on the *Titanic,* complete with his very own promenade deck, was also originally booked on the doomed voyage. But the "Napoleon of Wall Street" who helped create U.S. Steel and General Electric, opted for more time in the hot tub at the French resort of Aix. "Monetary losses amount to nothing in life," Morgan told a *New York Times* reporter after the disaster. "It is the loss of life that matters. It is that frightful death." Morgan died in his sleep at age 75, less than a year after the *Titanic* tragedy.

Novelist Theodore Dreiser's publisher talked him out of sailing on the *Titanic*, arguing that a cheaper ship might be better. Dreiser took the advice and was aboard the liner *Kroonland* when he learned of the tragedy. Dreiser, best known for his works *Sister Carrie* and *An American Tragedy,* died in 1945 at age 74.

Multi-millionaire sportsman Alfred Vanderbilt was so late in cancelling his passage on the *Titanic* that some newspapers reported him as one of the missing. But the heir to the Vanderbilt shipping and railroad empire wasn't so lucky three years later. He was one of 1,198 who perished when the *Lusitania* went down on May 7, 1915. He was 37.

 TRIVIA: In addition to the 700 passengers and crew who survived the *Titanic*, three dogs are also known to have been rescued.

CHAPTER 5

NO PEPPER GAMES ALLOWED

"Nobody remembers who came in second."
– Walter Hagen

UNREMEMBERED RECORDS

"Hit 'Em Where They Ain't."

They are etched in memory, the great baseball records of all time. There's Babe Ruth's standard 714 career homers, which stood until Hank Aaron raised the mark to 755 (but we won't mention the guy who broke *that* record). And even the most casual of baseball fans can tell you that Lou Gehrig held the most consecutive games played at 2,130 until Cal Ripken, Jr., raised it to 2,632. Then there's Joe DiMaggio's incredible 56-game hitting streak—what baseball fan doesn't know about that!—and Roger Maris's pre-steroid era record of 61 home runs in a season which erased Ruth's long-standing record of 60.

Thing is, who held those iconic records before these giants of the game came along?

Does the name Roger Connor ring a bell? Probably not. Before the Bambino came along, he was baseball's all-time home run king. Connor took over the all-time home run lead from Harry Stovey in 1895. He retired two years later with 138 round-trippers and remained baseball's all-time home run king until Ruth assumed the throne in 1921. A quiet player who was never involved in controversy, Connor got little press while his accomplishments faded into history. In fact, he wasn't even admitted to the Hall of Fame until 1976—and then only by the Veterans Committee. Such is Connor's anonymity that he was buried in an unmarked grave until a group of concerned citizens raised enough money for a tombstone in 2001.

Baseball's Iron Man used to be ... Everett Scott. *Who?* Yes, another forgotten star. Scott held the major league record for consecutive games played before Lou Gehrig. The slick-fielding shortstop played 1,307 consecutive games between 1916 and 1925 for the Boston Red Sox and New York Yankees. He more than doubled the previous record of 533 set by Fred Luderus of the Philadelphia Phillies. Scott's streak ended May 5, 1925 when he was benched in favor of Pee-Wee Wanninger. Ironically, it was Wanninger that Gehrig pinch-hit for when he began his record streak June 1.

When Joe DiMaggio went on a 56-game hitting streak in 1941, he broke a record set a generation earlier by Willie "Hit 'Em Where They Ain't" Keeler of the Baltimore Orioles. Keeler's 45-game hitting streak spanned the last game of the 1896 season and the first 44 of the 1897 campaign. Or maybe the record was held by Denny Lyons. He had a 52-game hitting streak with the Philadelphia Athletics of the American Association in 1887, the one and only season in major league history when walks counted as hits. On two occasions, Lyons needed a walk to keep his streak alive. But now Major League Baseball does not recognize his accomplishment (in fact his "record" was discovered by a Hall of Fame researcher a century after it happened, meaning Lyons went to his grave in 1929 without realizing he made history, of sorts).

When Babe Ruth hit 29 home runs for the Boston Red Sox in 1919, he broke a major league record that had stood since 1884 when Ned Williamson took advantage of a short right field fence (of less than 200 feet!) at Lake-Shore Park. Williamson hit 27 home runs for the Chicago White Stockings that year. Perhaps it's not surprising, then, that all but two of his round-trippers were recorded at the home-run friendly Lake-Shore. That year Williamson shattered the major league record of 14 home runs in a season set the previous year by Harry Stovey of the Philadelphia Athletics.

 TRIVIA: The St. Louis Cardinals have the second-most World Series championships with 11 (the New York Yankees are first with 27).

DEM BUMS!

"Brooklyn Dodgers, champions of the baseball world, Honest."

Wait 'til next year!
That was the cry of Brooklyn Dodger fans for decades—and for good reason.

The Dodgers were baseball's most frustrated bridesmaids, losing the first five World Series they played. Founded in 1883 as the Grays and later known as the Grooms, the Bridegrooms, the Superbas, the Robins and the Trolley Dodgers, Brooklyn's National League team finally settled on the Dodgers in 1931. They won their first NL pennant under that name in 1941 and faced the New York Yankees in the World Series. With the series tied 2-2, the Dodgers led Game Five 4-3 with two out and nobody on in the top of the ninth. The Yankees Tommy Henrich swung and missed at strike three, but made it to first as the ball scuttled past catcher Mickey Owen. The Yanks then scored four runs to win 7-4, then went on to take Game Six and the series.

The Dodgers made the World Series again in 1947, this time with the great Jackie Robinson in their lineup. Again, the opponent was the Yanks and again the Dodgers lost despite two historic moments that went their way. First, in Game Four, Brooklyn's Cookie Lavagetto broke up Bill Bevens' no-hitter by doubling home the tying and winning runs with two out in the bottom of the ninth. The second moment came in Game Six thanks to Brooklyn's Al Gionfriddo's grab of a 415-foot Joe DiMaggio drive. But it was *Close, But No Cigar* again as the Dodgers were sent home disappointed with a 5-2 loss in Game Seven.

Three more World Series losses to the Yankees followed over the next half-decade. In 1949, the Dodgers won the National League pennant but it was deja vu all over again as the Bronx Bombers eliminated the Dodgers in five games to win the first of a record five consecutive World Series. After the Dodgers blew a 13.5-game lead to lose the 1951 National League pennant to the New York Giants, they bounced back to make it to the World Series the next two years. In 1952, Brooklyn appeared ready to take the crown when it took a 3-2 lead in games. But the Yankees won Games Six and Seven and Brooklyn was once again crying in its beer. In 1953, the Yanks took another Series from the Dodgers on Billy Martin's Game Six RBI single in the bottom of the ninth.

In 1955 Brooklyn once again faced the Yankees for the sixth time in 15 seasons. Their record in the Fall Classic to date–0-5. But *this time* the Bums won it, taking Game Seven 2-0 helped by a sensational catch by Sandy Amoros. Shirley Povich would write in the *Washington Post,* "Please don't interrupt, because you haven't heard this one before. Brooklyn Dodgers, champions of the baseball world, Honest."

The Dodgers went back to their losing ways in the World Series the next year, dropping the 1956 Fall Classic to the Yankees who were helped by a perfect game by Don Larsen. In 1957, Major League Baseball in Brooklyn ended forever as Dem Bums moved to Los Angeles. It was the ultimate heartbreak for Brooklyn, which was to baseball what Green Bay is to football. But at least Brooklyn was able to celebrate one World Series championship.

TRIVIA: Brooklyn also lost the 1916 and 1920 World Series as the Robins.

FORGOTTEN TRAILBLAZER

"In the wrong place at the wrong time."

One gained immortality, the other obscurity.

In 1946, the Brooklyn Dodgers made history when they became the first major league team since the 19th century to sign an African-American player. That's when Jackie Robinson inked a minor-league contract with the Montreal Royals.

A few weeks later, the Dodgers signed a second player, but the name

John Wright is little more than a footnote in history right now.

John Wright was a good pitcher. The New Orleans native got his professional baseball start in 1936 at age 20 with the New Orleans Zulus, a baseball version of the Harlem Globetrotters. The right-hander then moved to the Negro Leagues, where in 1941 he began pitching for the Homestead Grays, the Negro Leagues equivalent of the New York Yankees. Described as being "as good as Satchel Paige" by long-time Negro Leagues observer George "Tex" Stephens, Wright joined the Navy in 1943 and two years later posted a 15-4 record for the Brooklyn Naval Air Base team.

Though it wasn't publicized, reports indicate the Dodgers signed Wright about a month after getting Robinson's name on a contract in October 1945. Despite his excellent credentials as a pitcher, it appears Dodger general manager Branch Rickey considered Wright as little more than a companion for Robinson and had no real plans for the pitcher. But, as Robinson summed it up, John had all the ability there was but he couldn't stand the pressure of going up into the Bigs.

While Robinson starred, Wright fared poorly with Montreal. Struggling with his control, he was soon demoted to the team's Class C outfit in Trois-Rivieres, Quebec. There he went 12-8 with a 4.15 ERA, capping his season by winning the championship game. He returned to the Grays in 1947–making the all-star team–before retiring the following season. Wright returned to New Orleans and worked at a gypsum plant, never publicly mentioning his baseball days.

John Wright, described by his team-mate Wilbur Fields as "a happy-go-lucky person who was in the wrong place at the wrong time," died in 1990 at age 73.

 TRIVIA: The first African-American player in Major League Baseball may have been William Edward White who played one game with the Providence Grays on June 21, 1879.

NO NO-NO

"It's part of the game."

S o close, so agonizingly close.

That was the story of Dave Stieb's quest for a no-hitter in the late 1980s. Not once, not twice, but three times (including two games in a row) Stieb came within one out of a no-hitter, only to have it broken up. He also had two other one-hitters (for a total of five), plus three two-hitters and eight three-hitters.

Stieb's first one-hitter was on May 31, 1988. He allowed only one base-runner—a fourth-inning single by B.J. Surhoff—as the Jays beat the Milwaukee Brewers 9-0. There was little drama in that game as it was broken up so early, but it was a much different story at Cleveland on September 24. Stieb held Cleveland hitless until two outs into the ninth when John Franco hit a seemingly routine grounder to Manny Lee. But the ball took a huge bounce and went right over Lee's head into right field. Lee didn't have a chance and the no-hitter was gone.

Stieb got another opportunity just six days later at Toronto's Exhibition Stadium. In his final start of the season against the Baltimore Orioles, the Jays right-hander again made it to two outs in the ninth with a no-hitter intact. But it was *Close, But No Cigar* for Stieb again, when pinch-hitter Jim Traber blooped a single past Fred McGriff into shallow right. Stieb became the first and only pitcher in major league history to lose a no-hitter with two out in the ninth in consecutive games. He then made it three one-hitters in four starts when, on April 10, 1989 at Yankee Stadium, Stieb allowed only one hit in an 8-0 Jays' victory. Jamie Quirk, who had only two hits for the Yankees the entire 1989 season, stroked the only New York safety.

But Stieb's close brushes with history weren't over. On August 4, 1989 at the brand-new Skydome, the Jays heartbreak kid retired the first 26 Yankees he faced before Roberto Kelly came to bat. You guessed it. Kelly ripped a double to left field to rob Stieb of what would have been the 13th perfect game in major league history. "It's part of the game," said Stieb afterwards, who finished with a two-hitter in the Jays' 2-1 win. Said Kelly, "I know he's got a no-hitter and a perfect game. I just wanted to break it up."

After the third two-outs-in-the-ninth miss, Stieb said, "If I hadn't got a no-hitter after three times, I doubt I ever will." But he did—after one more close call on August 26, 1989, against the Milwaukee Brewers. This time it was Robin Yount's sixth-inning single which marked Milwaukee's only hit as the Jays won 7-0. One year and one week later, Stieb's performance matched the title of his 1986 biography—*Tomorrow I'll Be Perfect*. On September 2, 1990, Stieb finally tossed a no-hitter in a 3-0 triumph in Cleveland. The final out was a Jerry Browne line drive to Junior Felix in right field. Close, and Finally a Cigar.

Stieb's no-hitter was #37's last big hurrah with the Jays. He saw limited duty the next two seasons due to shoulder and back issues, finally retiring in 1993 as a member of the Chicago White Sox. Stieb made a comeback attempt with the Jays in 1998 then left the field for good, but not before the seven-time all-star recorded the last of his 176 career victories.

 TRIVIA: In the history of Major League Baseball, 52 no-hitters have been broken up with two outs in the ninth inning. In addition, 12 perfect games have ended with two outs in the ninth (in two of those cases, the pitcher finished with a no-hitter).

STRIKE ONE!

It could have been one of the greatest seasons ever.

Instead it was the season that wasn't, but *mighta, coulda, shoulda, woulda.*

Looking back at the strike-shortened 1994 Major League Baseball season, one can't help but wonder, what if?

What if there was no strike and the Montreal Expos—owners of baseball's

CLOSE, BUT NO CIGAR

best record at the time—had won the World Series, perhaps even bettering their American League best-record counterparts, the New York Yankees, in a matchup for the ages. Would the Expos—boosted by their first-ever world championship—have thrived at the gate afterward and still be in Montreal? Would the extra revenue created by larger attendance in the wake of their World Series championship have helped the team keep its core of star players?

STRIKE TWO!

No one has hit over .400 in the majors since Ted Williams batted .406 in 1941 (and he wasn't even the MVP that year, but I digress). No one has come closer to that magic mark since Tony Gwynn in 1994. When the players walked out on August 12 to end the season, the Padre's Gwynn was hitting .394. "Everything was rolling," Gwynn remembered years later. Not only that, he was on a tear, having hit .475 over his last 10 games. Free of knee problems, and in the prime of his career, Gwynn might have done it. "To this day, I really believe I'd have hit .400," said Gwynn shortly before his death in 2014.

STRIKE THREE!

Then there are the career milestones not reached due to the strike shortened 1994 season. Consider Fred McGriff, who probably would have hit 500 career home runs—he only missed by seven—and sweetened his chances for the Hall of Fame had it not been for the strike. Reliever Lee Smith hasn't made the Hall of Fame despite 478 saves. Had he not missed six weeks of the 1994 season, he might have been a lot closer to 500, and possibly, the Hall of Fame.

 TRIVIA: The World Series was cancelled only once before the 1994 strike. That was in 1904 when John Brush, owner of the National League champion New York Giants, considered the American League inferior and refused to play its champion, the Boston Red Sox.

SECOND TWICE

"It was tough."

He was the second African-American major leaguer in modern times, yet Larry Doby has another important second to his credit. Not only did Doby follow directly in Jackie Robinson's footsteps, he was also the second African American to manage in the Bigs. When Doby was named manager of the Chicago White Sox in 1978, he went where only Frank Robinson had gone before (Robinson become the first African American to manage in the majors when he accepted the role of player-manager for Cleveland three years earlier).

Doby was born to baseball. Son of a semi-pro player, the South Carolina product lettered in baseball and 10 other sports (!) at Paterson (New Jersey) Eastside High School. Before he even graduated, Doby started playing Negro League baseball in 1942 with the Newark Eagles under the assumed name, Larry Walker. After a two-year stint in the segregated Navy during the Second World War, Doby returned to the Eagles where he hit a sparkling .348, leading Newark to the 1946 Negro World Series championship. Little did he know he was about to make history.

Bill Veeck, who had long wanted to integrate the American League, jumped at the chance to sign Doby. With little fanfare, Veeck purchased his contract from Newark and the 24-year-old center-fielder played his first major league game July 5, 1947 with Cleveland. He struck out in his first at-bat against Earl Harrist of the Chicago White Sox en route to hitting .156 with two RBI in part-time duty that season. Doby's team-mates didn't make it easy for him, averting their eyes and refusing to speak to their new outfielder when he entered the clubhouse. "I knew it was segregated times, but I had never seen anything like that in athletics," said Doby. "I was embarrassed. It was tough."

As Doby's on-field performance improved, his team-mates started to let down the barriers. He won the starting center-fielder job in 1948 and responded with 14 home runs, 66 RBI and a .301 average. That fall Doby became the first African-American player to hit a home run in the World Series, and the photo of Doby embracing white team-mate Steve Gromek after the game has become a classic. Doby went on to record 10 consecutive seasons of at least 14 home runs and 50 RBI. Doby played the final major league game of his Hall of Fame career with the Chicago White Sox in 1959.

Nearly two decades later, Doby made history again with his brief stint as manager·of the Chicago White Sox. He was fired after a 37-50 showing and never managed again. "I can't truly say what kind of manager I was or could have been because I didn't have enough time," Doby said. "I thought I could have been successful. I thought I had those intangibles."

Speaking years later of his battles with racial prejudice, Doby said, "I had to take it. But I fought back by hitting the ball as far as I could. That was my answer." At a 1997 ceremony to commemorate the 50th anniversary of he and Robinson breaking into baseball, home-run king Hank Aaron said to Doby, "I want to thank you for all that you went through, because if it had not been for you, I wouldn't have been able to have the career that I had."

 TRIVIA: Larry Doby was the first African-American to play in the American Basketball League, a forerunner of the NBA, with the Paterson Panthers in 1943.

BOMBED OUT

"First in shoes, first in booze and last in the American League."

Major League Baseball on the west coast in 1942?
Lights at Wrigley Field the same year?
It almost happened.

The St. Louis Browns were struggling just to make ends meet during the '30s and early '40s. How bad was it? To avoid having to pay a groundskeeper the Browns used a goat to trim the outfield grass. They paid their players so poorly they had to go on unemployment in the off-season. The league had to chip in to help pay their utility bills. Laying off their entire scouting staff and cutting five farm teams helped but they were still in dire financial straits. So in 1941, the Browns–"First in shoes, first in booze and last in the American League"–made plans to move to Los Angeles.

Everything was set: they had a park (Wrigley Field in Los Angeles) and territorial rights. Browns owner Donald Barnes had worked out a tentative schedule, made travel arrangements and had *de facto* approval from the other owners to move. Cardinals owner Sam Breeden was so happy to get the Browns out of town and have the St. Louis market to himself that he was going to give his cross-town rivals a going-away present of cash. The American League was set to unanimously OK the move at their annual winter meeting on December 8, 1941.

But the Browns never went west. The day before–December 7, 1941– the Japanese bombed Pearl Harbor forcing the U.S. into the Second World War. With the ensuing upheaval, St. Louis's move to the City of Angels was scotched. The Browns stayed put until they finally left, in the opposite direction, to Baltimore where they became the Orioles in 1954.

Pearl Harbor also ended the Chicago Cubs plans to put lights in Wrigley Field in 1942. Like many teams, the Cubs saw the installation of lights as a chance to boost sagging attendance. Cubs owner, Philip K. Wrigley, actually purchased steel supports and electrical cable and stored the material under the stands. But the day after Pearl Harbor, he donated it all to the war effort. So instead of becoming one of the first major league teams to install lights, the Cubs were the last, finally playing their first night game at home in 1988.

 TRIVIA: The last American League team to install lights was the Detroit Tigers, in 1948.

CLOSE, BUT NO CIGAR

FORGOTTEN BASEBALL TROPHIES

"Baseball's Lost Chalice."

It's a familiar sight after the final game of the World Series.

In a champagne-soaked dressing room, the winning team is presented with a snazzy trophy showcasing the pennants of all 30 major league teams. It's been awarded to the World Series champion since 1967. It didn't have an official name until 1985 when it was finally dubbed the Commissioner's Trophy. The winning team gets to keep their 24-inch-high trophy, and a new one is made every year.

But what did the World Series champ get *before* the Commissioner's Trophy?

They got rings, just as they do now, but no trophy. The tradition of giving rings to World Series winning members dates to 1922, when the New York Giants defeated the New York Yankees. Prior to this, World Series champion teams gave players pocket watches or pins.

The World Series itself started in 1903 following the formation of the American League two years earlier. But post-season championships were also played in the 19th century. The first of these was a "World's Series" between the National League and American Association in 1884. In 1887, the winning team received the Dauvray Cup, donated by actress Helen Dauvray. Winners also received gold badges, similar to military medals. The Dauvray Cup disappeared after the Boston Beaneaters won it for the third straight time in 1893, giving them permanent possession of the trophy. The tradition was for players on the winning team to pass it around, but somewhere along the line the trophy vanished and became "Baseball's Lost Chalice."

Major league teams then started playing for the Temple Cup in the World's Championship Series. Donated by lumber baron William Chase Temple–then part-owner of the Pittsburgh Pirates–the 30-inch-tall silver trophy went to the winner of a series between the first- and second-place finishers in the National League. The series was held from 1894 to 1897 but apathy from players and fans alike put the kibosh on the event so the silver cup was returned to Temple. The National Baseball Hall of Fame in Cooperstown, New York, later purchased it for display.

Perhaps the most obscure—and certainly the shortest-lived—of baseball's post-season trophies is the Chronicle-Telegraph Cup. It was only contested once. At the end of the 1900 National League season, the *Pittsburgh Chronicle-Telegraph* offered a silver cup to the winner of a series between the second-place Pittsburgh Pirates and the first-place Brooklyn Superbas. Brooklyn won it three-games-to-one despite the fact that all games were played in Pittsburgh. The team voted unanimously to give the cup to pitcher Joe McGinnity, who pitched two complete-game victories without allowing an earned run. It was the last time Brooklyn would win a post-season series until the 1955 World Series. It was also the last time anyone won the Chronicle-Telegraph Cup.

Lastly, there is the Hall Cup, the oldest world baseball championship trophy known to exist today. Donated by cigarette manufacturer Thomas H. Hall, the cup was awarded to the winner of the 1888 World's Series, taken by the National League's New York Giants who belittled the St. Louis Browns of the American Association. Like the Temple Cup and the Chronicle-Telegraph Cup, it is on display at the National Baseball Hall of Fame. Now, if only someone could find the Dauvray Cup.

 TRIVIA: The Commissioner's Trophy is the only championship trophy of the four major North American pro sports not named for an individual.

JAPAN'S JACKIE ROBINSON

"I just wanted to play baseball."

W hat took 'em so long? That's what a lot of people were asking in 1995 when the Los Angeles Dodgers signed Hideo Nomo, the second Japanese-born player in Major League Baseball.

That a major league team would finally sign a player from Japan was not in itself a surprise. What was amazing is that more than three decades had elapsed since the signing of the first Japanese-born player.

Japanese professional baseball began in the 1930s, but it wasn't until 1964 that the MLB reached across the Pacific and dipped into Japan's rich talent pool. Japanese businessman Tsuneo "Cappy" Harada, who had scouted for the Giants in Japan, believed that getting Japanese players into Major League Baseball was a win-win for the U.S. and Japan. Giants owner Horace Stoneman agreed, so in 1964 San Francisco signed three Japanese players to minor league contracts: 19-year-old pitcher Masanori Murakami, catcher Hiroshi Takahashi, and third baseman Tatsuhiko Tanaka.

By far the best was Murakami. He posted an 11-7 mark with a 1.78 ERA with Class A Fresno of the California League. Most impressive was his 159-34 strikeouts to walks ratio. Mixing his late-breaking curve with an effective fastball, "Mashi" soon got the Giants attention and on September 1, 1964 made his major league debut at New York's Shea Stadium. After Mets organist Jane Jarvis introduced Murakami with *Japanese Sandman*, the young lefty struck out the first Met he faced, Charley Smith. It was the first-ever appearance by a Japanese-born player in the Bigs. Chris Cannizzaro then singled for the Mets, but Murakami set down the next two men he faced to complete a scoreless eighth and walked off the mound to a standing ovation.

Murakami made eight more appearances for the Giants in 1964, going 1-0 with a 1.80 ERA and one save. Displaying stellar control, he struck out 15 and walked only one in 15 innings. The Japanese lefty's return to San

Francisco in 1965 was in doubt for a time while the Giants and his Japanese team, the Nankai Hawks, wrangled over his services. An agreement was reached whereby Murakami would play another season for the Giants then return to Japan. He pitched well, posting a 4-1 record with a 3.45 ERA and eight saves while averaging more than a strikeout an inning. Nearly 27,000 fans showed up at Candlestick Park for "Masanori Murakami Day" on August 15. He made his only major league start that night, but didn't make it past the third inning in a 15-9 Giant win over Philadelphia. Murakami returned to Japan in 1966 and pitched 17 more seasons in his home country. He attempted a comeback in 1983 with the Giants but was one of San Francisco's final cuts that spring. Oddly, it would be another 12 years before Hideo Nomo became the second Japanese player in the majors—and six more years before Ichiro Suzuki became the first Japanese position player in the Bigs. As of 2018, a total of 58 Japanese-born players have appeared in a major league uniform.

Even though he was called The Jackie Robinson of Japanese Baseball, Murakami said he never thought of himself as a pioneer saying, "I just wanted to play baseball." But while his own description of his career as "so-so" is up for debate, there's no questioning the importance of the role he played in paving the way for all the Japanese players who followed him into the big leagues.

TRIVIA: The Cincinnati Reds are the only major league team never to have had a Japanese-born player on their roster.

NOT READY FOR PRIME TIME

"It was a tragedy."

If there were separate Halls of Fame for baseball "coulda-beens," "shoulda-beens" and "mighta-beens," David Clyde would be in all three.

It was 1973 and Clyde was going to be the savior of the Texas Rangers. The 18-year-old was the #1 pick in the 1973 draft, following a stellar stretch at Westchester High School in Houston. There he went 18-0 in his senior year, with a jaw-dropping five no-hitters (two of which were perfect games), and a microscopic ERA of 0.18. After signing with the Rangers for $65,000–big money in those days–a bright professional baseball career appeared to lie ahead for big lefty.

Clyde's star never burned brighter than on June 27, 1973, the night of his professional debut before a season-best crowd of 35,698 at Arlington Stadium (another 10,000 were turned away). Just 20 days after his final high school game, the 6-1, 190-pound lefty allowed just one hit in five innings as Texas beat the Minnesota Twins 4-3. "It was literally a three-ring circus," Clyde told *SportsDay DFW,* noting that the game was delayed 15 minutes by a traffic jam caused by the incoming crowd. Hula girls danced in the outfield, and a giant paper mache giraffe and two lion cubs were on hand as part of Clyde's splashy debut. It was a promoter's dream.

After 33,000-plus spun through the home turnstiles for Clyde's second start–a six-inning no-decision–Ranger owner Bob Short considered sending the young man down to the minors for further seasoning. But with fans flocking to the gate and the money flowing in, things were never better for the Rangers. So they left him in the rotation.

It was a disaster. Clyde finished the season 4-8 with a 5.01 ERA on a dismal Ranger outfit that went 57-105, the worst record in Major League Baseball. Clyde finished 3-9 in 1974 after winning his first three decisions and then was inexplicably benched for 30 days by Billy Martin, who had replaced Whitey Herzog as Ranger manager. Clyde developed arm trouble in 1976 and was traded to Cleveland two years later.

On August 7, 1979, the curly-haired southpaw threw his last big-league pitch. His early departure had been hastened by a rotator cuff injury. Clyde finished just 37 days shy of a major league pension. He signed with his hometown Houston Astros in 1981 and was pitching in the fall instructional league when he decided to quit, saying, "I wanted to get on with my life."

"He was really mishandled," said Herzog, who had asked Bob Short to send Clyde to the minors in his rookie year. "He was wild and the other hitters started sitting on his fastball. He never had the advantage of going to the minors and pitching against kids his own age. And he was really a good kid himself. It was a tragedy."

 TRIVIA: The #2 pick after Clyde in the 1973 amateur draft was catcher John Stearns, who spent a decade in the majors with Philadelphia and the New York Mets.

CHAPTER 6

SPORTING TYPES

"Second place is just the first-place loser."
– Dale Earnhardt

CLEAN SLATE

"I believe we have the power to keep the World Football League out of Canada."

They never played a game, never lined up for the national anthem ... or anything else. These are the teams that never were.

If you blinked you missed them. The Baltimore Claws lasted all of three pre-season games in the fall of 1975. Having never played a regular-season contest, the Claws are the shortest-lived American Basketball Association franchise ever.

The Claws came to Charm City from the Home of the Blues in a convoluted way. First, a group of Baltimore businessmen who "bought" the team for a million bucks couldn't come up with the dough, so a Memphis group was awarded the franchise. One day later, Memphis withdrew. The Baltimore investors got a second crack, and with a break on financing swooped up the team. They promptly named their new acquisition the Hustlers–and then re-named the team the Claws after complaints that the team sounded too much like Larry Flynt's naughty magazine.

Now that they had found a home, the Claws went after talent. But you need money to get talent. And Baltimore had none. A deal to get former ABA rookie-of-the-year Dan Issel from Kentucky fell through because Baltimore couldn't come up with $500,000 cash. Food costs money too, and it emerged that not only were several Claws not being paid their salaries, they weren't even getting their per diem meal money either. The Claws didn't even have warm-up uniforms for their first exhibition game, so the hungry Claws slinked onto the court wearing their red Memphis Sounds uniforms with a green Claws logo sewn over "Sounds" (hey, Christmas colors!).

The Claws financial woes came to a head when ABA president Dave DeBusschere asked the team to post a $500,000 performance bond. They came up with half the dough but couldn't get their hands on some $320,000 held in escrow by the city of Baltimore because they hadn't been paying their bills. Both sides threatened to sue but the Claws finally gave up, folding operations and inviting players to take whatever furniture and office equipment they could find in lieu of salary. The sight of seven-foot-tall basketball players, rooting through office supplies, must have been surreal.

No one put the World Hockey Association on the map quite like the Miami Screaming Eagles.

The team from the Sunshine State got everyone's attention when they became the first WHA team to sign a big-name player, inking Toronto Maple Leaf goaltender Bernie Parent to a long-term deal. But owner Herb Martin couldn't find an arena to play in, so WHA president Gary Davidson terminated the Screaming Eagles in 1972. A Philadelphia group took over the organization, changed the name of the team to the Blazers, and brought the WHA squad to Philly. After a season, the Blazers moved to Vancouver, then went to Alberta to become the Calgary Cowboys. The star-crossed but well-travelled team folded in 1977.

Even though they never played a game, you can still purchase Screaming Eagles merchandise—the name is just that good.

For a while in 1974, it appeared American professional football was coming to Canada—in the form of the World Football League. Toronto sports and media baron John F. Bassett stunned the gridiron world on March 31 when he signed Miami Dolphins stars Larry Czonka, Jim Kiick and Paul Warfield to big-money contracts to play for his Toronto Northmen of the upstart WFL. The trio were to get a combined $3 million over three years, an unbelievable amount for the time. Four-down football in Canada was just around the corner, or was it?

Marc Lalonde would have none of it. The Canadian Health and Welfare Minister proposed a bill giving the Canadian Football League a government-protected monopoly over professional football in Canada. "I believe we have the power to keep the World Football League out of Canada, and we intend to use it," were Lalonde's exact words. In other words: stay out Yanks! While the bill never passed, the threat was enough to send the Northmen packing to Memphis. Here it remained for over one-and-a-half seasons until the WFL drowned in a sea of red ink.

One of baseball's most storied teams nearly went to Toronto in 1976. With his team struggling financially, San Francisco Giants owner Horace C. Stoneman had worked out a deal to sell the team to Hogtown interests for $13.25 million. But Bob Lurie intervened, buying the Giants for $8 million to keep it in Frisco. Toronto, though, picked up a nice consolation prize in the expansion Blue Jays who began play in the American League a year later. That said, the NL Toronto Giants would have had some pretty good players in 1976, including Bobby Murcer (their highest-paid player at $175,000), Gary Matthews, Darrell Evans, Chris Spier and John (The Count) Montefusco. And just consider what kind of rivalry that would have created with the Montreal Expos! Hey, the "Spos" might still be in Canada had the Giants moved north.

TRIVIA: The Giants finally played in Toronto on June 10, 2002, losing 6-5 to the Blue Jays.

HISTORY AT INDY

"Will you wear make-up?"

From skepticism—and even outright hostility—to acceptance. That's the difference between the reception given Janet Guthrie— the first woman to drive in the Indianapolis 500—and Lyn St. James, the second.

Janet Guthrie made history in 1977 when she became the first woman to race in the Indianapolis 500. But making it to the *Greatest Spectacle in Racing* wasn't easy for the 39-year-old native of Iowa City, Iowa.

CLOSE, BUT NO CIGAR

Sportswriters suggested Guthrie would give out physically at high speed, that she couldn't make it 500 miles, that she couldn't race at certain times of the month. "It was probably worse than she says," Humpy Wheeler, former president of Charlotte Motor Speedway, told ESPN in 2013.

Worse came in the form of a rubber chicken that an Indianapolis Motor Speedway track guard waved at Guthrie every time she passed him. Or Jane Pauley of the *Today* show asking her, "Will you wear make-up for the race." Or the welcome chant she received from fellow competitors at Charlotte Motor Speedway, "No tits in the pits." Still, Guthrie persevered, finishing 29th in that first Indy start.

Guthrie went on to post her best Indianapolis 500 finish–ninth–in 1978 before fading to 34th the following year. She failed to qualify in 1980 and retired from racing the same year, having competed on both the NASCAR and IndyCar circuits and recording top six finishes in both.

Fifteen years after Guthrie's breakthrough, Lyn St. James became the second woman to drive at the Indy 500. The Ohio native was an already established name in racing when she made her Indianapolis debut in 1992. She had twice won the 24 Hours of Daytona, and competed in the 12 Hours of Sebring and the 24 Hours of Le Mans.

"I'm proud of the fact I'm a woman, I'm extremely proud that I'm a race car driver, and I'm very glad that I'm not the first," St. James told *The Associated Press* after qualifying for the race (she would finish 11th and win the Indianapolis Rookie-of-The-Year award).

St. James made six more starts at the Indianapolis 500, with a best qualifier of sixth in 1994 (her 11th in 1992 remains her best finish). She raced in 15 Indy-style races overall, with one top-10 and two top-10 qualifiers. St. James held 20 national and international speed records over a 20-year period. At age 53, she was the oldest driver in the field at the 2000 Indianapolis 500.

 TRIVIA: Forty cars started the first Indy 500 in 1911–there have been 33 starters every year since.

A FRIEND IN NEED

"How can I ever thank you for all you've done?"

One day he was one of basketball's most promising players, a gifted athlete destined for stardom. The next day he was permanently paralyzed, confined to a bed with little hope of a full recovery.

Of all the "what-if" stories in sports, few are as tragic yet inspirational as that of Maurice Stokes. Born into poverty at the height of the Depression, Stokes spent his early years in tiny Rankin, Pennsylvania. He later moved to Pittsburgh where he honed his skills playing sandlot pickup games against the best in the city, and then attended Saint Francis College in Loretto, Pennsylvania, where he single-handedly turned the small liberal arts college into a powerhouse.

Described by NBA legend Bob Cousy as "the first great, athletic power forward," Stokes was drafted second overall by the Rochester Royals in the 1955 NBA draft (the Royals moved to Cincinnati in 1957). Stokes became an instant star, the first true three-way threat (points, rebounds, assists) in NBA history. But tragedy struck. In the Royals' final regular-season game in 1958 against Minneapolis, the 6-foot-7, 240-pound Stokes fell awkwardly and was knocked unconscious when he hit his head on the hardwood floor while driving to the basket. Despite the nasty fall, Stokes nevertheless returned to the game and would suit up for the team's first playoff game in Detroit three nights later. It would be Stokes's last game. Telling a team-mate, "I feel like I'm going to die," he became ill on the flight home and was rushed to hospital.

Stokes spent several weeks in a coma, a quadriplegic unable to speak or feed himself. He was diagnosed with post-traumatic encephalopathy—a brain injury that damaged his motor control. With the Stokes family unable to pay his medical care, team-mate Jack Twyman stepped up. "Things had to be done immediately," said Twyman. So the future Hall of Famer became Stokes' legal guardian. But with hospital expenses piling up they needed a

CLOSE, BUT NO CIGAR

regular cash flow since the Royals had cut Stokes after his injury. That's when a hotel owner and basketball fanatic in the Catskills named Milton Kutsher suggested an annual charity game—and the "Stokes Game" was born. The first contest in 1959 attracted 30 of the NBA's best players, including Wilt Chamberlain who had been a bellhop at Kutsher's hotel. Kutsher provided the rooms and food *gratis*. The game raised several thousand dollars and became an annual tradition with the biggest stars paying their own travel expenses and playing for free.

Meanwhile, Stokes began a massive rehabilitation program in hopes of regaining his mobility. He would work out nine hours a day, while Twyman worked tirelessly in helping Stokes communicate. Eventually Stokes learned to speak again, though his words came out in a stuttering moan that was difficult to understand. Stokes was also able to develop enough flexibility in his fingers to type. His first message was addressed to Twyman: "How can I ever thank you for all you've done?"

Stokes' condition deteriorated afterward and he died in 1970 of heart attack. He was 36. The Stokes Game continued until 1999 in support of other players but faded out after that. Stokes was inducted into the Basketball Hall of Fame in 2004, a true testament to his post-injury struggle. Twyman accepted the honor with an emotional speech. When Twyman died in 2012 at age 78, the NBA initiated the Stokes-Twyman Teammate of the Year award.

"I benefited more from being associated with Maurice than Maurice benefited from being associated with me," said Twyman at Stokes' Hall of Fame induction. "Whatever I've done for Maurice I've gained ten-fold from him, just to be exposed to the person he was, on one side, and what he went through and to be exposed to the wonderful charitable thoughts and acts of many people in this country."

 TRIVIA: The Royals—now known as the Sacramento Kings—have the NBA's longest non-title drought, having not won the championship since 1951.

NO SHAM

"A big horse with a big heart."

Had he raced in any other era, he would have been hailed as one of the greatest horses of all time.

But Sham had the misfortune of racing at the same time as perhaps *the* greatest horse ever, Secretariat.

Few horses have run so well and received so little recognition as "The Magnificent Sham." The big, brown bay colt was fast–very fast. He entered the 1973 Kentucky Derby as one of the favorites after winning the Santa Anita Derby in record-equalling time. Sham also won in the Santa Catalina Stakes and finished second in the Wood Memorial ahead of Secretariat.

On May 5, 1973, before a packed crowd of more than 134,000 at Churchill Downs, Sham ran one of the fastest times in the history of the Kentucky Derby. No exact times are available, but the horse ran the mile-and-a-quarter no slower than two minutes and possibly as fast as 1:59.80 despite losing two teeth on the starting gate at the bell. But incredibly, that was only good enough for second place, two-and-a-half lengths behind Secretariat whose time of 1:59.40 remains fastest in the history of the race.

Sham also finished second in the Preakness, again two-and-a-half lengths behind Secretariat. In the Belmont Stakes–the third jewel in the Triple Crown–Sham went head-to-head with Secretariat for about two-thirds of the race. Then Secretariat–the 1-to-10 favorite–pulled away like a jet to win by a record *31 lengths* in a world-record 2:24 for the mile and one-half. Sham faded badly to last, 45 lengths behind.

Sham was supposed to race Secretariat again that August at the Whitney Stakes, but he was sidelined by a hairline leg fracture. He was retired to stud and never raced again. Sham's final record was five wins, five seconds and one third in 13 starts. His progeny includes the Irish champion Jaazeiro and multi-stakes winner Arewehavingfunyet.

Sham died of a heart attack April 3, 1993–six days away from his 23rd birthday. A necropsy revealed that Sham's heart weighed 18 pounds, about twice that of the average thoroughbred. Since 2001, the Sham Stakes have been run every January at Santa Anita in his honor.

Pondered Tom Callahan in the *Washington Post,* "What did Sham represent? Nothing to speak of, really, maybe the putt that lipped out, the fly ball caught on the warning track, the touchdown drive that died at the one ..."

 TRIVIA: Sham was Secretariat's half-cousin.

THE NAME OF THE GAME

"Nobody's come up with anything better."

Pete Rozelle hated it. Lamar Hunt suggested it as a joke. But from those humble beginnings came the name of America's biggest sporting event.

NFL and AFL officials struggled to come up with a catchy moniker in 1966 when they agreed in principle to stage an annual championship game between the two leagues as part of the pro football merger. The official name for the inaugural contest between the Green Bay Packers and Kansas City Chiefs on January 15, 1967 was the "The First AFL-NFL World Championship Game." However, in a letter from Lamar Hunt to NFL commissioner Pete Rozelle in 1966, the Kansas City Chiefs owner wrote, "If possible, I believe we should 'coin a phrase' for the Championship Game ... I have kiddingly called it the 'Super Bowl,' which obviously can be improved on."

Rozelle had no enthusiasm for the name, which was inspired from the hyper-bouncy "Super Ball" so hugely popular in the mid-'60s. The commissioner thought "Super Bowl" was too colloquial—"it had no sophistication," explained NFL publicity director Don Weiss. Weiss said Rozelle would have preferred "Pro Bowl" except that name was taken by the league's all-star game. "The Big One" was also considered and turned down by owners. "Ultimate Bowl" and "Premiere Bowl" were also rejected in a mid-1969 contest aimed at re-branding the game. "Kinda silly, isn't it? I'm not proud of it," Hunt told an *Associated Press* reporter in 1970. "But nobody's come up with anything better."

The fact is, the media got wind of the "Super Bowl" moniker in the summer of 1966 and it stuck, for good. The *New York Times* led off its September 1966 sports section with the headline "NFL Set to Open Season That Will End in Super Bowl." The *Los Angeles Times* also referred to the Super Bowl by name that very same day, and a week later it appeared in the *Washington Post*. By the time the 1967 game rolled around, it was in common parlance (though some contemporary accounts called it "Supergame") and networks had already started calling the day of the game "Super Sunday."

The 1968 game was officially called the "The Second AFL-NFL World Championship Game" even though everyone was calling it the Super Bowl by then. Green Bay beat the Oakland Raiders 33-14 in what would be the last game for Vince Lombardi as coach of the Packers. While the Los Angeles Coliseum was only about two-thirds full for the first game in 1967, the second contest saw the first of many Super Bowl sell-outs as 75,546 jammed the Orange Bowl in Miami. The Grambling State University Marching Band provided the half-time entertainment (the days of mega superstar rock acts performing were decades away).

The NFL *officially* adopted the term for the third championship in January 1969. The first two games were *retroactively* named Super Bowl 1 and Super Bowl 2. The use of Roman numerals to designate the NFL championship game began with the fifth game and have been used ever since—except for the 50th game in 2016. It was promoted as Super Bowl 50 instead of Super Bowl L because the NFL was having difficulty incorporating the L in its logo.

Just as the Super Bowl was named rather casually, so was the championship trophy designed. Tiffany vice-president Oscar Riedner sketched what would become the trophy on a napkin while having lunch with Rozelle in 1966. When the Green Bay Packers won the first Super Bowl in 1967, they got to keep the trophy which was simply inscribed "World Professional Football Championship." It was renamed the Vince Lombardi Trophy after the death of the Packer legend in 1970. To this day the winning team gets to keep a copy of the original trophy—it is not a permanent artifact like the Stanley Cup.

TRIVIA: At the peak of its popularity in the mid-'60s, Wham-O was making 160,000 Super Balls a day.

FIT TO BE TIED

"I hope they aren't going over there for a tie."

What's perfect for a book about non-winners? Ties. And we're not talking the neckwear variety.

A sure way to get booed at a sports event is to announce that the game is about to be declared a tie. That's exactly what happened at the 2002 Major League All-Star Game. With the game tied 7-7 with one out in the bottom of the 11th—and no pitchers available in either bullpen—the PA announcer let it be known that if the National League failed to score in the bottom of the 11th, the game would be declared a draw. Outraged fans at Milwaukee's Miller Field tossed beer bottles on the field and screamed "Let 'em play!" and "Rip-off!" Things settled down but the mayhem resumed when the game actually ended without a winner. After the fiasco, a rule was put in place requiring an All-Star Game winner and giving that team home field advantage during the World Series. It was argued that the games would now be more meaningful. "It was embarrassing," then commissioner Bud Selig said of what has simply become known as "The Tie." "I was tremendously saddened by it."

The headline in the *Harvard Crimson* read "Harvard Beats Yale 29-29," neatly summing up what has been called "the most famous game in Ivy League history." The headline was not a typo–it trumpeted the fact that Harvard's football team had achieved a moral victory that fall of 1968 by scoring an incredible 16 points in the final 42 seconds of the game, thereby salvaging a 29-29 tie with their Yale Bulldogs rival. The result was a shocker. Even though both teams entered the game with perfect 8-0 records, Yale, led by future NFL quarterback Brian Dowling was the favorite, but he could do nothing about that historic last-minute comeback by Harvard. Not coincidentally, it was the last tie between the bitter rivals as draws were subsequently banned in Division 1-AA football.

It was November 19, 1966. There was a minute-and-a-half to go with Notre Dame holding the ball at its own 30-yard line. They were tied with Michigan State at 10-10. Fighting Irish coach Ara Parseghian now had a big decision to make: go for the win and for sure retain the #1 college football ranking in the season-ending polls, or run out the clock, play for the tie, and *most likely* keep the #1 ranking. Parseghian choose the latter, running ground plays instead of playing the risky passing game. The game ended in a tie. And Parseghian's strategy paid off–Notre Dame and Michigan State finished #1 and #2 respectively in the polls, ahead of #3 ranked Alabama. However, Parseghian's play-for-the-tie strategy earned him a barrage of criticism in an era when sportswriters, not playoffs, decided the national champion. "It was like seeing John Wayne parade around the room in high heels and a strapless gown," fumed Alabama coach Bear Bryant, acknowledging that several of his own players would soon be going to Vietnam. "I hope they aren't going over there for a tie." An unapologetic Parseghian explained, "We'd fought hard to come back and tie it up. After all that, I didn't want to risk giving it to them cheap." Meanwhile, Michigan State lineman Bubba Smith had his own explanation for Notre Dame's season ending #1 ranking: "All the sportswriters are Catholic."

The longest baseball game in major league history didn't have a winner. On May 1, 1920, Brooklyn's Leon Cadore and Boston's Joe Oeschger hooked up in a pitcher's duel for the ages–a 26-inning, 1-1 tie between the Robins and Braves before some 4,000 on a Saturday evening at Boston's Braves Field. The game ended when umpire Bill McCormick called it because of darkness at 6:50 p.m., when he saw lights going on in nearby buildings on this gray, damp afternoon. Reporters and telegraphers submitted their game reports by candlelight as there were no electric lights in the press box. Previously, the longest game in major league history was a 24-inning affair in 1904, won 4-1 by the Philadelphia Athletics over the Boston Red Sox. While pitch counts are not available for the Brooklyn-Boston game, Oeschger guessed he threw no more than 250 pitches–most of them fastballs–while Cadore figured he tossed "at least 300 curves." It was a week before either hurler could pitch again (Cadore couldn't even lift his arm to comb his hair–*three days later*). Mostly forgotten in all this was the plight of Braves second baseman Charlie Pick, who went 0-for-11 to set a major league mark that still stands.

It has been called the Greatest Tie Ever. On New Year's Eve 1975, the Montreal Canadiens and Soviet Red Army played to a sparkling draw at the Montreal Forum in a game that is still talked about with awe. The game pitted the Canadiens–a team just beginning a dynasty that would see them win four consecutive Stanley Cups–against the storied Red Army team that won 32 Soviet league titles from 1947 to 1992. The talent on the ice was so glittering it was almost blinding. Montreal had future Hall of Famers Guy Lafleur, Ken Dryden, Larry Robinson, Yvan Cournoyer, Jacques Lemaire, Bob Gainey, Steve Shutt, Guy Lapointe and Serge Savard. The Soviets had goaltending sensation Vladislav Tretiak along with Vladimir Petrov, Valeri Kharlamov, Vladimir Lutchenko and Alexander Maltsev. It was the unofficial Championship of the World–at the peak of the Cold War no less–and it didn't disappoint as fans were treated to a non-stop thrill-fest of clean, fast hockey. The fact that the Habs coughed up a two-goal lead despite out-shooting the Soviets 38-13 didn't seem to matter at the end. It was a masterpiece, described by Pete Mahovlich as, "the best hockey game I've been associated with, in terms of goaltending, puck possession and so on." International hockey writer Joe Pelletier called it, "An absolute joy to watch." Montreal Canadiens 3, Soviet Red Army 3. No winner, but certainly no loser.

 TRIVIA: The Philadelphia Flyers set an NHL record in 1969-70 with 24 ties.

WHITEWASHED

"He's beginning to annoy me."

Jimmy White won practically everything there is to win in snooker—but the game's greatest prize always eluded him.

For much of the '80s and '90s, White was one of snooker's greatest players. The London native won the English Amateur Championship and the World Amateur Championship in 1979 and 1980 respectively—all before his 19th birthday.

The man known as "The Whirlwind" because of his fluid, attacking style turned professional in 1981 and began to turn the game on its ear. He captured most of the sport's big titles, including the U.K. Championship, the British Open, the European Open, The Grand Prix, the Masters and the World Doubles. He completed more than 300 century breaks (100 or more points off the break), only one of a handful of players to achieve that milestone in competition.

But all that success is overshadowed by his string of near-misses at the World Snooker Championship. He did everything but win the sport's most prestigious event, losing six times in the final and four more times in the semis. Add in another five quarter-final losses and we have a player who made the final eight 15 times without winning snooker's oldest Triple Crown event.

White's string of losses in the final began in 1984 when he was beaten 18-16 by Steve Davis. He made the final again in 1990 but this time lost to Stephen Hendry. John Parrott nixed White in the 1991 final for his third loss in the big game. In 1992, White became only the second man—and the first southpaw—to record a perfect break of 147 at the World Snooker Championship. But for the fourth time it was *Close, But No Cigar* in the final, as he blew a six-frame lead to lose again to Hendry.

After being beaten yet again by Hendry in the 1993 final, White made it to the 1994 final where he suffered his toughest final loss yet. In the deciding match, White missed a routine shot on a black ball which would have virtually clinched the title. His old nemesis Hendry then ran off 58 consecutive points to win his fourth World Snooker Championship, while handing White his sixth defeat in the final, four of them to Hendry. Interviewed after the match, White said jokingly of Hendry, "He's beginning to annoy me."

White never made it to the final again but has gone on to win other championships including the World Series of Snooker in 2009 and the World Seniors Championship in 2010. But while he'll always be remembered for the one that got away, White believes he can still win snooker's biggest event. "If I didn't think I could win I wouldn't play."

 TRIVIA: A variant on snooker called "snooker plus," with orange and purple balls, was introduced in 1959 but never caught on.

SECOND BILL-ING

"I could not hear a sound."

It was the biggest field goal of Scott Norwood's career.

With 4:18 left in the 1992 AFC Championship, Norwood booted a 44-yard field goal to give the Bills a 10-0 lead over Denver in a tense struggle at Buffalo's Rich Stadium. It proved to be the difference as the Broncos scored a late TD to make the final score 10-7. The clutch three-pointer made a hero of Norwood—but no one remembers that now.

What Norwood is *really* remembered for—and will always be remembered for—is the 47-yard field goal he missed that cost the Bills Super Bowl XV against the New York Giants. The Bills haven't come that close since. They lost the next three Super Bowls by lopsided margins and have watched all the ones since on TV.

It was January 27, 1991. With time running out, Buffalo quarterback Jim Kelly marched the Bills down the field to get within Norwood's range (his longest field goal that season had been 48 yards). Running back Thurman Thomas ran 11 yards to the Giants 29 and Kelly intentionally grounded the ball on the next play and called time out. Eight seconds remained as Norwood stepped on the field hoping to become the first player since Baltimore's Jim O'Brien to win the Super Bowl on a game-ending field goal.

"I could not hear a sound," Norwood recalled later. Frank Reich took the snap, the kick was up ... but there was a problem ... the ball was headed right ... "No good! Wide right!" ABC sportscaster Al Michaels exclaimed. So *Close, But No Cigar*. The Bills lost 20-19—the first of four consecutive Super Bowl losses for Buffalo.

 TRIVIA: Scott Norwood is still the third-leading scorer in Buffalo Bills history.

DID HE, OR DIDN'T HE?

"The silence turned into unimaginable uproar."

Germany has won a lot of World Cups, but the one they *didn't* get still haunts the Deutschlanders.

On July 30, 1966, a crowd of 96,924 packed London's Wembley

Stadium to watch the World Cup final between Germany and England. The game was a thriller, as a late German goal forced extra time at 2-2 before an estimated world-wide television audience of 400 million.

Ten minutes into extra time, English forward Geoff Hurst fired a sharp blast at the German goal. The ball bounced downward off the crossbar to the ground, then back out to the playing field. But did the "whole of the ball" enter the goal, as soccer rules require of a goal? Swiss referee Gottfried Dienst couldn't tell, so he deferred to his linesman, Tofiq Bahramov. The Azerbaijani official said it was in and awarded the goal to England. Hurst scored again in extra time—his third goal of the game—and England won 4-2 to claim its one and only World Cup title.

Controversy has raged over Hurst's controversial goal ever since. In or out? English supporters say it was, citing the position of the linesman and the fact that Roger Hunt—the English player closest to the ball—made no effort to score on the rebound. But some German fans suggest that Bahramov may have been biased, and his call may have been connected to West Germany's victory over the Soviet Union in the semi-finals (in the aftermath of the goal, Bahramov was referred to as the "Russian linesman," to the extent his real name was virtually forgotten).

In his 1967 book *1,001 Matches,* Bahramov wrote, "Goal? When Dienst came up to me and asked this question in his brisk voice, it seemed to me that all the stands could hear, as silence had enveloped Wembley. I confidently pointed the flag to the center spot. In a second the silence turned into unimaginable uproar."

Bahramov was awarded the Golden Whistle by FIFA for his "distinguished and fair" performance as a linesman in the 1966 World Cup final. He officiated at the 1970 World Cup and continued to officiate into the '70s. After he died in 1993 at age 93, the Azerbaijan stadium in Baku was named Tofiq Bahramov Stadium.

Dienst went on to officiate many more important tournaments, achieving the rare feat of officiating both a World Cup and European Championship final. He said he had no idea if Hurst's shot was in, as he couldn't see it from where he was standing. Dienst died in 1998 at age 78.

Was it a goal? A 1996 study by the Department of Engineering Studies at the University of Oxford said it missed being in by six centimeters.

 TRIVIA: England's best finish since winning in 1966 is a fourth in 1990 and in 2018; Germany has won three times since.

SECONDARY SKILLS

"I'd rather play lacrosse six days a week and football on the seventh."

Sometimes an athlete is so good at one sport their accomplishments in another take second place.

Case in point: Jim Brown.

The Cleveland running back won eight rushing titles in a nine-year run highlighted by the Browns' victory in the 1964 NFL championship. He stunned the football world by retiring in 1966 at age 30 after a career that included four MVP titles, nine Pro Bowl selections and a still-standing NFL career record of 5.2 yards a carry. The former Syracuse star was named to the Football Hall of Fame in 1971. But Brown's football exploits overshadow his excellence in his first love, lacrosse. "I'd rather play lacrosse six days a week and football on the seventh," Brown famously said about a sport that saw him earn three All-State selections in high school and two All-America nods in college. He closed out his college lacrosse career with five goals in just one half of play at the 1957 Collegiate All-Star game. Brown was named to the National Lacrosse Hall of Fame in 1983.

Case in point II: Ted Williams.

No one combined pure hitting ability and power like the Splendid Splinter. He had a .344 career batting average, the highest of anyone with 500 or more home runs. Williams twice won the Triple Crown, leading the American League in batting average, RBI and home runs. He remains the last player to hit over .400 in the majors, having posted a .406 average in 1941. He played his last game in 1960 and was named to the Baseball Hall of Fame six years later. But it was retirement that allowed Williams to devote more time to his other love, fishing. Williams was a world-class angler, and like hitting he studied and practiced hard to be the best at it. His specialties were tarpon, bonefish and salmon, catching more than 1,000 of each but letting most of them go. "Releasing a great fish," Williams said, "is about the greatest thrill I get from fishing." Williams was inducted into the International Game Fish Association Hall of Fame in 1999.

Case in Point III: Walter Ray Williams, Jr.

Pro bowling fans are familiar with the man known as "Deadeye," Walter Ray Williams, Jr., the PBA's all-time leader in tournament wins and earnings. What they might be less familiar with is the fact that Williams originally received his nickname for his prowess in horseshoes. The native of Eureka, California, is a nine-time world horseshoe champion, having collected six men's and three junior titles dating back to the early '70s. He got so good at pitching right-handed that he switched to south-paw finishing second in the 2005 World Championships. Williams was named to the National Horseshoe Pitching Hall of Fame in 1988 and seven years later made it to the Professional Bowlers Association Hall of Fame.

 TRIVIA: Despite hitting .406 in 1941 and winning the Triple Crown, Ted Williams was not the American League MVP that year—that honor went to Joe DiMaggio, who had a record 56-game hitting streak.

A.W.O.L. TROPHIES

"A full-fledged NFL mystery ..."

C all it "The Curse of Ed Thorp."

The Minnesota Vikings were the last team to win the NFL championship but lose the Super Bowl in the same season.

Then the Ed Thorp Memorial Trophy disappeared.

How the Vikings managed to win the NFL Championship yet lose the Super Bowl in the same season requires some explanation. It was 1969, the final season before the merger between the NFL and AFL. While the merger was agreed upon in 1966, it didn't take effect until 1970. So the first four Super Bowls matched the NFL champion against the AFL champion. Green Bay, the NFL champion, won the first two Super Bowls but in Super Bowl III the AFL champion New York Jets beat the Baltimore Colts, who remained NFL champions despite losing the Super Bowl. Still with us? The Minnesota Vikings managed the same trick the following season after they won the NFL championship then lost the Super Bowl to Kansas City.

The Vikings didn't just lose the Super Bowl, but somehow the now-obscure trophy they earned for capturing the 1969 NFL championship vanished as well. The Ed Thorp Memorial Trophy was established in 1934. It was named after Ed Thorp, who in the 1930s was one of the best-known referees in the U.S., an expert on the rules and an assistant to the president of A.G. Spalding and Company. After Thorp died in 1934, the league commissioned a trophy in his honor.

After going AWOL for nearly half a century, the Ed Thorpe Memorial Trophy resurfaced in 2015, in of all places the Green Bay Packers archives. No one seems to know how it got there, but it is now on display at the Green Bay Packers Hall of Fame.

Believe it or not, the Ed Thorp Memorial Trophy is not the only pro football championship trophy to have disappeared. Anyone seen the Brunswick-Balke Collender Cup recently? If you have, call the NFL. In 1920, at the founding meeting of the American Professional Football Association–forerunner of the NFL–it was decided that the championship team would get a "silver-loving cup." If a team won it three years in a row, they could keep it. The cup was donated by the Brunswick-Balke Collender company (today known as the Brunswick Corporation).

The league decided that the first Brunswick-Balke Collender Cup would be awarded by a vote of the league's managers. The undefeated Akron Pros, whose big star was future Hall of Famer Fritz Pollard, won the vote and was awarded the cup at a ceremony in the spring of 1920. That's the last anyone's seen of it. Its whereabouts remain a mystery to this very day. The Pro Football Hall of Fame in Canton, Ohio doesn't even have a picture of it.

"We're intrigued by the possibility that a piece of football history this important cannot be located," NFL Films Senior Producer Ken Rodgers told packersnews.com in 2007. "If a few more of our leads come up empty, we might have a full-fledged NFL mystery on our hands."

 TRIVIA: The Vince Lombardi Trophy was originally engraved simply "World Professional Football Championship;" it gained its current name in 1970.

CONTINENTAL SHIFT

"As inevitable as tomorrow morning."

They never played a game, never even got nicknames and even the most avid of baseball fans would be hard-pressed to remember them. They were the teams that almost were, in a league that never was.

The Continental League was a proposed third major league that emerged from the mind of William Shea, a politically connected New York lawyer who wanted to lure a new team to the Big Apple to replace the departed Dodgers and Giants. The idea was to create a league with teams in cities that didn't have Major League Baseball, complementing–but not competing with–the existing National and American Leagues. Shea announced formation of the new league on July 19, 1959. He would also head up the New York franchise.

Continental League franchises were also originally granted to Toronto, Minneapolis, Houston and Denver; three more cities joined the roster later: Atlanta, Dallas-Fort Worth and Buffalo. The first games were scheduled for April 18, 1961. The new league was "as inevitable as tomorrow morning," said Continental League president Branch Rickey as planning progressed throughout the fall and winter of 1959-60.

But there was lots going on behind the scenes. What the Continental Baseball League owners really wanted, rather than a league of their own, was entry into the heavily owner-guarded major leagues. Getting into the majors wasn't easy as combined National and American League membership had remained rigid at 16 teams since 1903. The Continental League, which planned to fill its rosters with major league cast-offs and minor leaguers, was really just a bunch of MLB hopefuls masquerading behind a future league.

The Continental League died on August 2, 1960. Major league owners announced that agreement had been reached with the Continentals to take in four of their teams, and eventually let in the remaining teams if the new league folded. Toronto franchise owner Jack Kent Cooke said he was "deliriously happy" at the news, and optimistic he would get a major league franchise. But Toronto didn't. Not yet. Minneapolis, however, got an American League expansion franchise for 1961, as did Los Angeles, which wasn't even part of the Continental League fold. New York and Houston got National League franchises for 1962. Atlanta made it to the Bigs in 1966 when the Braves relocated from Milwaukee. Dallas got the Washington Senators in 1971, and Toronto began play in the American League in 1977. The Colorado Rockies played their first games in Denver as a National League expansion team in 1993. Of the eight Continental League cities, only Buffalo never made it to the majors.

The Continental League never played a game but it has an important legacy: it forced the majors—a closed shop if there ever was one—to add new teams for the first time since Theodore Roosevelt was president. Finally, more major league-worthy cities would get to see the national pastime first-hand. As Bill Veeck once said, "if the baseball owners were running the United States, Kansas and Nebraska would still be trying to get in ..."

 TRIVIA: The last *third* major baseball league to actually play games was the Federal League in 1914 and 1915–Toronto had a franchise in the early going but never played a game.

PERFECT TEN

"I believed I was the fastest skater in the world that night."

On February 7, 1976, Darryl Sittler made NHL history with a 10-point night against the Boston Bruins.

The Toronto Maple Leaf star shattered the record of eight points set by Maurice "Rocket" Richard in 1944 and equalled by Bert Olmstead in 1954.

But while Sittler set the NHL record, he only tied a professional record that was forgotten almost as soon as the ink dried on the score sheet.

On January 30, 1973, Jim Harrison became the first professional hockey player to amass 10 points in a game, scoring three goals and adding seven assists as the Alberta Oilers clobbered the New York Raiders 11-3. Harrison scored once in each period as part of a 52-shot Alberta assault. He broke the World Hockey Association record of seven points in one game set by Philadelphia's Danny Lawson earlier in the month.

"I believed I was the fastest skater in the world that night," says Harrison in David Ward's book *The Lost 10 Point Night: Searching for My Hockey Hero*. "The puck seemed to follow me around and I was able to pass and shoot at will." Harrison said nobody really took notice of his big game until he finished second to the undefeated Miami Dolphins for the Wilkinson Sports Award, honoring the biggest sports achievement of 1973. His game did make it into the Guinness Book of Records. Harrison also wound up with 39 goals and 86 points on the season, easily his best in a pro career that began with Oklahoma City of the Central Hockey League in 1968 and ended with his retirement a dozen seasons later with the NHL's Edmonton Oilers.

No one has matched the feats of Sittler and Harrison since, even though nine players have posted eight-point nights, including Mario Lemieux, three times. The last was Edmonton's Sam Gagner in 2012. Can the record hold up? "You never say never, but it's a longshot," Sittler said. "There are very few times when 10 goals are scored by one team, let alone for one player to be in on all 10."

 TRIVIA: The junior hockey record for most points in a game is 12, set by André Savard of the Quebec Ramparts on February 5, 1971.

CHAPTER 7

SECONDARY SCIENCE

"You have to bear in mind that Mr. Autry's
favorite horse was called Champion. He ain't never
had one called Runnerup."

– Dale Gene Mauch

MISSED CONNECTION

"The history of the telephone will never be fully written."

Ma Bell?

It could have been Ma Gray.

By a matter of hours, Elisha Gray may have missed out on being "The Father of the Telephone."

On February 14, 1876, Gray filed a caveat at the U.S. Patent Office to file a patent claim for the telephone. However, just two hours earlier, Alexander Graham Bell filed a patent application at the same office for *his* version of the telephone. Based partly on the earlier filing time, and the fact Gray had filed a patent caveat and Bell an actual patent application, the U.S. Patent Office awarded Bell the patent for the telephone. *Close, But No Cigar*, Mr. Gray.

It was later discovered that the device described by Bell in his patent application would *not* have worked, while Gray's would have. However, Bell was the winner in subsequent legal proceedings–and the telephone is his.

While he didn't get credit for inventing the telephone, Gray has many other inventions to his name. He's considered the father of the modern music synthesizer. He invented the "telautograph"–a forerunner to the fax machine–and he also conceived of an early closed-circuit television system called the "telephote." Gray founded the Western Electric Manufacturing Company, forerunner of Western Electric Company. Just prior to his death, he tested an underwater signalling device to transmit messages to ships. All told, Gray was granted more than 70 patents for his inventions but if he's remembered at all, it's for the one that got away.

After his death in 1901 at age 65, a note was found in Gray's belongings that read: "The history of the telephone will never be fully written ... it is partly hidden away ... and partly lying on the hearts of a few whose lips are sealed–some in death and others by a golden clasp whose grip is even tighter."

TRIVIA: The word telephone is derived from two Greek words: tele = far and phone = voice.

BRIGHT IDEA

"It beamed forth in beautiful light."

The list of Thomas Edison's inventions is astounding. Among his 1,093 U.S. patents are the phonograph ... the electric generator ... the movie camera ... the light bulb ...

The light bulb? You probably thought Edison invented it. So do a lot of people. But think again.

While widely credited with inventing the light bulb, the illumination device that we take so very much for granted did not come from the mind of Edison. Instead, the first to successfully produce and patent the electric filament bulb were a couple of Canadians, Henry Woodward and Matthew Evans. Their problem? Money, or lack thereof, a familiar situation for many an inventor.

As often happens, the invention of the light bulb was part genius, part luck. In 1873 Woodward and Evans, neighbors and part-time amateur scientists, were conducting lighting experiments in their Toronto laboratory. They noticed that a spark from an induction coil they were testing was lighting up their workbench. Soon a light went off (literally): the two realized that if you pass current through a high resistance filament it raises the temperature causing the filament to glow, and *voilà*, light!

Lots of work still remained to be done. After much trial and error, Woodward–a medical student–and Evans–a hotel worker–developed a crude light tube filled with nitrogen instead of air so the carbon rod inside wouldn't catch fire. In 1874 they tested the device by attaching the electrodes to an industrial battery. It took a while for the carbon rod filament to heat up, but when it did the immediate area around it lit up. As Evans later remembered:

> *There were four or five of us sitting around a large table.*
> *Woodward closed the switch and gradually we saw the*
> *carbon become first red and gradually lighter in color until*
> *it beamed forth in beautiful light.*

Woodward received U.S. and Canadian patents for their incandescent light tube, but he and Evans ran into that problem a lot of us folks can relate to: money. They needed cash—but instead were sneered at. "Who needs a glowing piece of metal?" guffawed potential investors. Unable to raise enough scratch to see their invention through, the pair sold their U.S. patent rights to Edison in 1879 for $5,000 ($119,000 in today's dollars). Six years later Edison bought the Canadian patent.

The light bulb—once the subject of ridicule—took off once Edison got behind it. U.S. sales of electric lights reached 300,000 by 1885 as "The Wizard of Menlo Park" got richer and more famous. Woodward and Evans, on the other hand, were forgotten. Both men died in obscurity.

Edison, who died in 1931, still holds the record for most U.S. patents held by a single person. He's also universally celebrated as the greatest inventor of his time. Which he was. But he didn't invent the light bulb.

 TRIVIA: Thomas Edison liked Morse code so much he proposed marriage to his girlfriend with it and nicknamed their first two children Dot and Dash.

OVERSHADOWED SCIENTIST

"Melancholy, mistrustful and jealous."

He's so obscure that not a single authenticated contemporary likeness of him is known to exist.

Yet Robert Hooke was one of the greatest natural philosophers of his time, his thunder stolen by one of history's most famous figures.

The Isle of Wight-born scientist, architect and all-around smart guy was the first to conceptualize the theory of gravity, draw the rings of Saturn and craters of the moon, construct the first wheel barometer and was the first to examine fossils with a microscope. He also speculated about extinction 150 years before it was confirmed; identified and named biological cells; and as a surveyor played a major role in the rebuilding of London after the Great Fire of 1666. He published a best-selling collection of illustrations and observations made through a microscope, *Micrographia,* which established the field of Microscopic Biology. Whew! When did this guy sleep?

Hooke got off to a rotten start in life. Born in 1635–the last of four children–he was so sickly as a child his clergyman father was forced to educate him at home (until he died when Robert was 13). His brother would later hang himself. But Hooke overcame his problems to assemble an incredible body of work as a scientist and inventor. He constructed the first prototype of a respirator, invented the universal joint and a diving bell, came up with a method of telegraphy 200 years before the real thing, discovered the red spot of Jupiter and was the first to report on the giant planet's rotation. He's responsible for Hooke's Law–which states that the stretching of a solid body is proportional to the force applied to it. He was the first to demonstrate the elliptical paths of planets in their orbit around the sun–and oh, he also founded the field of Meteorology.

So why wasn't Hooke famous? Well, he happened to be overshadowed by a colleague who became very famous: Sir Isaac Newton. It seems Hooke didn't get along with Newton to the point where Sir Isaac–who was president of the powerful Royal Society–is said to have destroyed (or failed to preserve) the only known portrait of the man. Hooke doesn't seem to have been very well-liked–his biographer Richard Waller describes him as "melancholy, mistrustful and jealous"–but his main problem was that he was good at *too many* things. While Newton could claim to be the greatest physicist of the century, and Christopher Wren the leading architect, Hooke was–to use a modern expression–a jack of all trades.

After Hooke died in 1703, his work fell into obscurity for centuries but recent efforts have been made to raise his profile. A memorial to Hooke was added to Westminster Abbey in 2005, as well as an inscription mentioning Hooke's role after the Great Fire of London. He even has a meteorite named for him: the 3514 Hooke.

 TRIVIA: The biological term "cell" was coined by Hooke.

UNNATURAL SELECTION

"It's indelibly Darwin and the monkeys."

Great minds think alike.

In the mid-19th century, Charles Darwin and Alfred Russel Wallace both came up with the idea of evolution completely independent of each other. However, while Darwin got all the fame and glory, Wallace has sunk into the primordial ooze.

Born in Wales in 1823, Wallace was drawn into the world of science by a naturalist named Henry Walter Bates. He and Bates went to the Amazon rainforest to collect and study animal species. After collecting thousands of specimens, mostly birds, beetles and butterflies, Wallace set sail for England but his ship sank and most of his research wound up at the bottom of the Atlantic. A good student never gives up and a year later Wallace sailed for the Far East where he collected more than 250,000 different specimens. It took him eight years. His book *The Malay Archipelago* opened the world's eyes to the fauna and native peoples of the area now known as Malaysia and Indonesia. The book is still in print today.

Wallace's idea about evolution came to him literally, in a flash. He was lying in bed with a fever in Indonesia when a revolutionary thought suddenly came to him on how species changed and evolved: it was survival

CLOSE, BUT NO CIGAR

of the fittest—the strongest survived and passed on their best characteristics to their offspring, who did the same to their offspring. He wrote about it to his colleague and fellow naturalist Charles Darwin, who had independently been working on the same theory. Both presented their findings to the Linnean Society in 1858. The following year Darwin published *On the Origin of Species,* spelling out his case for evolution.

Though both came up with the idea of evolution at virtually the same time, Darwin has completely overshadowed Wallace. One big reason is the popularity of Darwin's great book, while Wallace was a rather modest chap whose championing of other controversial causes, such as spiritualism, diverted people's attention away from his evolutionary work. That said, Wallace didn't lack for recognition in his day—he was given Britain's highest honor, the Order of Merit. But when natural selection was resurrected in the 1940s after years on the back (Bunsen) burner, it was Darwin and not Wallace whose name survived the battle of the fittest—and it has stayed that way ever since.

When it comes to evolution and natural selection, biologist James T. Costa, an expert on both men, said: "It's indelibly Darwin and the monkeys."

 TRIVIA: Alfred Russel Wallace published 21 books and more than 700 articles, essays and letters.

A CLOSER LOOK AT THE TELESCOPE

"For seeing things far away as if they were nearby."

No one really knows who invented the telescope, but one thing's for sure—it wasn't Galileo.

While he's the one most identified with the telescope, Galileo Galilei actually followed in the footsteps of others. The first person to apply for a patent for the telescope was a Dutch eyeglass maker named Hans

Lippershey (also spelled Lipperhey). In 1608, Lippershey asked the Dutch government for a patent for his instrument "for seeing things far away as if they were nearby." He called it a kijker ("looker").

As legend goes, Lippershey got the idea for the telescope when he noticed two children in his shop holding up two lenses that magnified a distant weather vane. However, some folks at the time accused him of stealing the idea from another inventor, Zacharias Janssen. And as if that weren't enough to obscure the stars, yet a third Dutchman—Jacob Metius—applied for his own patent for the telescope a few weeks after Lippershey.

Next Galileo entered the picture. He'd heard about these "Dutch Perspective Glasses"—they weren't calling them telescopes yet—and quickly whipped together his own version in 1609 and pointed it toward the skies. What set Galileo apart? He was the first to explore the heavens with the device *and* publish the results. He was also one of the first to observe sunspots with a telescope, and it was he who discovered the moons of Jupiter.

Galileo's findings convinced him that Copernicus was correct: the Earth and the other planets revolved around the sun—and he put it in writing to his later regret. The all-powerful Roman Catholic church screamed heresy and placed "The Father of Modern Science" under house arrest where he remained for the rest of his days. He died in 1642. One-hundred-and-sixteen years later the church realized its error and lifted a ban on most works supporting Copernican theory.

So where did the name "telescope" originate? It comes from two Greek words: *tele* = far, and *skopien* = to look or see. A Greek mathematician named Giovanni Demisiani coined the name at a banquet honoring Galileo in 1611.

 TRIVIA: The Vatican didn't officially clear Galileo of all perceived wrong-doing until 1992.

HEARTBREAKINGLY CLOSE

"You can't always be first."

It was a medical miracle.

Dr. Christiaan Barnard gained world-wide fame on December 3, 1967 when he and his team successfully completed the world's first heart transplant at Cape Town's Groote Schuur Hospital. The nine-hour operation saw the heart of car accident victim Denise Darvall transplanted into the chest of grocer Louis Washkansky. While Washkansky would only live another 18 days, Barnard's everlasting place in history was secure.

Dr. Adrian Kantrowitz says he was "stunned" when his daughter woke him to news of the historic transplant. You see, Kantrowitz had been working on heart transplantation for some time, having already done an experimental procedure on some 400 dogs and cats. In fact, he was ready to perform the very first human transplant 18 months earlier. At that time his team was waiting to transplant the heart of a one-day-old baby that had been born without a brain into the body of a baby suffering from a number of terminal heart defects. The parents of the donor had given their permission, but two members of his team said he should wait until the donor heart stopped beating. They waited an hour, but by then the heart was too damaged to use.

So three days after Barnard's historic surgery, Kantrowitz would have to nobly follow suit, this time with a pediatric heart transplant performed at Maimonides Medical Center in Brooklyn, New York. While the recipient of the world's first pediatric heart transplant lived only six-and-half hours, it was a breakthrough that led to thousands more such procedures.

Kantrowitz, who was known to work 18-hour days, six days a week, did his first adult transplant in January 1968 but soon abandoned the transplant field to work on artificial heart aids. Over a six-decade career, Kantrowitz developed more than 20 medical devices that helped with circulation and other vital functions. One of his devices, an intra-aortic blood pump, has been used by three million patients since it came into use in the 1980s.

Kantrowitz, who died in 2008 of heart failure at age 90, didn't outwardly seem to be bothered about Barnard so narrowly beating him to the history books. "You can't always be first. Some races you lose, some you win."

TRIVIA: About 3,500 heart transplants are performed every year world-wide, the majority of them in the U.S.

TWO HEARTS

"Pushed the seeds of a tree into the ground knowing he may never live in its shade."

For William Schroeder, it was literally do or die.

In 1984, Schroeder—52 and near death because of a heart weakened by three decades of smoking—was told he was too old to be a priority candidate for a transplant. With only days to live—and all other medical options exhausted—Schroeder had just one hope left: the experimental Jarvik-7 artificial heart. On November 25, 1984, the native of Jasper, Indiana, became the second person to receive an artificial heart. The procedure was done by Dr. William DeVries, who had operated on Barney Clark two years earlier when the Seattle dentist became the first to receive an artificial heart.

Schroeder's six-and-a-half-hour operation went so well he was sipping a beer four days later. He soon began an exercise program and was out of intensive care December 7. An excited Schroeder told an interviewer about two weeks after the procedure he felt "super" and the artificial heart was beating inside him like "an old-time threshing machine." President Reagan called and Schroeder asked where his Social Security cheque was (it was hand-delivered the next day). But a stroke and a couple of other seizures left him unable to speak by Christmas.

The gritty Schroeder was able to leave the hospital briefly for the first time on March 10, 1985. Six days later he broke Clark's world record of 112 days surviving with an artificial heart. Schroeder was able to move into an apartment across the street from the hospital for a while, even attended a Louisville Redbirds game in the summer and visited his hometown. But another stroke November 11 placed him back in hospital for good.

Schroeder hung on for another nine months before dying in August 1986 at age 54. He lived 612 days with a mechanical heart, a record that still stands. A memorial has been erected in Schroeder's honor in Jasper, and the headstone marking his grave is shaped like two overlapping hearts, one of which is engraved with a depiction of the Jarvik-7.

In his eulogy, Dr. DeVries praised Schroeder as a man "who pushed the seeds of a tree into the ground knowing he may never live in its shade."

Sometimes in instances like this there is really no first or second place.

 TRIVIA: The second-longest lived artificial heart recipient after Schroeder is Tom Christerson, who lived 512 days with the AbioCor heart from 2001 to 2003.

VINDICATED TOO LATE

"He was a genius."

Sixty-seven days after Louise Brown became the world's first test-tube baby in 1978, a team led by Dr. Subhash Mukherjee created the second.

But what should have been a triumphant time for the Indian physician turned out to be the beginning of a nightmare.

It was an historic moment when Mukherjee and his team followed in the footsteps of British doctors Robert Edwards and Patrick Steptoe by performing in-vitro fertilization in India. The procedure resulted in the world's second test-tube baby on October 3, 1978. The Indian baby was named Durga (a.k.a. Kanupriya Agarwal) marking a major triumph for Mukherjee, who first started work on the IVF technique in the 1960s. He was so dedicated that he convinced his wife that they should not have a child as it would impede his work. "He was a genius. Nothing could keep him down," remarked his associate years later.

Instead of praise, all Mukherjee received was criticism. The government and the medical profession in India didn't believe he had successfully performed in-vitro fertilization. A committee headed by a radiophysicist—not exactly an expert in such matters—ruled against Mukherjee's claims. Despite world-wide acclaim, he was banned from travelling internationally and even restricted from talking on the subject within his own country.

Mukherjee never recovered from the humiliation. He suffered a heart attack in 1980 after being denied a passport to go to Japan to present a paper on IVF. Then, after twice being transferred to work in different hospitals, Mukherjee stopped his experiments and research altogether. On June 19, 1981 his wife Namita returned to their Calcutta home to find her husband dead by hanging. His suicide note read, "I can't wait everyday for a heart attack to kill me."

Sixteen years later, Mukherjee finally received the public acclaim so long denied him. T.C. Anand Kumar, who was officially regarded as India's first test-tube baby doctor (he successfully performed IVF 8 years after Mukherjee), examined the late doctor's notes. He concluded that Mukherjee had been wronged. In 2003, the Indian Council for Medical Research agreed and the history books were rewritten.

What of Durga (a.k.a. Kanupriya Agarwal), India's first test-tube baby? She revealed her identity on her 25th birthday the year Mukherjee was finally recognized. She said she was "proud to be a living example of the work of a genius."

Another casualty of the controversy is Mukherjee's wife Namita. Paralyzed and bedridden since 2004, she lives for the hope that an institute named after her husband will be built.

The state government promised to name a medical facility in Mukherjee's honor, but decades later it does not exist. "That is the only reason why I'm alive," his widow lamented. "I still hope that I will be able to see the institute before I die."

 TRIVIA: "In vitro" is a Latin expression meaning "in glass."

CHAPTER 8

LOST IN SPACE

"Winning is habit. Unfortunately, so is losing."
– Vince Lombardi

MOON MISS

"Magnificent desolation."

I magine being first to go all the way to the Moon, coming within a few miles of the surface, only to pull up and go home, leaving all the fame and excitement to those on the next mission?

That was the fate of Thomas Stafford, John Young and Eugene Cernan, the crew of Apollo 10.

The May 1969 mission of Apollo 10 was a dress rehearsal for the historic Apollo 11 flight two months later. Stafford, Young and Cernan did practically everything Neil Armstrong, Buzz Aldrin and Michael Collins would do, except land on the Moon. Part of Apollo 10's mission was to test the Lunar Module space capsule, so Stafford and Young flew some manoeuvres and came within 8.4 miles of the Moon's surface while Cernan orbited it alone in the command module. *Close, But No Cigar,* or Moon in this case.

Young would return to the Moon in April 1972 as commander of Apollo 16, while Cernan went back in December 1972 on NASA's final lunar mission, Apollo 17 (since Cernan was the last to re-enter Lunar Module, he became the *last* man on the Moon). Stafford, however, never got to walk on the celestial body.

Public interest in Moon landings faded pretty quickly after Apollo 11. The second mission, Apollo 12, was launched later the same year, but only space buffs remember crew members Charles "Pete" Conrad, Alan Bean and Richard Gordon. Even less remember Conrad's first exclamation after stepping on the Moon: "Whoopie! That may have been a small one for Neil, but that's a long one for me." Not quite Armstrong's, "That's one small step for (a)* man, one giant leap for mankind."

Speaking of Armstrong, what were Buzz Aldrin's first words as he became the second man on the Moon? "Beautiful view. Magnificent desolation." As for Armstrong's next words on the moon: "Yes, the surface is fine and powdery. I can kick it up loosely with my toe. It does adhere in fine layers, like powdered charcoal, to the sole and sides of my boots. I only go in a small fraction of an inch, maybe an eighth of an inch, but I can see the footprints of my boots and the treads in the fine, sandy particles."

What did Aldrin think about Armstrong getting to the Moon's surface ahead of him? Well, according to Chris Kraft, head of Mission Control, "Aldrin desperately wanted that honor and wasn't quiet about letting it be known."

* *Armstrong claims he said, "a small step for a man," but the word "a" was obscured by static in the transmission and most heard it as "one small step for man."*

 TRIVIA: Alexey Leonov was selected in the mid-1960s to command the first manned USSR Moon mission which would have put him in-line to be first on the surface, but the Soviets never went after the U.S. got there first.

RUSSIAN RUNNER-UP

"The living symbol of Russian achievements in space."

The second man to orbit Earth had his share of firsts.

Less than four months after the USSR's Yuri Gagarin became the first man in space, Soviet cosmonaut Gherman Titov blasted off en route to a number of historic milestones.

Yuri Gagarin's historic flight in April 1961 proved that man could survive outside Earth's atmosphere. But the Soviets wanted to see how a longer flight would effect a human, so in August 1961 Titov became the first person to spend a whole day in space with a flight of 25 hours and 18 minutes.

Titov also became the first man to sleep in space (in fact he *overslept* by half an hour), the first to personally fly a spacecraft, the first to orbit the Earth multiple times (17 in his case) and the first to film the Earth from space. And by becoming the first to suffer space sickness, Titov also became the first to throw up in space.

Titov emerged as one of the two frontrunners from an original group of 20 test pilots vying to be the first Soviet in space. It was between him and Gagarin. Cosmonaut instructor Cesar Solovyov says that while Titov was brighter and more inquisitive, Gagarin got the nod because he had a winning smile.

After his flight, Titov went back to work as a test pilot but was banned from flying following the death of Gagarin in a 1968 plane crash. The Soviets didn't want to take a chance on another space hero dying, so Titov was bumped upstairs into a series of high-level administrative positions before retiring in 1991. He was elected to the Soviet lower house of parliament in 1995, wrote several books on spaceflight, and was given the highest Soviet honor, Hero of the Soviet Union. Titov died in a sauna in his Moscow flat in 2000 following an apparent carbon monoxide leak. He was 65.

"He was the living symbol of Russian achievements in space," his close friend Alexei Leonov said. "But sometimes he couldn't conceal his true feelings about it; sometimes he would reveal a kind of sadness that he was the second and not the first."

 TRIVIA: A month shy of 26 years old when he orbited the Earth, Titov is still the youngest person to fly in space.

NOT SOON ENOUGH

"A manned orbit of Earth ... in October 1960."

Buried deep in the gamma rays of history is a short-lived U.S. space program that preceded NASA but was completely overshadowed by it. The Man in Space Soonest program lasted only a few weeks but its ranks included one very famous future astronaut and quite a few forgotten pioneers.

Man in Space Soonest (MISS), introduced June 15, 1958 by the U.S. Air

Force, was a forerunner of NASA's Mercury 7 program. It had a bold four-part agenda. Phase One: "a ballistic capsule, first carrying instruments, then primates, then finally a man" with a goal toward "a manned orbit of Earth ... in October 1960." Phase Two was called Man-in-Space Sophisticated. It would utilize "a heavier capsule, capable of a 14-day flight" and would orbit the Moon. Phase Three, dubbed Lunar Reconnaissance, would "soft-land on the Moon." The final phase, called Manned Lunar Landing and Return, would accomplish a manned lunar landing by 1965. The price tag: $1.5 billion (about $123 billion in today's dollars).

The U.S. Air Force revealed its preliminary astronaut selections in 1958. In that first group were Neil Armstrong, then an obscure test pilot who 11 years later would become the first man on the Moon. Also included was Joseph Walker, a Pennsylvanian who made it to space twice in 1963 when he piloted two X-15 experimental rocket aircrafts beyond the 62-mile threshold of outer space.

Seven other incredible but long forgotten test pilots were chosen, none of whom ever made it to space. They were:

Iven Kincheloe, Jr.

The Detroit native won the Silver Star and the Distinguished Flying Cross during the Korean War. He was dubbed "America's No. 1 Spaceman" in 1956 after becoming the first to fly over 100,000 feet high. Kincheloe died when his military jet crashed at Edwards AFB on July 26, 1958 (a week before MISS was cancelled). He was 30.

William Bridgeman

Once known as "The Fastest Man Alive," the Iowa-born Bridgeman set world aircraft records in 1951 for speed and altitude. After MISS was cancelled, he tested commercial aircraft and went into real estate. Bridgeman died at 53 when in 1968 his plane fell into the Pacific Ocean during a leisure flight off the California coast.

John B. McKay

The Virginia native flew for the U.S. Navy during the Second World War and later worked for the National Advisory for Aeronautics and NASA. McKay died in 1975, aged 52. He was later inducted into the Aerospace Walk of Honor and posthumously awarded his astronaut wings.

Robert Rushworth

Born in Maine, Rushworth flew the X-15 more than any other test pilot. He also flew 189 combat missions in Vietnam, retiring as a major general. He died in 1993 at age 68.

Scott Crossfield

According to capmembers.com, Crossfield flew the X-15 to the edge of space on many occasions, suggesting that's why many consider him the "world's first true astronaut." The Californian also helped design the first astronaut suit. Crossfield died in 2006 at age 84 when his Cessna crashed into a mountainous region of Georgia.

Alvin S. White

The Californian flew for the Air Force during the Second World War and later worked as a military test pilot. In 1966, White narrowly escaped death in a mid-air collision that killed his co-pilot along with his fellow MISS member, Joseph Walker. White died in 2006, aged 87, after a career that included some 8,500 flying hours testing some 125 different aircraft.

Robert "Bob" White

Born in New York City, White was shot down over Germany in 1945 and was held as a prisoner of war. He flight-tested many types of aircraft for the U.S. Air Force in the 1950s. In 1961, White also became the first person in history to fly a winged aircraft at six times the speed of sound. When White died in 2010 at age 85, it left Armstrong as the only survivor of the original MISS program. The Ohio-born Armstrong died in 2012 at age 72.

His famous accomplishments, however, would have to come with another space program.

What happened to MISS? The Eisenhower Administration cancelled it August 1, 1958, replacing it with Project Mercury, which would also be run by the new civilian program, NASA. But for that decision, *who knows?* The names of Scott Crossfield, William Bridgeman, Joe Walker and others might have been just as famous as Mercury astronauts John Glenn, Scott Carpenter and Alan Shepard.

 TRIVIA: The X-15 still holds the world record for the highest speed ever recorded by a manned, powered aircraft at 4,520 mph (7,274 km/h) by William J. Knight in 1967.

DOG DAYS

"Remembered as heroes."

The second dogs in orbit barked down a very important first. Three years after Laika became the first dog in orbit in 1957, strays Belka and Strelka followed in his paw prints to make history of their own. While Laika suffocated just a few hours after the launch (a fact not revealed by the Russians until 2002), Belka and Strelka survived, thus becoming the first dogs to orbit Earth and return safely home. Less than a year later, Soviet cosmonaut Yuri Gagarin became the first human to accomplish that feat.

Belka and Strelka were not supposed to be the second dogs in orbit. That honor was originally scheduled to go to Chaika and Lisichka, but those two dogs were killed when their spacecraft exploded pre-flight. So Belka (Squirrel) and Strelka (Little Arrow) blasted off August 19, 1960 aboard Korabl-Sputnik 2. The two dogs were accompanied by 40 mice, two rats, a rabbit, some flies and several plants. All returned safe and sound the next day after 18 orbits of the Earth—the first living beings to orbit Earth and safely return.

Belka and Strelka became national heroes, touring the Soviet Union in little red and green spacesuits. Strelka went on to have six puppies, one of which, Pushinka, was given to U.S. President John F. Kennedy. Pushinka hooked up with JFK's dog Charlie and the canine couple had four Cold War puppies, which the president jokingly called "Pupniks."

 TRIVIA: The Soviets chose stray dogs because they were considered naturally hardy.

GENDER GAP

"When in orbit, one thinks of the whole of the Earth, rather than one's country, as one's home."

Nearly two decades separate the first female in space from the second.

Barely two years after Yuri Gagarin became the first man in space, Valentina Tereshkova became the first woman when she flew aboard Vostok 6 in 1963. Hoping to beat the U.S. to another space first, the Soviets began a selection process in mid-1961 headed by the first man in space, Yuri Gagarin. Tereshkova, a former textile worker, was chosen from among five candidates in a special woman-in-space program directed by Soviet Premier Nikita Khrushchev. The woman called "Gagarin in a skirt" never flew again after her historic 48-orbit flight.

Nineteen more years would pass before a second woman went into space. This time it was Svetlana Savitskaya. Like her predecessor Tereshkova, she was a skilled parachutist who had completed 450 jumps by her 17th birthday. Dubbed "Miss Sensation" by the British press, in 1982

Savitskaya became the second woman in space when she flew aboard Soyuz T-7. In 1984 she became the first woman to walk in space. Savitskaya was also supposed to command a first-of-its-kind all-female crew on Salyut 7 but that was cancelled. Twice named "Hero of the Soviet Union," Savitskaya was one of five cosmonauts selected to raise the Russian flag at the opening ceremonies of the 2014 Winter Olympics in Sochi.

"When watching the Earth from over there," said Savitskaya, "one can see the results of human activities, not just a beautiful bluish habitable planet, but because one can see just how habitable it is, with all of its floodlit streets and avenues, and its huge cities. When in orbit, one thinks of the whole of the Earth, rather than one's country, as one's home."

 TRIVIA: China became the third nation in space in 2003.

A WALK UNSPOILED

"I'm coming back in ... and it's the saddest moment of my life."

Edward White was the second man to walk in space—and he didn't want it to end.

In fact, White was enjoying himself so much that he had to be *ordered back* into the spacecraft by Mission Control. The June 3, 1965 exchange between him and fellow astronaut James McDivitt was one of the most memorable in the history of the U.S. space program:

McDivitt: *They want you to get back in now.*
White (laughing): *I'm not coming in. This is fun.*
McDivitt: *Come on.*
White: *Hate to come back to you, but I'm coming.*
McDivitt: *OK, come in then.*

White: *Aren't you going to hold my hand?*

McDivitt: *Ed, come on in here. Come on. Let's get back in here before it gets dark.*

White: *I'm coming back in ... and it's the saddest moment of my life.*

The four-day Gemini flight from which White sallied was by far the longest U.S. space voyage to date. The space walk wasn't in the original flight plan, but it turned out to be one of the most memorable moments of the Gemini program.

It was a perfect assignment for White, a photography buff who snapped pictures and chatted with McDivitt inside the space capsule as millions watched on TV or listened on radio around the world. His 20-minute walk was twice as long as that of Soviet Alexei Leonov, who made history's first space walk less than three months earlier. However, White became the first man to use jet propulsion to navigate through space. This time, however, his fuel ran out and he had to return along a 25-foot tether. On his jaunt White accidentally bumped into McDivitt's window, prompting his partner to comment in fake disgust, "You smeared up my window, you dirty dog."

The successful mission put the U.S. space program back on the map, and the two astronauts were honored with a ticker-tape parade in Chicago. But tragedy struck only a year-and-a-half later. White was killed along with Gus Grissom and Roger Chaffee on January 27, 1967 when a fire engulfed their cabin during a rehearsal for the Apollo I launch. White was 36.

 TRIVIA: Edward White nearly qualified for the 1952 U.S. Olympic track team.

BETTER LATE THAN NEVER

"We explore, we discover and we share."

Sometimes it's better to be number two.

Barbara Morgan's very existence is evidence of that.

In 1985, the California-born educator was selected as the back-up candidate for the just-introduced NASA "Teacher in Space" program. Morgan and Christa McAuliffe trained along with the crew of the space shuttle *Challenger* which blasted off from Cape Canaveral at 11:38 a.m. on January 28, 1986. Seventy-three seconds after take-off, *Challenger* exploded and McAuliffe and the rest of the seven-member crew died. They were the first in-flight fatalities in the history of the U.S. space program.

Morgan resumed teaching grade school in the fall of 1986. But her dream of going into space did not end–in 1998 NASA selected Morgan as a mission specialist and its first Educator in Space. She finally went into space in 2007 as a mission specialist on the STS-118, where her duties included transferring cargo with the robotic Canadarm. She also did several question-and-answer amateur radio sessions with young people.

Morgan, who received the George H.W. Bush Leadership award for her efforts, left NASA in 2008 to teach at Boise State University. Morgan says to this day she gets letters about her space experience. She says being an astronaut is not much different from being a teacher. "We explore, we discover and we share. And both are absolutely wonderful jobs."

 TRIVIA: NASA also had a Journalist in Space program–Walter Cronkite, Tom Brokaw and Sam Donaldson were among the candidates–but it was cancelled after the *Challenger* disaster.

CHAPTER 9

EXPLORERS CLUB

"The tragedy of life is not that man loses,
but that he almost wins."

– Heywood Broun

OUT-POLED

"An awful place."

Finishing second is bad enough, but for Robert Falcon Scott, it proved deadly.

In 1910, Scott and Norwegian Roald Amundsen were in a race for exploration's biggest prize–the South Pole. Earth's southernmost point had never been reached but this time two of the world's most renowned explorers were vying for it simultaneously. In one corner there was Scott– the English-born Royal Navy veteran who had failed to reach the pole a decade earlier. Then there was Amundsen, who gained fame as the first to successfully navigate the Northwest Passage a few years earlier.

Originally, Amundsen had planned to become the first to reach the North Pole. But after American explorers Frederick Cook and Robert Peary claimed the prize (though there's strong evidence neither made it), the Norwegian explorer turned his sights to the southern pole. Heavily in debt, Amundsen kept his plans secret, even from his own crew at first. They thought they were heading to Antarctica for research. But on September 9, 1910 he told his surprised men he was planning to go to the South Pole–and they were welcome to join.

Meanwhile, Scott was planning his own South Pole trek. Imagine his shock when he received a telegram on October 12 saying, "Beg leave inform you proceeding Antarctic. Amundsen." Suddenly the race to the Pole was on, though Amundsen had a huge head start. It was a long and arduous trek for both explorers and their parties. But 14 months later–on Friday, December 14, 1911–Amundsen and his team planted the Norwegian flag at the South Pole. They had made it!

Meanwhile, Scott trudged on. "One cannot see the next tent, let alone the land," he wrote in his journal about the "horrible" conditions he and his party faced that December. Finally, on January 16, 1912, they reached the South Pole but were stunned at what they saw–there flew the Norwegian flag. Amundsen had beaten them by a month. "Great God!" wrote Scott. "This is an awful place, and terrible enough for us to have labored to it without the reward of priority."

An exhausted, frozen and bitterly disappointed group began the return journey. The first to die, on February 17, was Seaman Edgar Evans. Lawrence Oates willingly walked to his death in a blizzard March 16, sacrificing himself because he was slowing down the others. One by one the rest of the party—Henry Bowers, Edward Wilson, Scott—all died, ravaged by extreme cold, starvation and exhaustion. This final trio was only 11 miles from a supply depot when they were socked in by a raging blizzard. The last entry in Scott's journal reads, "It seems a pity, but I do not think that I can write more. R. Scott. For God's sake look after our people." A search party found them in their sleeping bags, all dead, eight months later.

"Victory awaits him who has everything in order, luck people call it," said Amundsen, who didn't rest on his laurels. From 1918 to 1920, he became the second to navigate the Northeast Passage. In 1926, Amundsen and his crew became the first to fly over the North Pole in an airship.

Norway's most famous explorer disappeared while on a rescue mission in 1928. Amundsen's body was never found. He was 55.

 TRIVIA: Antarctica is the second-smallest continent after Australia.

REACHING FOR THE TOP

"We knocked the bastard off."–Edmund Hillary after conquering Everest

Their names are forever etched in the history books.

On May 29, 1953, New Zealand beekeeper Edmund Hillary and his Sherpa guide Tenzing Norgay became household names by becoming the first climbers to reach the summit of Mount Everest, the world's highest mountain. It ended a quest of more than three decades, dating back to the first British expedition in 1922.

To the victors go the spoils. The names of those on the second expedition to reach the summit of Everest have been all but forgotten, as are those of the pair who almost beat Hillary and Tenzing to the top in the first instance.

The fame and accolades enjoyed by Hillary and Tenzing almost went to Charles Evans and Tom Bourdillon. On May 26, 1953, the British team members came within 300 feet of Everest's summit—actually, within sight of it—before being turned back due to exhaustion, oxygen equipment problems and time issues. *Close, But No Cigar*. Three days later, Hillary and Norgay conquered Everest leaving Evans and Bourdillon to wonder "what if."

Three years after Hillary and Tenzing, Swiss explorers Ernst Schmied and Juerg Marmet became the second team to conquer Everest. Schmied, officially the third man to reach the summit, was a veteran climber. Marmet—a chemical engineer by profession—followed right behind Schmied to become the fourth person to conquer Everest.

Schmied and Marmet were followed a day later by two other members of their team, Dolf Reist and Hans-Rudolf von Gunten. No one else would reach the summit of Everest until 1960, when a Chinese expedition made it. Since then, there have been more than 5,000 ascents of Everest, including 169 on a single day in 2010.

 TRIVIA: Mount Everest was originally measured at exactly 29,000 feet, but publicly declared to be 29,002 feet so people would not get the impression that it was a rounded number (the actual height according to latest estimates is 29,029 feet).

FAMILY BEFORE FAME

"Short on curiosity."

H e could have been the first European to set foot in North America, but he wanted to see his parents.

Bjarni Herjolfsson was a wealthy seafaring merchant who alternated his time between Norway and his home in Iceland. A devoted son who visited his Icelandic parents every summer, Bjarni was unnerved when he came to visit in 986 CE and found out the family had packed up and moved west to Greenland. Without as much as a map, Bjarni ordered his crew to set sail for Greenland. He wanted to see his parents!

The big problem was that Bjarni and company had little idea where they were going—all they had were directions from a few locals in Iceland. Three days into their trip they were "beset by winds from the north and fog, for many days they did not know where they were sailing." Finally, the weather cleared and they spotted land. But this was no land they'd ever seen before. There were no typical glaciers, mountains or large rocks. Instead, there were low hills that were heavily wooded. But this *new found land* (that's a hint, folks) was of no interest to Bjarni. He sailed on.

Two days later, they found more new land. It was flat and forested and certainly not Greenland. Bjarni's crew wanted to go ashore but their boss refused—he wanted to visit his parents so he ordered them to keep going. A few days later, Bjarni's crew saw land that was high, rocky and had glaciers. It was the third land sighting of their journey, but Bjarni was adamant, they weren't stopping. Finally—four days later—they discovered a fourth landmass. Bjarni said it looked like Greenland from what he'd heard so they finally landed. Bjarni was right, and in fact was practically in his parent's backyard. The family was soon reunited but Bjarni was about to get a lifetime pass to the *Close, But No Cigar* hall of fame.

On his return to Norway, Bjarni mentioned that he'd sighted "various lands" during his journey, but did not go ashore to explore. Locals were confounded saying he was a man "short on curiosity." So today—just like before—we are left asking, where had he been? Historians suggest he first spotted Newfoundland, followed by Labrador then Baffin Island, all previously unexplored by Westerners.

Leif Erikson was not short on curiosity. He bought Bjarni's ship and around 1,000 CE took a 35-man crew to the lands the accidental explorer had described. Unlike Bjarni though, Leif went ashore. And so it was Erikson—not Bjarni—who entered the history books as the first European known to have set foot on North American soil. Nearly 500 years later, Christopher Columbus paid a visit.

 TRIVIA: The first European to set foot on the North American mainland was John Cabot in 1497.

PLANE ENVY

"Lindbergh was lucky and we were not."

Who's heard of Clarence Chamberlin? Like most of history's runner-ups, the name of the second person to fly from New York to continental Europe in a fixed-wing aircraft is pretty much forgotten. Chamberlin and his navigator flew from Roosevelt Field on Long Island to Eisleben, Germany a scant two weeks after Charles Lindbergh, their departure delayed by some needless dawdling. Their flight of 42 hours and 45 minutes covered 3,911 miles, beating by about 300 miles the record set by Lindbergh in his flight from New York to Paris. But no one remembers that of course—all history remembers is that Lindbergh got there first.

Clarence Chamberlin loved fixing things. His father owned the first automobile in Denison, Iowa and the young Clarence took on the role of mechanic for the family car. He would fix clocks and watches in his father's jewellery shop. When he saw his first plane at an air show it's not surprising that he took great interest in this fledgling mode of transportation.

Chamberlin got his engineering degree and started a successful Harley-Davidson dealership in his hometown. But he couldn't resist the lure of the air. Chamberlin enlisted with the Army Signal Corps in 1917 and soon decided to devote his life to flying. He gave flying demonstrations and charged folks to go up in his plane, worked as a flight instructor, delivered air mail and found employment in aerial photography. But fame and fortune beckoned in the form of a $25,000 prize offered by New York hotel owner Raymond Orteig to become the first to fly across the Atlantic non-stop in a fixed-wing aircraft.

Chamberlin might have won the prize had he settled faster on a navigator for his plane, *Miss Columbia*. The plane's owner Charles Levine replaced navigator Bert Acosta with Lloyd Bertrand then dumped Bertrand. An angry Bertrand got a court injunction stopping the plane from taking off for Europe unless he went. Lindbergh took advantage of the group's dallying by taking off May 20, 1927 in *The Spirit of St. Louis* for points east. Thirty-three-and-a-half hours and 3,600 miles later, he landed to a hero's welcome at Le Bourget Field in Paris.

Exactly two weeks after Lindbergh's flight, Chamberlain and Levine—who jumped in at the last minute—became the second aviators to accomplish the feat. President Coolidge cabled congratulations and the Brooklyn Chamber of Commerce awarded Chamberlain and Levine $15,000 for the first successful New York to Berlin flight. Chamberlin got an additional $25,000 from his boss who raged about the strong headwinds he and Chamberlin faced during their flight "Lindbergh was lucky and we were not. If we had only one-tenth of Lindbergh's luck, we'd have done much better."

His exploits in the air behind him, Chamberlin went into aircraft manufacturing. He designed New York's first municipal airport, Floyd Bennett Field, and helped train pilots in the Second World War just as he did in the First World War. Chamberlin died in 1976 at age 82 just a few months short of the 50th anniversary of his historic Atlantic crossing.

TRIVIA: The first transatlantic flight in a fixed-wing aircraft was made in 1919 by John Alcock and Arthur Brown, who flew from St. John's, Newfoundland, to Galway, Ireland.

POLAR OPPOSITES

"Not proven."

I t's tough to say who was second to the North Pole since no one knows for sure who was the first.

On September 2, 1909, the *New York Herald* greeted its readers with an astounding headline: "The North Pole is Discovered by Frederick A. Cook."

Five days later the *New York Times* trumpeted a completely different story: "Peary Discovers the North Pole After Eight Trials in 23 Years."

So which was it? Cook or Peary? Or neither. More than a century later no one can say for sure.

Robert Peary and Frederick Cook had a long history as friends and rivals. Cook, a New York physician, was Peary's surgeon on the American explorer's expedition to Greenland in 1891-92. A decade later, Cook rescued Peary who was lost in the Arctic, and treated his fellow explorer for heart troubles and scurvy. The two parted ways again, with Peary failing to make the North Pole in his sixth attempt in 1905-06. Meanwhile Cook—having claimed to have become the first to scale Mount McKinley in 1906—set his sights on the North Pole.

In July 1907 Cook established a base camp in Greenland, some 700 miles from the pole. He then set out for the top of the world in February 1908 with a team of nine locals and 103 dogs pulling 11 sledges. As had been planned, most of Cook's support team turned back as they moved northward, except for a couple of local hunters named Etukishook and Ahwelah. They pushed on despite heavy winds. Finally, on April 21, 1908 Cook used his sextant to calculate that they were "at a spot which was as near as possible" to the pole. Barely surviving the return journey, Cook and his guides returned to camp in April 1909, more than a year after leaving the pole.

Meanwhile, Peary had already left for the pole before Cook. Peary took along an army of 50 men and nearly 250 dogs pulling some two dozen sleds. Only 134 miles from the Pole, Peary sent everyone back except his long-time aide Matthew Henson and four Inuit guides. On April 6, 1909, believing he had reached the top of the world, Peary planted the American flag.

The race was on for both explorers to tell the world their story. On September 9, 1909, Peary wired the *New York Times* with the triumphant words "Stars and Stripes Nailed to North Pole." Two days later he added: "Don't Let Cook Story Worry You. Have Him Nailed." On September 21–the same day Peary arrived in Nova Scotia–Cook was greeted by hundreds of thousands of cheering supporters in New York. But while the public initially supported Cook's claim, a Peary campaign to discredit his Arctic rival was underway. Working against Cook was his lack of documentation: three boxes of what he said were detailed exploration records were left behind in Greenland and never seen again. Public opinion began to shift against Cook while the National Geographic Society put their weight behind Peary. Meanwhile, the University of Copenhagen examined Cook's claim and pronounced it "not proven." It seemed Cook lost the public opinion race.

So who reached the North Pole first? Peary's claim also came under suspicion after a U.S. congressman examined his diary in 1911 and pointed out its pristine condition–shouldn't it have some finger markings or more indications of use? A U.S. bill signed by President Taft to honor Peary left out the word "discovery" in reference to the North Pole. Peary never showed his papers again and rarely spoke publicly about the North Pole. He died in 1920 at age 63. Cook, on the other hand, went into the oil business but spent seven years behind bars on mail-fraud charges. Paroled in 1930, he died a decade later at age 75, a few months after he was pardoned by President Roosevelt.

 TRIVIA: There is a North Pole in Alaska, New York and Idaho, and a North Pole City in Oklahoma.

MATTERHORN MATTERS

"The last great problem of the Alps."

Tragedy overshadowed triumph in the race to conquer the Matterhorn.

On his eighth attempt, London-born Edward Whymper became the first to lead a team to the summit of one of the world's most recognizable peaks, planting the English flag atop the Matterhorn on July 14, 1865. But it was the Whymper team's descent that is better remembered because it was marked by a terrible calamity: one of his men fell and dragged three others with him to their deaths. The tragedy haunted Whymper the rest of his days.

Whymper and his team were on a race to the summit against a seasoned group of Italian climbers. When Whymper's team reached the summit, they could see their competitors–headed by Jean-Antoine Carrel–scrambling up behind them, unaware that Whymper had reached the summit. So Whymper and his group hurled rocks down the mountain at the Italian group just to let them know who was king of the hill (crazy bunch, those mountaineers). Carrel and his men gave up but would make it a couple of days later with the footprints of the Whymper party still fresh at the summit.

The conquest of the Matterhorn came during an incredible time in mountaineering known as the "Golden Age of Alpinism." It started in 1854 when Briton Alfred Wills scaled the Wetterhorn, an achievement which sparked an avalanche (OK, bad choice of words) of interest in mountain climbing. Over the next decade, many of the great alpine peaks were reached for the first time, leaving just the Matterhorn, "the last great problem of the Alps."

One can sense that Carrel carried a case of sour grapes, and would be less than thrilled with his membership in the *Close, But No Cigar* club. After his climb, he said, "Although we have been forestalled by Whymper, the victory from a practical point of view is ours, because we have now proved that the peak is accessible [from the Italian] side." That said, it would be another thorn in Carrel's side to know that today, Whymper's route up the Swiss side of the Matterhorn remains the most popular.

Carrel died in 1890, collapsing from exhaustion as he guided a group on the Matterhorn. He was 61. Whymper passed away in 1911 at age 71 having conquered many other mountains, including what is now known as Mount Whymper in the Canadian Rockies. So we'll leave the last words to Whymper, who penned one of the most famous passages in mountaineering history:

Climb if you will, but remember that courage and strength are naught with prudence, and that a momentary negligence may destroy the happiness of a lifetime. Do nothing in haste, look well to each step, and from the beginning think what may be the end.

 TRIVIA: Over 60,000 people have climbed the Matterhorn, including the first woman–Lucy Walker of England–in 1871.

CHAPTER 10

RING AROUND THE OLYMPICS

"Winning may not be everything,
but losing has little to recommend it."

– Dianne Feinstein

GOOFY GAMES

"It's a miracle that the Olympic Movement survived."

T he first modern Olympics were a rousing success.
Nearly 300 athletes–all male–from 14 countries participated in the 1896 Games in Athens. Overflow crowds at Panathenaic Stadium were estimated at 80,000 for the opening ceremonies. It was an encouraging start for the modern Olympic movement.

The second modern Olympics were a disaster.

Held in Paris at the same time as the massive World Exposition, the 1900 Games were at best a sideshow, at worst a joke. Conditions were terrible–track athletes found themselves running on uneven grass instead of a cinder track. So short were the discus and hammer throw grounds that sometimes their shots wound up in the trees. Swimmers were slimed in the muddy waters and buffeted about in fast-moving currents of the Seine. Scheduling was so chaotic that many athletes missed events.

The marathon was a complete zoo. The course was so poorly marked that some runners found themselves fighting for their share of the road with cars, cyclists, casual runners, even animals. Some runners got lost and had to double back. Beer proved too big an obstacle for one competitor–he stopped for a cold one and then dropped out. There was even controversy surrounding the marathon winner. Several competitors claimed Michel Théato took shortcuts en route to victory (they were later proven wrong). Also, at the time of his win, everyone thought Théato was French. But research decades later showed he was actually born in Luxembourg.

The lowest point for the 1900 Olympics might have been the Live Pigeon Shooting. How this "sport" wound up on the Olympic program is anyone's guess. Nevertheless, for the first and fortunately only time in the history of the Games, live animals were deliberately killed in an event. As American sports historian Andrew Strunk wrote years later, "The idea to use live birds for the pigeon shoot turned out to be a rather unpleasant choice. Maimed birds were writhing on the ground, blood and feathers were swirling in the air and women with parasols were weeping in the chairs set up nearby." More than 300 birds were reportedly killed in this most gruesome of Olympic events.

One major problem for organizers, athletes and fans alike was figuring out which events were part of the Olympics and which were part of the World Exposition. Competitions like fire fighting, motor racing, kite flying, cannon shooting, angling, ballooning and motorcycle racing were all a jumble of confusion. As a result, some athletes didn't even know if they were participating in the actual Olympics or not.

There were a couple of significant firsts at these second-rate Olympics. It marked the first time women competed in the Games, and the first time events were contested on a Sunday. But as Olympic president Baron de Coubertin later commented, "It's a miracle that the Olympic Movement survived that celebration."

TRIVIA: Winners at the 1900 Olympics received silver medals; second-place finishers got bronze.

ON YOUR MARKS, GET SET, PROSE!

"A long-divorced couple: Muscle and Mind."

Jesse Owens ... Nadia Comaneci ... Michael Phelps ... Carl Lewis ... Jean Jacoby.

Jean Jacoby?

If you think the name out of place, you're not alone. But Jacoby is an Olympian too, albeit from a long-forgotten side of the Games.

From 1912 to 1948, medals were actually given to folks who battled it out for supremacy... in the arts. The art competition, brainchild of modern Olympics founder Baron de Coubertin, was to "reunite in the bonds of legitimate wedlock a long-divorced couple: Muscle and Mind." He proposed medals be given in five categories: architecture, literature, music, painting and sculpture. But there was one caveat: the entries had to be inspired by sport.

The first crop of Olympic art medallists in 1912 included none other than de Coubertin himself. His poem "Ode to Sport" would win gold in literature in a field of 33 contestants. While greatly overshadowed by the athletics, the art event did have a following–some 400,000 visited the art displays at the Los Angeles Museum of History, Science and Art during the 1932 Games. A number of prominent names actually threw their hats into the Olympic rings over the years, including John Russell Pope (architect of the Jefferson Memorial), American illustrator Percy Crosby (his comic Skippy was said to have been an inspiration for Charles Schultz's Peanuts), and Irish author Jack B. Yeats (younger brother of W.B. Yeats). Only one woman ever won an arts gold, the Finnish poet Aale Tynni.

This is where Luxembourger Jean Jacoby comes in. He was the only art Olympian in history to win two gold medals, taking the middle podium in painting in both 1924 and 1928.

The art competition was cancelled in 1949, and since, all 151 art medallists from the Olympics have been stricken from the official record. Rumors that this decision was met by angry hordes of abstract expressionists have not yet been verified.

 TRIVIA: If art medallists were still on official Olympic record, then John Copley of England–73 at the time he won silver at the 1948 Games–would be the oldest Olympic medallist in history.

FORGOTTEN HERO

"He suffered to the day he died."

He was the third man on the podium.

It was 1968. Race riots raged on U.S. streets. Civil rights icon Martin Luther King had been assassinated, as had civil rights supporter Robert F. Kennedy. With an opportunity to dramatize the fight, American sprinters Tommie Smith and John Carlos took the cause to the world's biggest sporting stage.

After winning gold and bronze respectively in the 200-meter dash, Smith and Carlos prepared to go to the podium and give the "Black Power Salute." But there were a couple of problems. First, Carlos had left his black gloves at the Olympic Village. That logistical issue was solved when silver medallist Peter Norman of Australia suggested they wear black gloves on alternating hands. The second problem was Norman himself.

Norman was white, with no obvious connection to the U.S. civil rights movement. But he was a staunch supporter of civil rights, and wanted to support his podium mates. So the Aussie sprinter borrowed an "Olympic Project for Human Rights" badge from a member of the U.S. rowing team to show solidarity with the U.S. athletes.

As "The Star-Spangled Banner" played, Smith and Carlos raised their clenched fists, hushing the crowd. "I couldn't see what was happening," said Norman, whose back was to the two Americans during the playing of the anthems. "I had known they had gone through with their plans when a voice in the crowd sang the American anthem but then faded to nothing. The stadium went quiet."

Smith and Carlos were sent home and never again ran for the U.S., but Norman's actions also ended his own track career. In the odd ways racism manifests itself, the Melbourne-born physical education teacher was considered a pariah and the forgotten man of the Black Power Salute never ran in the Olympics again. He wasn't even invited by his own country to ceremoniously participate in the 2000 Olympics in Sydney. (When the U.S. team heard this, they invited him instead.) In 2012, the Australian government issued an official apology, but it was too late for Norman who passed away six years earlier at age 64. "He suffered to the day he died," his nephew Matthew Norman says.

"It took inner power to do what he did, inner soul power," said Tommie Smith of Norman. "He was a man of solid beliefs, that's how I will remember Peter. He was a humanitarian and a man of his word."

 TRIVIA: Peter Norman still holds the Australian national record for the 200 meters.

QUICK STUDY

"Nobody was more surprised than I was."

The second person to win Olympic gold was the last survivor of the original U.S. Olympic team.

Just hours after James Connelly became the first person to win an Olympic gold (in the hop, skip and jump), fellow American Robert Garrett became the second gold medallist in Games history when he scored an amazing victory in the discus.

The Greeks were heavy favourites to win the discus at the first modern Olympics in 1896. After all, they were performing on home turf in Athens, and they were masters of the craft that dated back to the ancient Games. But they weren't counting on Garrett, a student at Princeton.

Urged by a professor to enter the discus (even though Garrett had never held one before), the 20-year-old Maryland native had a blacksmith fashion a 12-inch, 30-pound disk that resembled a manhole cover. He practiced with the monstrosity on the boat ride across the Atlantic. When Garrett arrived at Panathenaic Stadium lugging his oversized discus, he discovered that the instrument the Greeks used weighed only five pounds (25 pounds less than his) and was only eight inches in diameter. He borrowed one from a Greek competitor and with little time to prepare, entered the world's first Olympic discus event.

Eleven competitors wearing overcoats started the competition on the chilly March evening. The wheat was soon separated from the chaff, however, leaving only Garrett and the Greek, Panagiotis Paraskevopoulos, vying for top prize. Paraskevopoulos appeared to have it won with a toss of 28.95 meters. But Garrett, despite his scant experience, tossed it an astonishing 29.15 meters for gold—and a world record to boot.

"I got into the discus thing," Garrett recalled, "never figuring I'd do anything but finish in absolute last. The technique of throwing it was all new to me. I threw the thing 95 feet 7 1/2 inches, which was high school distance later on. But it was better than anyone else, so I won, and nobody was more surprised than I was when they gave me the prize."

Garrett also won the shot put at the 1896 Games and took second in both the high jump and the long jump. Garrett later went into banking while also founding and financing a series of outdoor gymnasiums in Baltimore. When he died in 1961 at age 85, he was the last survivor of the original 13-man American team that participated in the first modern Olympics.

"All were stupefied," Burton Holmes, a witness at those first Games would say. "The Greeks had been defeated at their own classic exercise. They were overwhelmed by the superior skill and daring of the Americans, to whom they ascribed a supernatural invincibility enabling them to dispense with training and to win at games which they had never seen before."

 TRIVIA: Only 14 countries participated in the first modern Olympics, with the U.S. taking the most first-place finishes (11).

CLOSE, BUT NO CIGAR

OVERLOOKED PERFECTION

"There are moments, when a natural smile is worth more, than triumph."

Romania's Nadia Comaneci stole the show at the 1976 Montreal Olympics, winning three gold medals and becoming the first female gymnast in Olympic history to record a perfect 10.

But another gymnast at those same Games won just as many golds, and also achieved perfection in gymnastics.

Her name was Nellie Kim—and she's a forgotten star of the Olympics.

Born in Kazakhstan in 1957, Kim was nine years old when she started in gymnastics. She began to get international recognition in 1974 when she won a bronze medal on the balance beam at the World Gymnastics Championships. Kim burst into prominence a year later when she captured four medals at the European championships. The stage was set for the 1976 Montreal Olympics.

Everyone should have been talking about Kim after the Games. Her trio of golds included wins in the team, vault and floor exercise events. She also recorded perfect 10s in the vault and floor exercises. But her success was overshadowed by Comaneci, who became the *first* Olympic female gymnast to record a perfect 10. Comaneci followed with six more perfect 10s to etch her name into the Olympic annals (she also burst into maybe the most memorable smile in Olympic history when she ran onto the floor after a perfect 10 in the uneven parallel bars to take a bow as the crowd roared).

Despite her incredible success, it is Comaneci and not Kim who is remembered from the 1976 Montreal Olympics. Soviet gymnastics coach Larisa Latynina may have expressed it best: "there are moments, when a natural smile is worth more, than triumph."

 TRIVIA: Albert Seguin of France was the first gymnast to earn a perfect 10 at the Olympics, in the side horse vault at the 1924 Games (he also earned a perfect 10 in rope-climbing).

NO SILVER LINING .

"The biggest (Olympic) farce of all-time."

S ince 1972, a dozen Olympic silver medals have been gathering dust at a vault in Lausanne, Switzerland.

They likely will never be claimed, thanks to one of the most controversial games in Olympic history.

The U.S. was the heavy favorite heading into the gold medal basketball game at the Munich Olympics, and for good reason. The Americans had won seven consecutive gold medals dating back to the first Olympic basketball tournament in 1936, never losing a game in the process. With a strong lineup that included future NBA stars Doug Collins and Tom McMillen, the U.S. seemed poised to make it eight.

Their opponent in the gold medal game, however, would be no pushover. "They had a great team," U.S. assistant coach John Bach said of the Soviet Union. "Their team, it was reported, had played almost 400 games together—400 games. We had played 12 exhibition games and the trials." In addition, the Soviets had been a regular contender in the Olympic basketball tournament, with four silvers and a bronze in the last five Games.

The gold medal game proved to be a thriller. Confounded by the Soviet slow-down game, the U.S. trailed by 10 points with less than 10 minutes to play. But a tremendous rally pulled the U.S. to within one point with 10 seconds to play. The U.S. led by one after Collins was fouled, and the American star made his two pressure-packed free throws.

Three seconds remained on the clock. The Soviets in-bounded the ball, but the refs halted the game with one second left and put the clock back to three seconds. The Soviets claimed they had asked for a time-out between Collins's two free throws. So the ball was in-bounded a second time. It clunked off the backboard, the horn sounded and a wild victory celebration began for the Americans. The game was over, the gold belonged to the U.S. Or did it?

It didn't. The head of FIBA, basketball's ruling body, came out of the crowd and ordered that the three seconds be put back on the clock again. The reason given was that the three seconds had not been restored *properly*. The players went back on the court, and on their third try Alexander Belov grabbed a full-court pass and tossed in a lay-up between two American defenders. Final score: the Soviets 51, the U.S. 50. *Close, But No Cigar*–or gold–for the Americans.

The U.S. had just lost a basketball game at the Olympics after 63 straight wins. And the controversy was just beginning. Referee Renato Righetto–who was later quoted as saying the result was "completely irregular"–refused to sign the scoresheet. The U.S. protested to the International Basketball Federation, but was rejected. Another appeal to the executive committee of the International Olympic Committee went nowhere.

The Americans voted not to accept their silver medals. More than four decades later, they still haven't. Two U.S. players–captain Kenny Davis and team-mate Tom Henderson–have even stated in their wills that none of their descendants can ever accept a silver medal from the 1972 Games. Since the medals must be awarded to a team as a whole, it's doubtful that they will ever be claimed.

"It was sort of like being on top of the Sears Tower in Chicago celebrating and then being thrown off and falling 100 floors to the ground," Collins said. "That's the kind of emptiness and sick feeling I had." But Ivan Edeshko, who completed the winning pass for the Soviets, counters that "the Americans didn't want to lose and admit loss. They didn't want to lose in anything, especially basketball."

We'll leave the last word to U.S. lawyer Donald "Taps" Gallagher, who started a campaign to restore the gold medal to the U.S.: "It's still the biggest (Olympic) farce of all-time."

 TRIVIA: The Lithuanian men's basketball team in the 1992 Olympics was sponsored by the Grateful Dead.

DRESSING FOR SUCCESS

"A piece of Olympic history."

The second woman to win an individual gold at the Olympics never knew that she in fact, had even won.

Nevertheless, Margaret Abbott actually won gold in Paris at the first-ever Olympic golf competition. She shot a 47 over nine holes to best 10 other competitors, including her mother, who placed eighth (the only time a mother and daughter have competed in the same Olympic event). Abbott became the first *U.S.* woman to win Olympic gold.

The 1900 Games were so poorly organized, however, that none of the golfers even knew they were competing in the Olympics, including Abbott, who had been studying art in Paris and entered the tournament on a whim. Even though the various Olympic events were being held in Paris, decisions on what events would be officially included in the Games were made after the fact. Abbott didn't get the memo and her golden accomplishment faded into history. She passed away in 1955 not knowing that she had won Olympic gold. However, a University of Florida professor named Paula Welch uncovered Abbott's gold after spending a decade doggedly digging through the Olympic archives. "It was a piece of Olympic history that I felt people should know more about," said Welch, whose efforts got Abbott featured in the official program at the 1996 centennial games in Atlanta.

A major reason for Abbott's success may have been her choice of clothes. She told relatives afterward that her fellow competitors had, "apparently misunderstood the nature of the game scheduled for the day and turned up to play in high heels and tight skirts." Abbott dressed for the occasion and earned her place in history.

 TRIVIA: Women were banned from competing at the first modern Olympics in 1896 in Athens.

SILVER STREAK

"Bridesmaid laurels."

Just color them silver.

Soviet gymnast Viktor Lisitsky holds the record for most silvers won by a male at the Olympics without capturing a gold, that is, five runner-up prizes over two Olympics.

Lisitsky got the silver ball rolling by capturing four bridesmaid laurels at the 1964 Games in Tokyo: the individual all-around; the floor exercises; the vault; and the team competition.

He added a fifth silver at the 1968 Games in Mexico City, again in the team competition. Lisitsky never competed in an Olympics again.

Lisitsky's female counterparts in most silvers won with no golds are: American Kara Lynn Joyce (four silvers, team swimming), Erika Zuchold of Germany (four silvers, gymnastics), and Hilkka Riihivuori of Finland (four silvers, cross-country skiing).

But wait! Someone has more silver medals in their drawer (or wherever they put them) than this group. Soviet gymnasts Alexander Dityatin and Mikhail Voronin won six silvers each (though both also won gold), and American Shirley Babashoff also won six in swimming, along with two gold. Bobsledder Bogdan Musiol matches Lisitsky's total of five silver medals at the Winter Olympics, though he also won a gold.

Now that we're on the subject, the country with the most silver medals and no golds at the Summer Olympics is Namibia, with four. Its Winter Games counterpart is Latvia, which also has four silvers and no golds. The U.S. leads the all-time Summer Games silver table with 758, while Norway leads the all-time Winter Games silver medal list with 111.

 TRIVIA: Silver medals (plus an olive branch and diploma) were given to the winners at the first modern Olympics in 1896; runner-ups were awarded a copper medal, a laurel branch and a diploma.

CHAPTER 11

RUB OF THE GREEN

"There is no such thing as second place.
Either you're first or you're nothing."
— Gabe Paul

SECOND-BEST FRIEND

"If you wouldn't have been born, I'd have been known as a pretty good player."

If it wasn't for his best friend, Jug McSpaden might have had golf's greatest season.

Byron Nelson set the golf world on fire in 1945 when he won 18 PGA events in one season, including *11 in a row*. Both records are likely to stand forever, as is an obscure mark put up that very same season: Jug McSpaden's PGA record of 13 runner-up finishes over one season.

For about two decades, Harold Lee "Jug" McSpaden was a consistent threat on the PGA Tour. The native of Monticello, Kansas, won 17 times on tour between 1933 and 1945. In 1939, he became the first pro golfer to shoot 59 on a par-71 course. In an era that included stiff competition from Nelson, Ben Hogan and Sam Snead, among others, McSpaden finished second 30 times and third on 18 other occasions.

McSpaden almost ended Nelson's 1945 streak at six consecutive wins. At the Philadelphia Inquirer Open, McSpaden was in the clubhouse looking like a sure winner, but Nelson birdied five of his last six holes to win by a couple. It was the narrowest margin of victory during Nelson's magical streak. Throughout the tournament Nelson had been a house guest of McSpaden, who quipped to his friend afterward, "You not only beat my brains out but you eat all my food, too."

Ironically, Nelson's streak started when he and McSpaden teamed to win the Miami International Four-Ball. The two finished one-two in tournaments so often they became known as The Gold Dust Twins. But as McSpaden once told Nelson, "If you wouldn't have been born, I'd have been known as a pretty good player."

 TRIVIA: Jug McSpaden was the oldest player to better his age in a Champions Tour event—at age 85 he shot 81 in the 1994 PGA Seniors Championship.

MISSING MAJOR

"The Impregnable Quadrilateral."

I t's the major that was, then wasn't, but maybe should be.

As the defunct Western Open golf tournament recedes into history, let's not forget what it once was. For much of the first half of the 20th century, the Western Open was considered by pro golfers to be a major championship before that "major" designation became popular. First played in 1899 at the Glen View Golf Club in Illinois, the tournament attracted most of the top players of the day. Its list of champions reads like a Hall of Fame honor roll: Jack Nicklaus, Arnold Palmer, Sam Snead, Ben Hogan, Billy Casper, Tom Watson, Walter Hagen, Gene Sarazen, Byron Nelson and Tiger Woods.

Like all majors except the Masters, the Western Open moved around a lot in its early days. Between 1899 and 1961, it was held in 16 different states—three more than the U.S. Open over the same period. Sixteen of those Western Opens were held in Illinois, with nine in Ohio, eight in Michigan, five in Missouri and three in Wisconsin. The Western Open was then held in the Chicago area from 1962 until the last one in 2006. The tournament was renamed the BMW Championship the next year.

The definition of a "major" has changed a lot over the years. In 1930, Bobby Jones completed "The Impregnable Quadrilateral" by winning the U.S. Open, the British Open, the U.S. Amateur and British Amateur in the same year. In 1960—after winning the Masters and the U.S. Open—Palmer mused aloud to *Pittsburgh Press* writer Bob Drum about the possibility of a modern-day professional Grand Slam, including the two he had already won, plus the Open Championship and the PGA Championship. Palmer's comments came as the two flew to that year's Open Championship and Drum—intrigued by the idea—started talking it up with British golf writers. The concept took hold and the modern-day Grand Slam was born. But left out in the cold: the Western Open.

So what really pushed the Western Open to the sidelines? The Masters. First played in 1934, the annual tournament at Augusta National gained immediate stature due to the support and involvement of Bobby Jones. It then grew into one of golf's crown jewels under the careful tutelage of Cliff Roberts. At some point in the '40s or the '50s, the Masters surpassed the Western Open in importance and the tour's second oldest tournament was no longer considered a major.

Such revisionism changed the course of golf history. Walter Hagen's five Western Opens, for instance, were stricken from the major record, reducing him to 11 major titles instead of 16. By the same token, if the Western Open counted as a major, Hagen would have a career professional grand slam because he also won the U.S. Open, British Open and the PGA Championship. Ditto for Tommy Armour and Jim Barnes, who both won the Western Open and the other three professional majors at the time.

Should men's pro golf count defunct majors? The LPGA does. Discontinued LPGA majors like the Titleholders, the Women's Western Open and the du Maurier Classic are still rated as majors and the winners of those tournaments are still considered major champions. Once a major, always a major—at least on the women's pro tour.

We'll leave the last word to two-time Western Open champ Arnold Palmer. "When I started playing on the Tour, the Western Open was on its way to being a major championship, but it never happened. I don't know why. I always enjoyed playing in it."

TRIVIA: The village of Golf, Illinois—where the Western Open was first played—got its name from a sign that directed train riders to the nearby Glen View Golf Club.

NORMAN THE CONQUERED

"Lay on the beach and cried."

He won two British Opens and nearly 100 tournaments world-wide, but Greg Norman is mostly remembered for the ones that got away.

No one found more ways to lose than Norman during his spectacular run as one of the world's top golfers in the '80s and '90s. The Shark blew big leads; he would make incredible comebacks only to get magically beaten at the end; guys holed shots from every place possible to deny him victory; putts he needed to win would spin out or stay out seemingly against the laws of gravity ...

Norman's string of nail-biting losses in majors started at the 1984 U.S. Open. The Aussie holed a 45-foot putt on the final hole of regulation only to lose in a playoff to Fuzzy Zoeller. At the 1986 Masters, Norman needed to birdie the final hole to beat his hero, Jack Nicklaus. Instead, he bogeyed and tied for second with Tom Kite, one stroke behind the Golden Bear. But the worst was yet to come.

Bob Tway says of his bunker shot on the 72nd hole of the 1986 PGA Championship, "I was just trying to get it close to the hole." Tied with Norman on the final hole of regulation, Tway's ball sat in a sand trap, with the green sloping away from him. But Tway miraculously holed the shot to win by two shots. "Don't go saying the monkey's back on my back," Norman growled to a reporter afterward.

Norman looked like a sure winner the following spring at the Masters. On the second hole of a sudden-death playoff, he was on the right edge of the 11th green facing a birdie putt, while his opponent, Larry Mize, faced an incredibly difficult 140-foot uphill chip onto a nasty, down-sloping green. In one of the most famous shots in golf history, Mize amazingly holed it and the Augusta native leaped into the air with glee. The stunned Norman missed his long putt giving Mize the Green Jacket. "All I could do was take it," Norman said. "It was the hardest 45 seconds of my life."

Lady luck gave Norman the cold shoulder again, this time at the 1989 British Open. Norman entered the playoff after shooting a spectacular 64. His opponent, Mark Calcavecchia, had holed a 40-foot birdie putt and a 60-foot wedge shot for birdie on the back nine of his final round to put himself in playoff position. Norman and "Calc" were tied on the final hole of the four-hole playoff when Norman launched a tremendous drive that–unluckily–bounced into a fairway bunker. The Shark beached himself again on his approach, and then hit the next one out of bounds to hand his opponent the title. "How lucky can you be?" asked the astonished Calcavecchia.

Norman had another narrow brush with victory at the 1993 PGA Championship. In his bid to win his first major on U.S. soil, the Shark twice lipped out putts in a playoff to lose in agonizing fashion to Paul Azinger. "I'm happy for him, but I wish it was me," said Norman who also narrowly missed a 20-footer on the final hole of regulation that would have given him the win. But once again it was *Close, But No Cigar* for the Shark.

But it didn't end there as the golf gods had one more major heartbreak in store for Norman. The big Aussie held *a six-shot lead* over Nick Faldo going into the final round of the Masters. Norman was now poised to finally slip on a Green Jacket. But Norman absolutely collapsed with a final-round 78–including an implosive water shot on 16–while his English rival shot a 67 to win by five. Afterward, Norman said he went home and "lay on the beach and cried, because I felt like I'd completely screwed up winning a golf tournament I wanted to win."

All told, Norman finished second eight times in majors, with four thirds and an astounding 30 Top 10s. But his many failures cut him to the core. "I hid it inside me and wouldn't admit how much it hurt me. I was in denial."

 TRIVIA: Jack Nicklaus holds the record for most runner-ups in professional majors with 19, but he also won a record 18 times.

ROBERTO'S REGRET

"Roberto was popular, Bob wasn't."

It's a rare case where the runner-up is better remembered than the winner. In 1968, Roberto De Vicenzo was one stroke away from a playoff for the Masters crown–a pencil stroke, actually. The Argentinean bogeyed the 18th hole then went to the scoring area to sign his card. Still angry with the bogey, De Vicenzo barely looked at his scorecard before signing it. Big mistake. His playing partner, Tommy Aaron, had entered a four as De Vicenzo's score on the 17th hole, instead of the birdie three he actually scored.

It was Aaron who noticed the mistake first. He idly picked up the card and realized that someone–probably an official–had added up De Vicenzo's score and given him a 66. *That can't be right,* thought Aaron, who knew his playing partner had shot 65. Aaron alerted the official who scooted off to a cabin where tournament president and co-host Bobby Jones was watching on TV.

A few minutes later, Bob Goalby finished his round with a 65. He assumed he'd be heading to a playoff with De Vicenzo the next day. Consider his shock then, when commentator Cary Middlecoff came down from the TV tower and told Goalby he'd won. "What the hell you talking about?" asked the stunned golfer. Meanwhile, as De Vicenzo entered Butler Cabin for the annual TV presentation of the Green Jacket which in those days, was attended by the runner-up, the crestfallen player muttered the line he would become famous for, "What a stupid I am." He then added, "But in my country, what you get is what you shoot." Following the presentation, Goalby told the media, "I'm very, very happy to win the Masters. I'd be a liar if I said anything else. But I deeply regret the way it had to be done."

Despite the fact he had done nothing wrong, many thought that Goalby really hadn't earned his Masters victory, that he was an accidental champion. No one wanted to talk about the 11-under-par he shot to win at Augusta. Instead, the focus was on De Vicenzo's scoring error and how wrong it was for him to have lost that way. As a result, the personable De Vicenzo drew sympathy while the more reserved Goalby was seen as the bad guy. As CBS-TV producer Frank Chirkinian noted, "Roberto was popular, Bob wasn't."

The gaffe overshadowed the careers of both players. De Vicenzo should be remembered as the guy who won the 1967 British Open and more than 230 tournaments world-wide, including eight on the PGA Tour. Goalby should be recalled for his 11 wins on the PGA Tour, and seven other Top 10s in major tournaments—in addition to his star-crossed Masters. But a scoring error on a Sunday afternoon at Augusta changed all that.

"For me, the Masters hasn't ended," De Vicenzo told *Golf Digest* in 2006. "Technically, the ending was legal. But there was something missing. The winner hasn't yet emerged. It lacks an ending. Sometime, maybe in another place, it will be decided."

TRIVIA: Roberto De Vicenzo won tournaments in six consecutive decades, from the 1940s to the 1990s.

A SIXSOME OF SECONDS

"I am such an idiot."

It's a big hole in Phil Mickelson's record, and it has left an even bigger hole in his heart.

"Lefty" has been the heartbreak kid at the U.S. Open, with a record six runner-up finishes in three decades. It's the only one of the four Grand Slam tournaments Mickelson has never won.

Mickelson's tales of woe at America's oldest professional tournament began in 1999 at Pinehurst #2 in North Carolina. Not only was he chasing down Payne Stewart, he was also racing against the clock. His wife Amy was due with child and Phil said as soon as he got the word she was in labor, he'd rush to the hospital in Scottsdale, Arizona. Mickelson's pager never went off the whole tournament which culminated at the 72nd hole, with Mickelson in a bid to win his first major just one stroke behind Stewart. Phil left inches short a 25-foot putt that would have guaranteed him no worse than a spot in a playoff. Then Stewart stepped up and miraculously canned a 15-foot par putt to capture his second U.S. Open crown. The jubilant Stewart punched his fist into the air, then cupped Mickelson's face in his hands and exclaimed, "You're going to be a father!" The next day Phil was at his wife's side as she gave birth to a daughter. Meanwhile, Stewart never got to defend his U.S. Open title—he died four months later in a plane accident.

U.S. Open runner-up #2 for Mickelson came three years later at Bethpage Black on Long Island. Tiger Woods—a career nemesis for Mickelson—was at the height of his golfing prowess and was the heavy favorite to win his second U.S. Open crown. He didn't disappoint, playing nearly flawless golf to finish five under and coast to a three-shot victory over Mickelson. Lefty trailed by eight shots entering the weekend and battled back with rounds of 67 and 70, but it was another case of *Close, But No Cigar* for the San Diego native.

Mickelson came to the 2004 U.S. Open at Shinnecock Hills having just won the first major of his career at the Masters two months earlier. But Mickelson faded after a 66-68 start to record his third second-place U.S. Open finish, two shots behind Retief Goosen of South Africa. Any hope Mickelson had of winning ended when he double-bogeyed the 71st hole, three-putting from five feet.

Two years later and another U.S. Open reboot, this time with Mickelson concluding, "I just can't believe I did that. I am such an idiot." That's after he out-and-out blew that tourney. Here, Mickelson stood on the 18th tee at Winged Foot needing only a par to finally nail down his first U.S. Open crown. But he inexplicably hit a hospitality tent with his drive and proceeded to double-bogey the hole, handing victory to Geoff Ogilvy. Mickelson, Montgomery and Furyk tied for second, one stroke behind Ogilvy, who exclaimed afterward, "I think I was the beneficiary of a little bit of charity."

In 2009, Mickelson returned to Bethpage, where he had lost to Tiger in 2002. He had a share of the lead with an eagle on #13 on Sunday. But it was the same *Close, But No Cigar* story for Lefty as he gave it away by missing a short putt for birdie on #14, three-putted #15, missed another short putt on #16 on his way to bogey #17. Lucas Glover beat him by two shots. For Lefty, it was U.S. Open runner-up #5.

More heartbreak was in store in 2013 at Merion. Lefty took a one-stroke lead into the final round but lip-outs on #1, #2 and #9 didn't help his cause. After eagling #10 from the rough, Mickelson gave away three strokes on the back nine to lose by two to Justin Rose of England. "Heartbreak," the now six-time U.S. Open runner-up told NBC after the round. "This was my best chance of all of them."

Despite all the disappointment, Mickelson still believes he can win the last leg he needs for a career Grand Slam. "I played some of my best golf in this event, and I should have the opportunity—and more than one opportunity—to close one out here in the future."

 TRIVIA: Sam Snead finished second four times in the U.S. Open without ever winning his national championship.

WRONG NUMBER

"I went from getting congratulated, literally, to missing by one."

He passed the golf exam, but failed the accounting test.

Jaxon Brigman was on the brink of qualifying for the PGA Tour in 1999. All he needed was a par on the final hole at the PGA qualifying school in Miami and he would achieve his Tour dream. He got his par, signed his card, and started celebrating with his family. Then a grim-faced tour official pulled up in a golf cart and Brigman thought, "this can't be good."

It wasn't. The official told Brigman he had signed for the wrong score. Brigman's knees buckled and he fell to the ground, crying, after learning his playing partner, Jay Hobby, mistakenly wrote down a "4" for his tally on the 13th instead of the "3" he actually scored. Under the Rules of Golf, the score you sign for is the score you get, no exceptions. So one stroke was added to Brigman's score–and that one stroke cost him a spot on the PGA Tour.

Brigman never came close to qualifying for the tour again after his *Close, But No Cigar* moment. He now plays the mini-tours still chasing his PGA card. The former Oklahoma State golfer says people still talk to him about his close call. "They usually say, 'I'm sorry to bring this up ...' or, 'Was that you?' And I say, 'Yes, it was me but I'm fine to talk about it.' The scar's still there but the wound's gone."

 The PGA Tour Qualifying Tournament, or Q-School, was first held in 1965.

DALEY'S DISASTER

"I rolled that putt so good."

You've heard of "Tin Cupping" it? Well, Joe Daley "Plastic Cupped" it. In the fourth round of the 2000 PGA Tour qualifying school, the Pennsylvania native had a four-foot putt for double-bogey on the final hole. He stroked it perfectly–right in the center of the cup–but it somehow popped back out. Daley looked on in disbelief, slamming his hat to the ground in anger as the ball sat tauntingly, just on the lip of the cup.

It would have just been another missed putt–albeit a strange one– except for the fact Daley missed qualifying for the PGA Tour in the six-round "Q-School" event by one stroke. Yes, *that* stroke. Daley never again came close to making it to the big show, toiling in relative obscurity in pro golf's minor leagues before moving to the senior ranks and winning the Constellation Seniors Championship–considered a major event–in 2012.

But despite that success, Daley will always be remembered for the lousy break that cost him a spot on the PGA Tour.

The question remains—how did the putt miss? The reason can be found in the way golf holes are made. First, golf superintendents cut a hole in the turf, then a plastic cup is inserted so the hole will keep its shape. The likely explanation for Daley's miss is that the cup had become misaligned during the tournament. When Daley's ball dropped into the hole, it hit the top edge of the plastic cup just under the turf, and popped back out.

"I rolled that putt so good," Daley said afterward. "I wish I could roll every putt I ever had that good."

 TRIVIA: Daley didn't turn pro until he was 32.

LAURA'S LAMENT

"I found more ways to get beat than you can imagine."

She seemed to have it all.

Talent, looks, personality. Yes, Laura Baugh was going to be the next big star in women's professional golf.

But the wins never came, despite coming oh-so-close many times.

From an early age, Baugh was a golf natural. She won the first of five National Pee Wee Championships at the age of three. At 14 she won the first of back-to-back Los Angeles Women's City Amateurs, followed by the Junior World Amateur in 1970. But Baugh really burst onto the scene in 1971, when at 16 she won the U.S. Women's Amateur, becoming the youngest winner of that prestigious event at that time.

After being named the *Los Angeles Times* "Woman of the Year" in 1971, and *Golf Digest's* "Most Beautiful Golfer" in 1972, Baugh seemed to be on her way. She finished second in her first official LPGA event in 1973, and after yet another runner-up finish that same year was named LPGA Rookie of the Year. After starring in a Clio Award-winning commercial for Ultra Brite toothpaste, Baugh was becoming a household name.

Originally planning to play only five years and then settle down, that plan was put on hold as the endorsements continued to roll in. The money was good and retirement was pushed back. She figured the wins would come later, but they never did and Baugh's problems with drink proved problematic. The LPGA's one-time Golden Girl quit drinking in 1996 but by then her best days in pro golf were over.

Baugh, who finished second 10 times on the LPGA Tour without winning, told Golf Digest, "I found more ways to get beat than you can imagine." She came closest in 1979, when she lost a playoff to Hollis Stacy at the Mayflower Classic.

Baugh left the LPGA tour in the early 2000s to work as a commentator for The Golf Channel. Nowadays, she sells real estate in central Florida while sometimes playing the senior tour.

Despite the many ups-and-downs, Baugh describes her career as "blessed." Says Baugh, "I've had a chance to see the world and meet great people. And I've had some real, real good tournaments."

 TRIVIA: Laura Baugh's brother Beau Baugh played on the PGA tour for a couple of years in the late '80s.

PENCILLED OUT

"I've learned a lesson."

Jackie Pung went from hero to zero with the stroke of a pencil.

In 1957, the native of Honolulu appeared to have won the U.S. Women's Open. A final-round 72 at Winged Foot in Mamaroneck, New York, had apparently given her a one-stroke victory over Betsy Rawls.

But 40 minutes after she walked off the 18th green Pung's tears of joy turned to tears of despair–she had been disqualified for signing an incorrect scorecard. Rawls was declared the winner.

In the post-round excitement, Pung failed to notice that her playing partner, Betty Jameson, had written her down for a five on the fourth hole when she actually had a six. There was no attempt to cheat–it was strictly a clerical error as her total score of 72 on the card was correct. But the Rules of Golf are unyielding and in an instant, Pung went from being the 1957 U.S. Women's Open champion to being disqualified.

At the presentation ceremony Pung said, "Winning the Open is the greatest thing in golf. I have come close before. This time I thought I'd win. But I didn't. Golf is played by rules, and I broke a rule. I've learned a lesson. And I have two broad shoulders."

Pung got another surprise, but this time a good one. Members of the Winged Foot golf course passed the hat taking up a collection that netted her $3,000–exactly $1,200 more than the winner's purse.

Hounded by reporters, Pung describes her post-Open experience as "an ordeal." She says she spent the next week hiding out in a New York hotel while the media constantly hounded her about it over the next year.

"You know," Pung told *Hana Hou!* magazine years later, "Whenever I get together with the gals I used to play with on the old tour, they always tell me: 'Jackie, you were the real winner that day.'"

 TRIVIA: While she never won the U.S. Women's Open, Pung did win the U.S. Women's Amateur in 1952.

INCHES FROM IMMORTALITY

"It's all been close but no cigar."

I t was one of the greatest sand saves in golf history.

But nobody remembers it.

On the 71st hole of the 1970 Open Championship, Doug Sanders made a sensational up-and-down for par from the feared greenside Road Hole bunker to take a one-stroke lead into the final hole at St. Andrews.

On the next hole, needing only a par on the par-4 finishing hole, Sanders hit a perfect drive. His adrenaline-fuelled approach shot, however, landed 35 feet past the hole while his first putt stopped about three feet above the cup. The stage was now set for the dapper American to claim his first major golf crown, and do so at the storied Home of Golf.

Sanders carefully examined his putt, got himself set, but then paused to remove a blade of grass in his line. He addressed the putt again, and after a few more seconds, made an awkward jab at it. The crowd gasped–Sanders missed it badly and blew the most glorious opportunity of his golf career. The next day he would lose a playoff to Jack Nicklaus by one stroke.

"If I had made that putt, all the endorsements, the clothing lines, the golf-course designs," Sanders recounted to the *Philadelphia Inquirer,* his voice trailing off. "I never got set. I was thinking about which side I would bow to," Sanders admits. "It's all been close, but no cigar." Asked once if the missed putt ever bothered him, he responded, "No, sometimes I don't think about it for five minutes." So instead of being remembered as the player who won 20 PGA Tour events including the Canadian Open, Sanders is famous for missing one short putt that lost him a major.

Scott Hoch has a similar legacy. He and Nick Faldo were in a playoff in the 1989 Masters when disaster struck. After Faldo bogeyed, Hoch needed to make a simple two-foot putt to win the Green Jacket. After studying the virtual tap-in for a full minute, Hoch blasted it five feet past the hole, throwing his putter in the air in disgust. He made the comebacker but lost to Faldo's birdie on the next hole.

Fourteen inches separated another golfer, I.K. Kim, from her first major at the 2012 Nabisco Championship. A mere tap-in. But somehow Kim missed the putt–horseshoeing it completely around the cup as the crowd groaned. It was golf at its cruellest. "I'm not sure I have seen a short putt like that missed in a moment like this," Golf Channel commentator Terry Gannon told his audience. "This was just a formality." The shaken Kim went on to lose a sudden-death playoff to Sun Young Yoo on the first hole.

"It's life," Kim told golf.com a year after her devastating defeat. "You can't control everything. You can learn from things. You can work and practice. You can try to do better and move on." And move on she did– winning the Women's British Open in 2017 for her first major victory.

 TRIVIA: Hale Irwin whiffed a one-inch tap-in in the third round of the 1983 Open Championship. He would go on to lose the major by one stroke.

NEVER UP, NEVER IN

"I was lucky in life but not really lucky in golf."

A t least he won once.

That's about the only consolation for Fred Hawkins, one of golf's most frustrated bridesmaids.

The native of Antioch, Illinois, officially finished second 19 times on the PGA Tour while winning only once. He also took third spot 12 times and finished in the top ten 107 times in a career that ran from 1947 to 1965. Hawkins's only official tour victory was a two-shot triumph over Gardner Dickinson at the 1956 Oklahoma City Open.

Hawkins's most memorable runner-up finish came at the 1958 Masters. He missed out on a playoff with Arnold Palmer when he lipped out an

18-foot birdie attempt on the final hole. "He hit the greatest putt I've ever seen," fellow runner-up Doug Ford said. "The ball looked like it was going in the hole and went around the edge and stopped directly behind the hole, about half an inch. Impossible."

Hawkins did win something quite rare, however–the friendship of Ben Hogan. He was one of the few close friends of the reclusive legend. "He could be as gracious as he wanted to be," Hawkins told the *Milwaukee Journal Sentinel* in 2009.

Alcoholism forced Hawkins from the game in 1965, ending a career that included 21 holes-in-one and two double eagles. He quit drinking for good in 1978 and two years later, Hawkins–who Ray Floyd called the best chipper he ever saw–helped found what is now known as the Champions Tour. But little changed for the star-struck golfer–he finished third twice on the new senior tour. Hawkins died in 2014 at age 91.

Hawkins told *Armchair Golf Blog* in 2008, "I've always said I was lucky in life but not really lucky in golf."

TRIVIA: Fred Hawkins was the only U.S. player to win a singles match at the 1957 Ryder Cup, which the Americans had lost for the first time in 24 years.

CHAPTER 12

FORGOTTEN FIRSTS

"There is no room for second place."
– Vince Lombardi

MONOPOLY ON SUCCESS

"The game has cost her more than she made from it."

It was one of the great (and few) success stories of the Depression.
Charles Darrow lost his job as a salesman in the stock market crash of 1929 but became history's first millionaire game designer when he invented Monopoly.

It's a great rags to riches story. But there's just one problem with it: Darrow didn't invent Monopoly.

The origins of the game can be traced back to 1903 and a woman named Elizabeth Magie, whose contributions toward inventing one of the world's most popular games were forgotten for decades.

Born in 1866 in Illinois, Magie was influenced by a book her newspaper publisher father shared with her at a young age, *Progress and Poverty* by Henry George. The American writer believed that land and only land should be taxed, a popular concept at a time when many were struggling financially. Why not shift the tax burden to the wealthy landlords? The book inspired Magie—a stenographer by day and a comedic performer by night—to develop a game based on George's teachings. She called it the Landlord's Game, which was actually two games in one. The first was an anti-monopolist's version in which everybody shared in the wealth; the second was a pro-monopolist's version which encouraged one to accumulate as much wealth as possible and bankrupt everyone else. It was this second version that caught on.

Magie got a patent for The Landlord's Game in 1904—and the game spread. It was especially popular on university campuses in the northeast, including Harvard, Columbia and the Wharton School of Finance in Pennsylvania. The game was also adopted by Quakers in Atlantic City who simplified it, and named the properties after local streets.

Enter Charles Darrow. Like many Americans, he had seen and played the Quaker version of the game. He published his own version of it, which

CLOSE, BUT NO CIGAR

he called Monopoly, and sold it to Parker Brothers in 1935 after Milton Bradley rejected it. By this time, Parker Brothers had purchased Magie's patent and two other game ideas. But while Darrow went on to fame and fortune as the inventor of Monopoly, Magie reportedly only earned $500 for The Landlord's Game. "Probably, if one counts lawyer's, printer's and Patent Office fees used up in developing it," the *Washington Evening Star* opined, "the game has cost her more than she made from it."

Magie died a forgotten figure in 1948. She likely would have remained that way had an economics professor named Ralph Anspach not uncovered Magie's role in the Monopoly story in 1973 while doing research for a legal battle against Parker Brothers over a game he had developed called *Anti-Monopoly*. Anspach won in court, but some would say the bigger victory was his uncovering Magie as the true inventor of Monopoly.

 TRIVIA: The man with the moustache and top hat on the Monopoly game is named Rich Uncle Pennybags, or Mr. Monopoly.

THE FIRST WINSTON CHURCHILL

"He began his political career early in the 20th century, served as an officer in his country's military, and painted in his spare time."

His name was Winston Churchill, but you've probably never heard of him.

Winston Churchill—not be confused with that *other* guy who just happened to be prime minister of England—was one of the best-selling novelists of the early 20th century.

Born in St. Louis in 1871, Churchill landed on the literary map with his second novel, *Richard Carvel,* which sold a startling two million copies after its release in 1899. The book paved the way for two more successful historical novels, *The Crisis* (1901) and *The Crossing* (1904). Churchill, who liked to insert political opinions into his books, eventually went into politics himself. He was twice elected to the New Hampshire state legislature and ran unsuccessfully for governor of the Granite State. He also took up landscape painting, and some of his works can be found in the Hood Museum of Art in Hanover, New Hampshire. He also served with the U.S. Navy in the First World War.

Winston Churchill withdrew from public life in 1919, but that wasn't the last the world would hear from Winston Churchill. The *other* Winston Churchill that is, whose star was surely rising at that point. By the early 1920s he was already a two-decade veteran of the House of Commons, having served with distinction as First Lord of the Admiralty during the First World War. One of the 20th-century's most famous leaders, he led England through the Second World War. No one-trick pony either, he also received the Nobel Prize for Literature in 1953 for, among other things, his six-volume work *The Second World War*. "Winnie" died in 1965 at age 90.

Though not related, the two Churchills met and sometimes wrote to each other. In one of those exchanges, the British Churchill wrote, "I propose to become Prime Minister of Great Britain. Wouldn't it be a great lark if you could be president of the U.S. at the same time?" In order to differentiate himself from the American Churchill, the British Churchill agreed to sign his books Winston S. Churchill (his full, rarely used surname was Spencer-Churchill). His American counterpart had no middle names so he remained plain old Winston Churchill. Plain old Winston Churchill died in 1947 at age 75.

 TRIVIA: The American Churchill wrote a book called *The Crisis;* the British Churchill wrote a book called *The World Crisis.*

OF MOUSE AND MEN

"The greatest animator in the world."

So you think Walt Disney drew the first Mickey Mouse cartoon? Think again.

Ub Iwerks, a partner of Disney during his early years in animation, created the first Mickey Mouse cartoon. It was a silent 1928 film called *Plane Crazy* where Mickey emulates the flight of Charles Lindbergh. Working in secret during the evening while his Disney colleagues completed a contract at Universal Studios, Iwerks averaged an amazing 600-700 drawings a night during a six-week flurry of activity in 1928 to complete the 'toon. *Plane Crazy* was shown before a test audience on May 15, 1928– the first time the public ever saw Mickey Mouse. Later that year, Mickey appeared in his first short film, *Steamboat Willie*. This was the first of some 130 films involving the world's most famous mouse.

Iwerks met Disney in 1919 while working as a commercial artist in his hometown of Kansas City. The two became friends and Disney made Iwerks his first employee when he started his own animation company in the early '20s. Iwerks broke away from Disney in 1930 to start his own studio under film pioneer Pat Powers, but it closed six years later. Labelled "the greatest animator in the world" by none other than Disney himself, Iwerks never animated again. When he returned to Disney in 1940, Iwerks switched his focus to special effects, live-action films and Disney theme parks (the Haunted Mansion at Magic Kingdom is his handiwork). He twice won Oscars for his technical work, and was nominated for his effects in the infamous bird-attack scenes in Alfred Hitchcock's *The Birds*.

With the success of Mickey Mouse, most people forgot about an even earlier Disney character named Oswald the Rabbit. This star-struck critter, whose name was picked out of a hat, was also drawn by Iwerks and became Universal's first cartoon series and Walt Disney's first success. The inaugural *Trolley Troubles* came out in September 1927. But in the spring of 1928–deciding never again to work with a character he didn't own–Disney quit Universal, began a global entertainment empire and became one of the most famous persons in the world. And to think, as Disney himself later said, "it all started with a mouse." But then again, it might all have started with that crazy rabbit.

What made Iwerks tick? He was fascinated with machines and what made them work. It's said that Iwerks once disassembled an entire car and reassembled it over a weekend. He never tired of new challenges and got bored with old ones he had mastered (he once bowled a perfect game then gave up the sport). It was the same with animation–once he felt he had mastered it, he gave it up but not before revolutionizing the craft. He infused his characters with real personality making them come alive for audiences and influencing animators for years to come.

But why didn't he become more famous? Disney says Iwerks was simply too shy to promote himself.

 TRIVIA: In 1978, Mickey Mouse became the first cartoon character to get a star on the Hollywood Walk of Fame.

PACIFIC PIONEERS

"Boy are we glad to get here."

Charles Lindbergh became an American icon after becoming the first to fly solo non-stop across the Atlantic.

Ditto for Amelia Earhart who became the first solo female aviator to cross the Atlantic non-stop.

Clyde Pangborn and Hugh Herndon, Jr., on the other hand, became the first to fly non-stop across the Pacific–yet these names have long fallen by the wayside.

Pangborn, dubbed "Upside-Down Pangborn" for his ability to fly, well, upside-down, was a nationally known exhibition flyer who co-owned and flew with Gates Flying Circus during the 1920s. When the Flying Circus folded during the Depression, Pangborn and his co-pilot Hugh Herndon, Jr.–playboy son of an oil heiress–tried to beat the world record for flying around the world. Backed by $100,000 from Herndon's mom, they set out to make history, but their plane, *Miss Veedol,* became bogged down in Siberia after sliding off a runaway. What to do next?

The adventure-seeking pair decided they would try to be the first to fly across the Pacific non-stop, their interest piqued by a $25,000 prize being offered by the Japanese newspaper *Asahi Shimbun.* But they were in for a rude awakening when they landed at Tachikawa Airfield–they didn't have landing papers and the Japanese took a dim view of the pictures they'd been taking of military installations. Pangborn and Herndon spent the next seven weeks under house arrest, which the Americans put to good use planning their Pacific flight aboard *Miss Veedol.*

Finally released from detention, Japanese authorities gave them one chance to take off or lose their plane and go back to jail. Burdened down with excess fuel, the pair took off for America on October 4, 1931 barely clearing some logs at the end of the runway. "I was determined to get off or pile into those logs," said Pangborn. "We had permission for only the one attempt and in no way was I going to spend any more time in Japan." Before they left, a little Japanese boy gave the flyers a gift of five apples, a gesture Pangborn never forgot.

It was a wild ride to say the least. To save on weight, they had no radio, or survival gear, not even a seat cushion. An attempt to cut loose the landing gear to reduce drag partially failed, as the struts remained attached. So– with the inexperienced Herndon at the controls–Pangborn literally walked on the wings in bitterly cold temperatures and high winds to free the struts. Later the engine stopped after Herndon forgot to pump fuel from the main tank to the wing tanks. To restart the engine they had to dive the plane in hopes the propeller would windmill. So the fearless Pangborn dove the plane from 14,500 feet to 1,500 feet before the propeller spun and the engines popped to life again.

Pangborn then went for a nap, telling Herndon to keep an eye out for Vancouver, the next big city. But when Pangborn woke up, they had already flown right past Vancouver, and Seattle, and were headed straight toward Mount Rainer. Pangborn took the controls and with Boise, Idaho and Spokane, Washington, fogged in, he was forced to belly-land *Miss Veedol* in a field in his hometown of Wenatchee, Washington. Waiting for them were his mother, brother and a representative from *Asahi Shimbun*—with a cheque for $25,000. Forty-one hours and 13 minutes after they left Japan— as dawn broke on October 5—Pangborn and Herndon became the first to fly non-stop across the Pacific. "Boy are we glad to get here," Pangborn told the *Wenatchee Daily World,* whose young reporter, Carl M. Cleveland, got a world scoop because he had access to the only local phone.

Pangborn got only $2,500 for his achievement (despite doing about 95% of the flying by his own estimation). Most of the prize money and cash from the sale of the plane was taken by Herndon and his mother, who financed the flight. Meanwhile, Pangborn and Herndon won the prestigious Harmon Trophy, an aviator-of-the-year award previously given to Charles Lindbergh and later to Howard Hughes and Jimmy Doolittle.

Remembering the Japanese boy's gift of five apples, Pangborn had five cuttings from Washington state's renowned Richard Delicious apple trees sent to Misawa City, Japan to be grafted onto trees. The descendants of those five cuttings are today found in Richard Delicious apple trees found all over the Land of the Rising Sun.

 TRIVIA: *Miss Veedol* disappeared while on a New York to Rome flight in 1932 and has never been found.

WAYNE'S WORLD

"The greatest there's ever been."

He was the Duke before the Duke.

John Wayne became a film icon not just for his acting but for his mannerisms. His slow yet pronounced way of talking, his distinctive walk, even the way he threw a punch or jumped on a horse, all became deeply imbedded in 20th-century pop culture. Who hasn't done or heard a John Wayne impression? But all of what you've seen and heard of the Duke was borrowed from another man whose name isn't nearly as well known.

Born in 1895 in the Snake River Hills of Washington State, Yakima Canutt was a rodeo champ who got into films after working an event in Los Angeles. He appeared in dozens of silent movies in the 1920s but the advent of talkies threatened his career–he admitted that he sounded like "a hillbilly in a well." So Canutt switched course and became the world's first full-time stuntman. With Westerns all the rage, "Yak" soon became the king of the stuntmen. Borrowing on his rodeo techniques, Canutt became legendary for spectacular daredevilry. In 1939's *Stagecoach,* for instance, he scrambled from his horse and onto a stagecoach team, then slid under the horses and down under the coach completely unscathed. Yak's stunt was copied in the 1981 film *Raiders of the Lost Ark,* this time with a Nazi truck instead of a stagecoach.

Canutt doubled for all the big names in Hollywood in the 1930s–that's him driving a wagon through flames for Clark Gable in *Gone with the Wind.* But all said he's most identified for being John Wayne's stuntman. Wayne, who called Canutt "the most magnificent man I've ever met," was mentored by Yak as he was first getting started in the business. "I spent weeks studying the way Yakima Canutt walked and talked. He was a real cowhand. I noticed that the angrier he got, the lower his voice, the slower his tempo. I try to say my lines low and strong and slow, the way Yak did."

Aside from his innovative stunts and the influence he had on Wayne, Canutt made another big contribution: to safety. He invented a stirrup that allowed stuntmen to fall off horses but not get hung. He developed cable rigs, harnesses and other equipment that made other stunts safe, thus cutting down on injuries and saving studios time and money. In the 1940s, Yak started directing stunt crews becoming one the greatest action directors in film (he was behind the famous chariot scene in 1959's *Ben-Hur*). That, and his other work, helped Canutt win a special Oscar in 1966 for contributions to film. The legendary stuntman and action scene director died in 1986 at age 90.

"He was the first guy to make a science of it," says Vic Armstrong, the guy who copied Canutt's stunt in *Raiders of the Lost Ark*. "Yakima Canutt was the daddy of them all–the greatest there's ever been."

 TRIVIA: John Wayne was an avid chess player, often playing the game on set.

THE LOST NETWORK

"The little network that could, could do no more."

It was one of the first U.S. television networks, and one of the most innovative, yet the DuMont Television Network is virtually forgotten today.

Founded by Allen B. DuMont in 1931, DuMont Laboratories rose to prominence by producing the first all-electronic television set in 1938. The sets were displayed at the 1939 World's Fair in New York but there was a big problem for potential buyers: there was almost nothing on TV. So in 1939 DuMont launched its own TV station in New York–the experimental outlet W2XVT–broadcasting from a former pickle factory in Passaic, New Jersey. In the early '40s Dumont added experimental stations in New York and

Washington and pressed on with test broadcasts during the Second World War while NBC and CBS cut back. DuMont did its first network broadcast in 1946, albeit with only two stations. Three years later DuMont shows were airing in 32 cities across the U.S. At its height in 1954, DuMont was affiliated with some 200 stations, but many of those were rarely watched UHF outlets. Just two years later the network was history, and it would be three more decades before FOX emerged as a viable fourth network.

So why did DuMont fail? Unlike NBC, CBS and ABC, it didn't have a radio division. Therefore, the television network didn't have a roster of radio stars to draw on, nor did it have the advantage of having a profitable radio division to balance out losses on the TV side. Another advantage the Big Three networks had is that while they were each allowed to own and operate five TV stations, DuMont was limited to three. Network owner Allen B. DuMont sold 26% interest in his company to Paramount in 1939 and Paramount's wholly-owned stations in Los Angeles and Chicago were still treated by the FCC as DuMont properties, even though they were actually competitors.

Another problem was DuMont's decline as a TV manufacturer. The company that boasted "First with the Finest in Television" was falling behind GE, RCA and Westinghouse. ABC's 1953 merger with United Paramount Pictures pushed it deeper into fourth place, and money was wasted when DuMont needlessly sank $5 million into a New York production center in 1954. But the death knell for Dumont was the sale of its highly profitable Pittsburgh station to Westinghouse to raise needed cash. When Paramount decided to take over complete control of DuMont in 1955, its days as the fourth network were as good as done.

Despite its short life, DuMont made its share of TV history. It was the first network to have shows with many different advertisers, rather than a single sponsor. DuMont also broadcast the first TV soap opera, *Faraway Hill*, the first game show, *Cash and Carry,* the first science-fiction series, *Captain Video and His Video Rangers,* the first regularly scheduled children's show, *The Small Fry Club*. And 17 years before Monday Night

Football, live prime-time telecasts of the NFL. They pioneered shows hosted by minorities: *The Gallery of Madame Liu-Tsong* was the first show hosted by an Asian-American (Anna May Wong); *The Hazel Scott Show* was the first TV program hosted by an African-American woman, the singer-pianist Hazel Scott. DuMont was also the birthplace of one of TV's most popular sit-coms, *The Honeymooners* starring Jackie Gleason (it moved to CBS after less than a year), and it was also the only network to broadcast the Army-McCarthy hearings.

The end of the spunky DuMont Television Network came on August 6, 1956 with the airing of *Boxing from St. Nicholas Arena,* hosted by Chris Schenkel. As Jeff Kisseloff wrote in his book, *The Box,* "The little network that could, could do no more."

 TRIVIA: Reruns of the DuMont program, *Life is Worth Living,* hosted by Bishop Fulton Sheen, are still aired to this day on the Eternal Word Television Network.

VICTORIA WAS NO SECRET

"Women are the equals of men."

With all the buzz about Hillary Clinton's historic run for the presidency, we shouldn't forget the nearly forgotten woman who was the first of her gender to run for America's top office–a century-and-a-half earlier.

Victoria Woodhull made history in 1872 when she ran for president on the Equal Rights Party ticket. Born Victoria Claflin in 1838 in Homer, Ohio, she married Canning Woodhull when she was only 15 years old. The marriage didn't last, but she kept the name. In 1868 Woodhull and her sister Tennessee got involved in the popular spiritualist movement, and Victoria got rich touring the country entertaining audiences as a clairvoyant.

CLOSE, BUT NO CIGAR

So impressed was tycoon Cornelius Vanderbilt with their psychological prowess that he set the sisters up in business. Thus started Wall Street's first female-run stock brokerage nicknamed the "Bewitching Brokers."

Woodhull wasn't afraid to champion controversial causes, including women's rights, communism, licensed prostitution and free love (she once lived with her ex-husband, husband and lover all in the same apartment). In 1870, she began putting her ideas into print through the *Woodhull & Claflin's Weekly*. One of Woodhull's regular concerns was women's suffrage. "Women are the equals of men before the law, and are equal in all their rights," she exclaimed. She ran for president the next year, even though women were not allowed to vote and she was younger than the constitutionally-mandated minimum age of 35.

Woodhull's presidential platform included some pretty progressive ideas for the time, including welfare, regulation of monopolies, an eight-hour workday and abolition of the death penalty. In the end it didn't matter– while her name was on the ballot in some states no one knows how many votes she received because they weren't counted.

Woodhull divorced her second husband in 1876 but married a wealthy English banker seven years later. She moved to England, wrote a book, *Human Body: The Temple of God* (1890), published a magazine with her daughter and helped preserve the English home of George Washington's ancestors. She returned to the U.S. to run for president again in 1892, saying she was "destined" by "prophesy" to become president. However, she didn't do any better than the first time. Woodhull lived long enough to see ratification of the 19th Amendment, which gave women the right to vote. She died in 1927 in England, aged 88.

Despite her efforts on behalf of women's rights, Woodhull was disowned by the American suffrage movement. Her political ambitions and public persona (among other things, she had been charged with sending obscene material through the mail) made her persona non grata with leading suffragists such as Susan B. Anthony and Elizabeth Cady. Huffed Anthony in a letter, "Both sisters are vile and indecent."

TRIVIA: The second woman to run for president was Belva Ann Lockwood of the National Equal Rights Party in 1884. She and her running mate Marietta Stow were on the ballot in six states and received 4,149 votes.

LATE-NIGHT BEGINNINGS

"The heckler of all hecklers."

L ong before Johnny Carson, Jack Paar and Steve Allen, there was *Broadway Open House.*

Network television's first attempt at late-night programming–the grand-daddy of them all–aired on NBC for about a year in the early 1950s. But the show and the names of the first hosts have disappeared into the mists of history.

TV in its early days was a blank slate filled with possibilities. No one really knew what would work, so they tried everything. NBC president Pat Weaver had been a production assistant on Fred Allen's radio show *Town Hall Tonight,* the longest-running hour-long comedy-based show in the history of early radio. Weaver thought a late-night variety/talk show on television might be a winner too, and planned *Broadway Open House* to air live on weeknights from 11 p.m. to midnight.

The first host was supposed to be comedian and novelty pianist Don "Creesh" Hornsby, whose wild and crazy act was described by *LIFE* as "a five-hour marathon of surrealist madness." However, he died of polio shortly before *Broadway Open House* was scheduled to debut and the network had to scramble for a replacement, or–as it turned out–replacements. Morey Amsterdam–who would later star as Buddy Sorrell on the *Dick Van Dyke Show*–would host the show two nights a week while brash comedian Jerry Lester–whose background included vaudeville, Broadway, film and radio–

would carry the ball the other three nights.

The show debuted May 29, 1950. It was a mish-mash of comedy bits, music and dance numbers and occasional informal chatting with celebrities, less a talk show than a variety show. Lester—a master of low comedy (he called himself "the heckler of all hecklers")—interacted with orchestra leader Milton DeLugg and the shapely blonde Dagmar. Amsterdam left in November 1950 leaving Lester to host all five nights. But Dagmar—a former chorus girl whose real name was Virginia Lewis—became such a big star in her own right that Lester got jealous and left the show in May 1951. Sarcastic comic Jack Leonard—who made Don Rickles seem kindly—took over as host until the show was cancelled in August 1951.

Tonight would debut in September 1954—three years after *Broadway Open House* was cancelled. Steve Allen was host. As *Broadway Open House* receded in memory, the public began to assume *Tonight* was the original late-night talk show. As for Lester, he left network TV and moved to Los Angeles where he resurfaced in 1959 as host of a late-night comedy-music revue on KTTV Los Angeles. He went on to star in several films and appear in the touring stage version of *A Funny Thing Happened on the Way to the Forum*. Lester retired from performing in 1975 after forgetting his lines at a New Year's Eve show. He died of Alzheimer's 20 years later.

Lester said likeability was more important than talent. "If they like you, you don't have to worry whether every gag goes over big or if every sketch is the best thing they've ever seen," Lester told an interviewer during *Broadway Open House's* heyday in 1950. "And if it isn't, I don't beat the audience over the head. I never tell them they're wrong. I just apologize."

 TRIVIA: *The Tonight Show* is the third-longest running TV show in history behind *Meet the Press* and *Today*.

RICHARD'S REVENGE

"I'll be damned if I don't do it."

Lee Harvey Oswald. John Wilkes Booth. John Hinckley.

If you know American history, you're familiar with these names because all were involved in the assassination or the attempted assassination of a president.

But the name of the man who *first* attempted to shoot the president has been forgotten by all but the most astute students of U.S. history.

Richard Lawrence first set foot in America at age 12 when his family came over from England. He worked as a house painter but was forced into unemployment by the early 1830s as his mental state declined. Lawrence thought he was King Richard III, which was odd because that British monarch had been dead for about 350 years. Soon, Lawrence started dressing flamboyantly, grew a moustache and believed President Andrew Jackson was holding back money that would eventually allow him to take over the English throne. Lawrence also blamed the president for the death of his father in 1832 (his pop actually died a decade earlier and was never in America; but no matter).

While Lawrence's problems with the president were imagined, his determination to kill him was very real. He got his chance January 30, 1835 when the president attended the funeral of South Carolina congressman William R. Davis at the Capitol Building. After telling himself, "I'll be damned if I don't do it" (Lawrence talked to himself a lot), the would-be assassin headed toward the Capitol and hid behind a pillar to await the end of the funeral.

When Jackson gave his leave, Lawrence left his hiding place, approached the president, then fired at his chest from just eight feet away. The gun misfired, so Lawrence took out a second pistol. But it too failed to fire. Lawrence was quickly subdued by a crowd that included legendary frontiersman Davy Crockett. Jackson survived the attack unscathed. The president got lucky that day; it's been estimated that the odds of both guns failing were 125,000-1.

Brought to trial two-and-a-half months later, the jury deliberated just five minutes before finding Lawrence not guilty by reason of insanity. He spent the rest of his life in mental institutions, where he painted landscapes while enjoying celebrity status among his fellow patients. Lawrence died in 1861 at what is now known as St. Elizabeth's Hospital in Washington, D.C. President Jackson, who for the rest of his life was paranoid that his enemies were out to get him, predeceased Lawrence by 16 years.

 TRIVIA: In 1933, Jackson was slapped in the face (or had his nose pulled, accounts vary) by a man named Robert B. Randolph on the U.S.S. *Cygnet.* Seems he was upset Jackson had dismissed him from the U.S. Navy for embezzlement. The president, though bloodied, was not seriously injured. He declined to press charges and refused a military guard. The Randolph incident is believed to be the first physical attack on a sitting president

CHAPTER 13

MORE SPORTING TYPES

"Shoulda, coulda and woulda won't get it done."
– Pat Riley

CAPTIVE COMPETITION

"They were all perfect gentlemen."

There were no TV cameras, turnstiles or refreshment stands.

There were lots of razor wire, watchtowers and armed guards.

Long before the NHL started making it an annual spectacle, the Detroit Red Wings became the first NHL team to play an outdoor game— and they did it at a prison.

It happened February 2, 1954. The Red Wings fulfilled a promise made by general manager Jack Adams to play a team of prisoners at maximum security Marquette (Michigan) Branch Prison. Months earlier, Adams— caught off guard by the warden's invite to have the Red Wings play a game at his pen—said he would do it if the warden paid for the plane, meals and hotel rooms. Warden Emery Jacques agreed and the Red Wings were soon set to faceoff at the "Alcatraz of the North."

The game was held on a cold, overcast afternoon in front of a (captive) crowd of some 600 inmates. Despite the setting, Gordie Howe said it was the best ice he had ever played on. Nevertheless, there were no surprises to report. The game was predictably a one-sided affair with the Red Wings scoring at will. It was 10-0 after 10 minutes and 18-0 after the first period (they stopped keeping score at that point). As losing defenceman Oakie Brumm said, "The only time I touched the puck was when I pulled it out of the back of the net."

To balance the talent somewhat after the opening frame, the Wings loaned a few players to their inmate squad, including star goalie Terry Sawchuk. On the other side a convict centered a line between Howe and "Terrible Ted" Lindsay. "I was viewed as a hero," remarked Lindsay, "because I was leading the league in penalties, so I fit right in with the boys." Marquette's inmates were a dangerous lot, and the NHL tough guy remembers asking the guards about safety. "Oh no," one guard told Lindsay. "If anyone thought of doing anything, they would be dead before he took two steps."

The Wings won a "honey bucket"—a refuse pail prisoners used in their cells—and some great memories. "It was an experience that I thoroughly enjoyed," Lindsay would later say.

The Red Wings didn't play outdoors again until they met the Blackhawks in the 2009 Winter Classic at Wrigley Field. Jack Adams continued to donate hockey equipment to the prison but the Wings never again played the Marquette big house. Says Brumm, "He got busy, we got busy, and for some reason it never happened."

TRIVIA: Marquette Branch Prison was added to the National Register of Historic Places in 1977.

THE TEAM THAT ALMOST WASN'T

"We weren't sure if we'd make it."

One of basketball's greatest franchises almost never happened.

In the pre-dawn hours of January 18, 1960, the Minneapolis Lakers—set to move to Los Angeles the following season—crashed into an Iowa cornfield during a raging blizzard. Miraculously, no one was killed or seriously injured. The Lakers, struggling through their final season, had gathered at the St. Louis airport for their flight back to Minneapolis. They had just played the Hawks in St. Louis the previous afternoon. However, the plane was delayed for a few hours because of icy conditions and light snow. Finally, at 8:30 p.m. the 1930's vintage twin propeller DC-3, owned by their tightwad boss Bob Short, took off.

Just minutes later, the plane suffered an electrical failure. Suddenly, the flight crew's radio went down. Also gone was their heating unit and navigation system. They were flying blind and the fates of the nine Lakers, plus interim coach Jim Pollard and 13 others, rested on the skills of pilot

Verne Ullman, co-pilot Harold Gifford and trainee Jim Holtznagel.

The pilots were in a tight spot. They couldn't return to St. Louis because the radio was out. They tried to fly above the storm but the higher they flew the worse the conditions got. Since the windshield wipers weren't working the pilots had to open the cockpit windows to swipe the snow away. They were completely lost. In fact, things got so bad they started following above the headlights of a car hoping it would lead to civilization. "For a time," admits co-pilot Gifford, "we weren't sure if we'd make it."

With fuel running low and no airport in sight, the DC-3 set down in a cornfield in Carroll, Iowa. It was "the smoothest landing I ever had," said Laker forward Elgin Baylor. The plane slid 100 yards before stopping when the tail wheel luckily hooked onto a barbed wire fence. Ullman–against regulations–had ordered the wheels to remain down during the emergency landing. Had he not done so, the plane would have plummeted into a ravine, which would have meant certain death. Despite that fact, Ullman's flying license was suspended by the FAA.

The first townspeople to greet the dazed but happy survivors was the local mortician, who according to Lakers rookie Tommy Hawkins, told the players, "Thought I had some business tonight, boys." The players spent the night at a local retirement home before busing it back to Minneapolis.

Their next game was in Cincinnati–and incredibly–they flew there on the same plane. Assured that everything was fine, the players got another shock when an engine caught fire after a fuel leak. Emergency measures were needed but the plane landed safely. Even more amazingly, the same cursed plane showed up again–a couple of years later–while the team was in the mid-west for an exhibition game. Seems the new Laker owner had bought it from the old one.

While the near-tragic crash remains a passing memory, the people of Carroll still remember it well. On the 50th anniversary of the crash, 2010, the town unveiled a marker showing a spot close to where the plane went down. The appreciative Lakers also donated $25,000 to a basketball court near the crash site.

TRIVIA: The Minneapolis Lakers were formed after the purchase of the Detroit Gems of the National Basketball League in 1947.

TRIPLE UNCROWNED

"They would stare at each other, their manes flicking in the breeze."

Not once, not twice, but three times Alydar stood on the brink of glory.

Three times the three-year-old chestnut colt finished second—to the same horse no less—on thoroughbred racing's greatest stages.

The story of Alydar is one of close calls, tragedy and a rivalry for the ages.

Alydar may have been the greatest horse never to win a Triple Crown race. But it wasn't through lack of effort, or an absence of skill. The speedy stallion entered the 1978 Kentucky Derby as a 6-5 favorite following wins in several major races including the Flamingo Stakes and the Florida Derby. Affirmed was installed as second choice at 9-5.

What followed was one of the greatest Triple Crown runs ever. In the Kentucky Derby, Affirmed held off a hard-charging Alydar by one-and-a-half lengths to win the Run for the Roses. Next up was the Preakness, won again by Affirmed by a mere head over Alydar. Then Affirmed edged Alydar by a nose after what is still the fastest closing mile in the history of the Belmont Stakes. The great Affirmed became the 11th Triple Crown winner, while Alydar was consigned to the *Close, But No Cigar* hall of fame as the first and only horse to finish second in all three Triple Crown races.

Undaunted, Alydar came back to win the Arlington Stakes and the Whitney Stakes that summer. And the rematch with Affirmed in the Travers Stakes proved anticlimactic, as Alydar finished second by one and three-quarter lengths but was handed first after Affirmed was disqualified for interference. It was their 10th and final meeting on the track—with the rivalry ending 7 to 3 in favor of Affirmed.

Alydar's racing career ended after injury in the 1979 Suburban Handicap. He was retired to stud and would go on to become one of the most successful sires ever—his offspring included Alysheba, the Kentucky Derby and Preakness winner in 1987—along with other top horses like Easy Goer, Turkoman and Althea.

Alydar died in 1990 under mysterious circumstances. He shattered his leg and was euthanized after apparently kicking and breaking a roller on his stall door. Suspicions were raised that Alydar might have been killed for insurance money. An engineer brought in to investigate the death speculated that the horse was injured when someone tied a rope to his hind leg before driving off with the other end tied to a truck. J.T. Lundy, who owned debt-riddled Calumet Farms at the time of Alydar's death, denies any involvement in the horse's demise and a judge declined to pursue charges.

One of the great ironies of this story is that Affirmed and Alydar were reunited in 1990 at Calumet Farms. As Skip Hollandsworth noted in his excellent *Texas Monthly* story "The Killing of Alydar," the two horses would stare at other, "their manes flicking in the breeze," and, always the competitors, would race each other from the opposite sides of the fence.

TRIVIA: Alydar jockey Jorge Velasquez was inducted into the National Racing Hall of Fame in 1990.

RUNNERUP FOR THE ROSES

"The bitter is a lot worse than the sweet."

Fifteen years after Diane Crump became the first female to ride in the Kentucky Derby, P.J. Cooksey became the second.

With considerably less ballyhoo than Crump's debut in 1969, Cooksey rode So Vague to an 11th-place finish in 1984's Run For The Roses. The native of Youngstown, Ohio, broke into racing in 1979, winning her very first race at Waterford Park aboard Turf Advisor. She briefly held the crown as racing's all-time female wins leader in 1988 until she was surpassed by Hall of Famer Julie Krone.

The all-time female wins leader at Louisville's Churchill Downs and the first woman to ride in the Preakness, Cooksey's greatest triumph came in the early 2000s when she survived breast cancer. She also came back from a 2003 racing spill in which she broke both legs.

Cooksey retired in 2004, ending a career which saw her win 2,137 races. "It's the old bittersweet. But I feel like the bitter is a lot worse than the sweet," she said following her last race at age 46. "I'm sad. I'm real sad."

 TRIVIA: Barbara Jo Rudin was the first woman scheduled to ride in the Kentucky Derby in 1969, but her horse was scratched.

RUNNER RUNNER-UP

"Legs like an ostrich."

He was one of the greatest runners of his time, but John Landy was destined to live in the shadow of another.

Landy came into running quite by accident. He ran to keep in shape for Australian rules football but began to take running seriously while at Melbourne University. The turning point came when Landy came under the tutelage of coach Percy Cerutty. In less than five weeks, Landy improved from 4:43 for the mile to 4:17. "He has legs like an ostrich," said Cerutty of his prize pupil. "He moves over the ground in the same effortless manner and is amazing just to watch."

Landy's time soon improved to 4:11 which landed him a spot on the Australian track and field team for the 1952 Helsinki Olympics. Landy ran a new personal best of 4:10 but finished a disappointing fifth in his 1,500-meter Olympic heat. Better things would be ahead, however. But also out there was a man named Roger Bannister.

Aided by European running shoes and training, Landy inched closer to the four-minute mark with a time of 4:02:1 in December 1952. It was the third-fastest mile in history. Now the race was on, who would be the first to run the four-minute mile? On May 6, 1954 Bannister beat him to it, reaching running's hallowed ground with a time of 3:59:4 (which some say was a time trial against two pacers and not a real race). Just 46 days later, Landy became the second man to break the four-minute mile with a world record time of 3:58.

Next up: the Miracle Mile. Bannister and Landy were scheduled to meet in August 1954 at the British Empire and Commonwealth Games in Vancouver. *Sports Illustrated* called it the "most widely heralded and universally contemplated foot race of all time." It didn't disappoint. On a hot, sunny day at Empire Stadium, Bannister edged Landy 3:58:8 to 3:59:6–the first time two runners had broken four minutes in the same race. A bronze sculpture outside Empire Stadium captures the moment when Landy glanced over his left as Bannister overtook him on the right. "I don't have the temperament of a race winner," Landy said afterward. "I just like to run fast."

Landy said he would have retired had he won, but decided to go for the 1956 Games in Melbourne which were practically in his own backyard. Incredibly, he won his qualifying heat after stopping to help another runner who had fallen. Like his Miracle Mile moment, that effort is commemorated with a sculpture in Melbourne (how many athletes are portrayed in two sculptures?). However, hampered by an Achilles heel problem, he only managed a bronze in the 1,500 meters on home soil.

Landy retired after the Olympics, became a highly sought-after public speaker, wrote two books on natural history, and served as governor of the Australian state of Victoria. He was inducted into the Sport Australia Hall of Fame in 1985. He was never bitter about the controversy about Bannister's historic feat. "The four-minute mile had been run," Landy said simply.

 TRIVIA: Who won the *bronze* medal in the Miracle Mile? It went to a Canadian, Rich Ferguson of Toronto, with a Canadian record time of 4:04:6.

20-20-20 VISION

"Babe Ruth leading the league in sacrifice bunts."

Wilt Chamberlain made history in 1962 when he became the first—and so far, the only—player to score 100 points in an NBA game.

But mostly forgotten is yet another incredible achievement by The Stilt, one that also stands alone in the annals of pro basketball.

On February 2, 1968, Chamberlain achieved the first and only 20-20-20 game in NBA history, scoring 22 points, stuffing 22 rebounds and dishing out 21 assists as the Philadelphia '76ers defeated the Detroit Pistons 131-121. It was part of an amazing season during which Chamberlain decided to show critics he could be a team player. He then went out to become the first and only center to lead the NBA in total assists, something Chamberlain likened to, "Babe Ruth leading the league in sacrifice bunts."

Had any other player done this, it would have stood out. But Chamberlain's 20-20-20 was just one of many astounding feats Wilt achieved during his amazing career. Aside from the 100-point game, Chamberlain holds several eye-popping NBA records, including single-season scoring average (50.4), most career 50 point or more games (118), career per-game rebound average (22.9) and most average career minutes played (45.8). The Big Dipper's number 13 has been retired by six teams, including three NBA squads.

 TRIVIA: Wilt Chamberlain never even fouled out in a game, not one, in high school, college or pro.

FOREVER IN SECOND

"I never thought of winning."

In cycling, they even have a name for a serial second-placer.

Eternal Second.

Raymond Poulidor was the original Eternal Second because he was the first to finish second three times in the Tour de France without ever winning. (He was also third *five times!*) His big problem? His career coincided with those of French legend Jacques Anquetil and Belgian great Eddy Merckx.

In 1964, the man they called "Pou Pou" lost his first epic Tour battle to arch-rival Anquetil—in fact, the 55-second margin of victory was the closest in Tour de France history to that point. Anquetil's record fifth victory also marked the end of an era—the cycling legend would never win it again and soon retired. But for "Pou Pou," the pain was just beginning.

The next year Poulidor finished second again, this time to Felice "The Phoenix" Gimondi. The Italian, who was in his first professional season, had been a last-minute substitute. Gimondi became a national hero while Poulidor could only wonder, "what if?"

Despite the hiccup with Gimondi, the way should now have been clear for Poulidor to finally win the Tour de France. But the Eddy Merckx era was just beginning. Nicknamed "The Cannibal" because he wanted to eat up the road and win everything, Merckx became the second rider after Anquetil to win five Tour de Frances. Poulidor finished third behind the Belgian great in 1969 and 1972 and was runner-up to Merckx in 1974. This made it "Pou Pou's" third second-place finish in the Tour. He finished third the next year at age 40 but would never grace the podium of the 3,500-km, 23-day race again.

Poulidor—who was also second once and third three times in the World Championships—did win his share of titles, including the Criterium International five times. He's in the Hall of Fame. But his name has become synonymous in France where athletes and politicians who finish second are said to have pulled "a Poulidor."

Though bitter rivals, Poulidor nonetheless visited Anquetil in his final hours as he lay dying of cancer in 1987. "He said to me that the cancer was so agonizingly painful it was like racing up the Puy de Dôme all day, every hour of the day. He then said, 'I will never forget it, my friend, you will come second to me once again.'"

TRIVIA: In 1904 a cyclist at the Tour de France was disqualified for covering part of the event—in a train.

BOB BOOTS IT

"We were world champs for seven seconds."

For a few brief moments, it appeared Bob LaBonte was world curling champion.

Then it all slipped away.

It was the final regulation end of the 1972 World Curling Championship at Garmisch Partenkirchen, Germany. The Canadian team, skipped by Orest Meleschuk, were heavy favorites to win. But they were trailing the American squad, led by North Dakota's Bob LaBonte, by two points with the hammer, or last rock. Meleschuk had a hit-and-stick for two on his last rock, but his rock appeared to roll too far. Before a measurement could be called to verify who won the points, the American vice, Frank Aasand, started to jump up and down to celebrate the apparent victory. LaBonte followed suit. For those of you unfamiliar with the game, curling is played on ice. Jumping up and down is not recommended.

Then, sure enough, it happened. LaBonte's feet came out from under him. He landed on his backside and grazed the Canadian rock, moving it closer to the button. A measurement was made that now showed that Canada had scored two points to tie the game as a stunned and embarrassed LaBonte looked on. Canada then won this very controversial game with a steal of one in the extra end.

"We were World Champs for seven seconds," LaBonte said years later. "At least I got to feel what it was like to win."

The infamous game spawned what was known as "The LaBonte Curse." Legend has it that following LaBonte's ice capades, he put a hex on future Canadian teams who played at the Worlds (though the curse appears to have been invented by a sports writer). That said, it was eight years before the regularly dominant Canada won another World Championship, and another 25 years before North Dakota made it to that stage.

Was the American rock closer than the Canadian rock? It appears quite possible, and two of the Canadian players had already taken off their gloves to shake hands and concede defeat. But we'll never know for sure, and Canadian vice-skip Dave Romano never had a chance to check the position of both stones before the rock was kicked.

LaBonte never again represented the U.S. at the World Curling Championship, but "Boots," as he was now nicknamed, would still show up at the tournaments to jokingly "hex" the Canadian team.

 TRIVIA: Canada has won the World Men's Curling Championship more times than all other countries combined.

MINORITY LEADERS

"People looked at me like I was a Martian."

When Mike Marson became the second black man to play in the NHL, he had big skates to fill.

That was because Mike was following "The Jackie Robinson of Ice Hockey," a visible minority with a hidden handicap.

Willie O'Ree not only overcame racial prejudice to become the first black player in the NHL, but he also concealed the fact that he was blind in one eye.

O'Ree lost sight in his right eye when he was struck by a puck in junior hockey. Determined to play in the NHL some day, O'Ree kept his disability a secret when he joined the minor league Quebec Aces for the 1956-57 season. In January 1958 O'Ree became the first black player in the NHL when the Boston Bruins called him up for a couple of games. O'Ree would play more than two decades in professional hockey—most of it in the minors—before retiring in 1979. All this time he hid the fact that he was blind in one eye.

It was 16 more years before another black player skated in the NHL. Mike Marson was a promising Sudbury Wolves left winger taken in the second round of the 1974 draft by the expansion Washington Capitals. He was picked ahead of future stars Bryan Trottier, Mark Howe and Tiger Williams. But his success in junior hockey never translated to the pros. One problem was his age—at 18 he just wasn't ready for the demands of professional hockey. Another was his weight—at 5'9", 200 pounds, Marson was considered too big to be a skill player at the time. Then there was the biggest problem of all: Race.

"I found out that people looked at me like I was a Martian," Marson told author Cecil Harris in *Breaking the Ice*. "Not Mike Marson. Mike Martian. Because I was a black hockey player."

Marson started well with Washington, scoring 16 goals in his rookie season and establishing himself as an enforcer. But it was downhill from there and he was soon out of pro hockey. Only 25 when he left the game, Marson got work as a bus driver but found a new outlet for his athleticism: martial arts. The one-time junior hockey star has become a 5th degree black belt in Shotokan, a Japanese style of karate, and has attained the status of Master-Shihan (expert or senior instructor). Marson also developed a martial arts training program for hockey players; one of his students is former NHL player Rick Nash.

"There was just so much garbage I had to deal with that I just wasn't used to," Marson said. "The accumulation of all that garbage just made me uneasy."

 TRIVIA: The first black player to sign an NHL contract was Art Dorrington in 1950 with the New York Rangers, but he never got called up.

STIRLING SILVER

"I had the respect of other drivers."

H e's been called the greatest driver never to win the World Championship.

Stirling Moss was close so often to the Formula One title he could practically touch it. The son of a London dentist finished second in the points race over four consecutive years (1955-58), then was third each of the next three seasons. Three times he was runner-up to Italian Juan Manuel Fangio; the other time he was second to fellow Englishman Mike Hawthorn.

Moss could have easily beaten out Hawthorn in 1958, but his sportsmanship got in the way. At the Portuguese Grand Prix in August 1958, Moss finished ahead of Hawthorn to tighten up the points race. But race officials received a complaint that Hawthorn had broken the rules because he wasn't on the actual course when he restarted his car. Moss argued in support of his opponent, saying Hawthorn shouldn't be penalized. The stewards agreed but the points Hawthorn kept proved to be crucial as he went on to win the World Championship by one point over Moss. Had Moss not spoken up, he would have held the title.

"It gives me my exclusivity, and makes me different, so it's been a bonus," said Moss in a 2012 interview with *The Telegraph*. Hawthorn, on the other hand, retired from auto racing immediately after winning the title, but died in a car accident three months later.

Of course, they wouldn't be calling Moss a great driver if he hadn't won a lot of races, and he won a lot. He captured 16 Formula One races between 1955 and 1962, culminating in a near-fatal crash that ended his career. He's still 16th on the all-time F-1 list, ahead of some pretty big names including Graham Hill, Emerson Fittipaldi and Mario Andretti, all of whom had longer careers. Overall, he won 212 of the 529 races he entered between 1948 and 1962 (including non-F-1 races). Moss was inducted into the International Motorsports Hall of Fame in 1990, and Prince Charles knighted him 10 years later.

Moss relished the dangers of racing. "To race a car through a turn at maximum speed is difficult," he once said. "But to race a car at maximum speed through that same turn when there is a brick wall on one side and a precipice on the other–ah, that's an achievement."

 TRIVIA: Alain Prost finished second four times in the Formula One drivers race, but he also won four times. .

OUTMUSCLED

"It's just one of those things you accept."

Ken Rosewall won just about everything there was to win in tennis. But he may be most remembered for the one that got away. Despite winning the Australian Open four times, and the U.S.

and French Opens twice each, the speedy, crafty Australian faced a road block at Wimbledon.

Rosewall never won Wimbledon despite making it to the final four times over 20 years. His first brush with glory at the All-England Club came in the 1954 final when Rosewall was just 19. "The Doomsday Striking Machine" faced Czech veteran Jaroslav Drobny. In what would be his last appearance in a Grand Slam final, Drobny defeated his young Australian opponent in four sets.

Rosewall again stood on the brink of Wimbledon glory two years later. This time the face on the other side of the net was a familiar one: Lew Hoad, a fellow Australian who was also Rosewall's doubles partner. The result was also familiar—Rosewall lost in another four-setter, the first all-Australian final since 1922. "People ask me about those two finals," Rosewall told an interviewer years later, "and I always say jokingly that I lost the first two of my Wimbledon finals because I was too young, and lost the last two because I was too old."

Rosewall turned pro in 1957 which was good for his bankroll but not for his Wimbledon hopes. That's because professionals were shut out of the amateur-only Wimbledon and other Grand Slam events until 1968, the period in which Rosewall was at the peak of his form. It was also a time when he was regarded as one of the game's best grass court players—and grass courts are Wimbledon's signature playing surface. That said, two years after Wimbledon opened up to professionals, Rosewall made it a career 0-for-3 there in the singles finals, losing to fellow Aussie John Newcombe at the home of strawberries and cream.

The diminutive Rosewall, nicknamed "Muscles" because he lacked them, got one more crack at the Wimbledon singles crown. In 1974—just months away from his 40th birthday—Rosewall fought his way to the finals with his "old-fashioned" wooden racket. His reward was a match against rising star Jimmy Connors and his "ultra-modern" metal racquet. Connors, at 21 nearly half Rosewall's age, beat the elder statesman in straight sets to win the first of his eight Grand Slam crowns.

Rosewall finally retired from pro tennis in 1980. He was 46—ancient by tennis standards. The man with the deft backhand (he was a natural left-hander who played right-handed) won eight Grand Slam singles titles and achieved a career Grand Slam in doubles. A member of four winning Davis Cup teams for Australia, Rosewall is credited with 133 tournament singles titles including 35 ATP crowns. All said, though, it was the big one that kept slipping away.

Rosewall's most amazing feat may have been his longevity. He was ranked #5 in the world in the 1951-52 season and was still #12 in 1977 at age 43. "The longevity of his playing will never be repeated," former Australian Davis Cup captain Neale Fraser asserts. "In terms of longevity and quality, Muscles is the greatest to ever play the game," adds former Australian tennis star Paul McNamee.

 TRIVIA: To give you an idea of how many Slams he might have won, Ken Rosewall won 15 "Pro Slam" events during the 11 years he was banned from the regular Grand Slams for being a professional.

AFTER THE BELL

"A very determined guy."

Marilyn Bell made history and captured the imagination of Canadians everywhere when in 1954 she became the first person to swim Lake Ontario.

Her 21-hour, 52-kilometer marathon made Bell a national hero and ensured her name would be remembered for decades to come.

The second person to do it, not so much.

Two years after Bell conquered the waves and charmed a country, John Jaremey made his bid for history. At 5:47 a.m. on July 22, 1956, the 26-year-old Toronto resident plunged into the water at Niagara-On-The-Lake with his coach and navigator in tow. His goal was "to swim the lake if it kills me." Blessed with ideal conditions and fortified by his usual breakfast of steak and eggs, Jaremey was halfway across the lake by noon.

Slowed by fatigue, stomach cramps, sore eyes, aching muscles and water temperatures that dipped to 57 degrees Fahrenheit (14 degrees Celsius), Jaremey considered quitting but kept thinking, if "that little girl" (Bell) had made it, then so could he. Finally, the steamfitter saw a large searchlight his union brothers had set up for him and he knew he'd make it. At 3:02 a.m. the next day, just over 21 hours after he started, Jaremey touched the Toronto shoreline before a cheering crowd of 12,000 to become the second person (and first male) to swim Lake Ontario.

Jaremey inherited his love of swimming from his father, who used to swim across the Dniester River in his native Ukraine. Growing up in Port Arthur, Ontario (now Thunder Bay), he would often swim against his brothers in a creek at the family farm. Jaremey swam competitively after moving to Toronto, training at local pools during the winter, then tackling Lakes Wilcox and Simcoe until Lake Ontario warmed up. His only son Chester recalls walking up and down the boardwalk all day long watching his father swim in Lake Ontario.

Jaremey—still relatively unknown to the public despite being the second to swim Lake Ontario—left competitive swimming in 1990 but continued as a recreational swimmer until he was felled by a stroke in 1992. John Jaremey—described by his wife Mary as "a very determined guy"—died at age 83. He was inducted into the Ontario Aquatic Hall of Fame in 2004.

 TRIVIA: The first double crossing of Lake Ontario was achieved by Vicki Keith in 1987.

NO GLITTER FOR GARY

"It's hard to lose."

Not surprisingly, Gary Ross's favorite NFL team is the Minnesota Vikings.

What a better fit for curling's greatest bridesmaid than to

cheer for one of the two NFL teams to have gone 0-4 in the Super Bowl (the Buffalo Bills are the other).

Ross may be the best player never to qualify for the Brier, Canada's national men's curling championship. Six times Ross came within one game of winning the Manitoba title—which would have qualified him for the Brier—and six times he fell short. He lost in 1964 and 1967 to Bruce Hudson, in 1972 to Orest Meleschuk, in 1974 to Don Barr, in 1978 to Doug Harrison and in 1982 to Mel Logan. But there's more. Ross also lost three Manitoba senior finals and one Masters final for a total of 10 final losses without a win.

"It's hard to lose, but I don't play for that alone ..." said Ross, a Winnipeg contractor. "If I were playing for just one reason, I would have quit a long time ago."

Ross's perseverance finally paid off after nearly 40 years, albeit on the senior circuit with his Brier days long behind him. In January 2001, he made it to his 11th provincial final, meeting Doug Armour for the Manitoba senior championship. With all the pressure of his past failures weighing on him, Ross made a clutch draw to the four-foot to win his first provincial title and advance to his first national championship. He took advantage of the long-sought opportunity to beat Tom Reed of Alberta 7-6 in 11 ends to capture the Canadian men's senior championship.

"It's been a long time coming," said Ross, who was inducted into the Manitoba Curling Hall of Fame in 2005 after a career that saw him appear in 32 provincial championships. "I always wanted to come to a Canadian championship to see how we stacked up against the rest. I guess we're all right."

 TRIVIA: The term Brier comes from a brand of tobacco made by the tournament's original sponsor, Macdonald Tobacco.

CHAPTER 14

ODDS 'N' ENDS

"Once you say you're going to settle for second,
that's what happens to you in life."

– John F. Kennedy

LATE FOR THE LOTTERY

"I was kind of numb."

If anyone belongs in the *Close, But No Cigar* club, it's Clarence Jackson. The Connecticut native literally held a fortune in his hands–yet let it slip all away. Jackson's woes began Friday, October 13, 1995 when he bought a ticket for the Connecticut lottery. It was the winning ticket–worth $5.8 million–but Jackson didn't know it. The ticket gathered dust in his home until *exactly* one year later–Sunday, October 13, 1996–when his sister saw a newscast mentioning that the winning ticket was about to expire that midnight. She decided to check the old lottery tickets around the house and lo and behold, she found the winner.

It was now 11:15 p.m.–45 minutes before expiration. All Jackson needed to do was go to any location that sold lottery tickets–and he was a multi-millionaire. But he didn't, thinking instead that he had to go to the lottery office. So he waited. Next day it was Columbus Day. The office was closed. So he waited some more. "When he finally went to the lottery office with his lawyer a couple of days later, they gave him the official word: rules were rules and his ticket was worthless. "I was kind of numb," Jackson concluded.

The story might have ended there except for State Representative Chris De Pino. He introduced a bill in legislature that would extend the grace period in cases such as Jackson's. It passed the state legislature and just needed to get by the senate. But state Senator Alvin Penn blocked it in committee, explaining, "If I'm playing blackjack and someone's allowed to win with 23, then that doesn't make it fair for those of us who have 21 or 19."

Jackson refuses to give up. Year after year, he shows up at the state Capitol to plead his case. He carries a large, black bag with articles about lottery winners in other states who managed to circumvent the rules. But year after year, his pleas go unanswered and Jackson continues his life as the lottery winner who almost was.

TRIVIA: Nevada is one of seven states without a lottery (the casinos don't want the competition).

ROLL OUT THE BARREL

"Who's for a sip o' gin?"

B obby Leach survived a plunge over Niagara Falls.

But he couldn't get past an orange peel.

Leach, a British-born circus stuntman and restaurant owner in Niagara Falls, Ontario, was the second person to go over the Falls in a barrel and survive. He did it nearly 10 years after former Michigan schoolteacher Annie Edson Taylor became the first, spilling over the Horseshoe Falls in 1901 on her 63rd birthday—all in a custom-made barrel.

After Taylor's plunge, Leach bragged he could do anything Taylor could do, and then some. So he set about completing a "Triple Challenge." Part 1 was accomplished in 1908 when he jumped with a parachute from the Upper Steel Arch Bridge (known as the Honeymoon Bridge—located below the Falls—which collapsed in 1938). This jump landed him in the Niagara River, upstream of the foaming rapids. The second part of the challenge was to make a barrel trip through the actual rapids all the way to the Whirlpool—a truly harrowing adventure. He had to be rescued on his first attempt, but was successful in three others in the summer of 1910. That left him with the trickiest part, the plunge over the Falls.

On July 25, 1911, Leach climbed into his eight-foot-long steel barrel upstream of the Horseshoe Falls. The contraption included heavy wooden planks at each end plus a harness and hammock for him to rest on. Towed to Hog Island, the barrel was released and Leach plunged, feet first, over the Falls. Twenty-two minutes later—despite Annie Taylor's prediction that "he will never do it"—Leach emerged from his barrel alive, but pretty banged up.

Reportedly his first words to rescuers were, "Who's for a sip o' gin?"

Leach spent the next six months in hospital having broken his jaw and both kneecaps. Unlike Taylor–whose manager embezzled all the money made from her stunt–Leach cashed in by touring vaudeville theaters and lecture halls, posing for pictures and selling a pamphlet called *Over Niagara Falls in a Barrel*. Looking for more headlines, Leach later parachuted off the Upper Steel Arch Bridge twice more, then in 1919 rode in his barrel through Niagara's actual Whirlpool rapids.

Ironically, after surviving numerous stunts that could have easily killed him, Leach was done in by a seemingly innocuous piece of fruit. In 1926, Leach broke his leg when he slipped on an orange peel on a street in Christchurch while on a publicity tour of New Zealand. The leg became infected and had to be amputated when gangrene set in. Leach died of complications. He was 69.

 TRIVIA: The highest falls in the world–Angel Falls in Venezuela–is about 19 times higher than Niagara Falls.

ANTHEM ICON

"Hum the anthem very loudly."

Roger Doucet is a Canadian icon, but what's forgotten is that the long-time Montreal Canadiens anthem singer had considerable fame in another country–the Soviet Union, of all places.

In 1976, Doucet was tapped to be the sole national anthem singer at the inaugural Canada Cup hockey tournament. He knew the Canadian and American national anthems of course, and he easily obtained the lyrics to the national anthems of Czechoslovakia, Sweden and Finland. But there was a problem with the Soviet Union's anthem–there were no lyrics.

The lyrics to the "Hymn of the Soviet Union" were quietly dropped in

1956 because of the regrettable references to Josef Stalin. So with nothing to sing, Doucet was instead asked to "hum the anthem very loudly." But that didn't fly with Doucet who set out to find the old Stalinist lyrics, which he did, then he took them to the Russian Department at the University of Montreal with instructions to "fix them up!"

Doucet showed Soviet officials the new lyrics prior to the September 3 game between the Soviets and Canada. The officials were surprised–yet quite amenable. Doucet then sang the new version of "Hymn of the Soviet Union" in public for the first time ever that night in Montreal. And the Soviets liked it so much they officially adopted them the next year.

Doucet received the Order of Canada in 1980, a year before he died, "in recognition of the pride he has instilled in his fellow citizens." His ad hoc lyrics inspired pride, however, in another country, the Soviet Union, a fact overshadowed by the Canada Cup–one of the premiere hockey events of all time.

 TRIVIA: Roger Doucet also sang the national anthems before Montreal Expos and Montreal Alouettes games.

AS NOBEL TOLLS

"No suitable living candidate."

One led India peacefully to independence.
Another wrote two of the 20th century's most celebrated works.
A third invented the Periodic Table of Elements.

Yet Mahatma Gandhi, James Joyce and Dmitri Mendeleev never won a Nobel Prize.

It's hard to believe that the man who developed the Satyagraha– "devotion to truth"–a non-violent method of redressing wrongs–never won the Nobel Peace Prize. "The Father of India" became a leader in his country's independence movement, and to this day his name is synonymous with peace. That said, Gandhi was nominated for the Peace Prize an incredible five times without winning. His last nomination came in January 1948, two days before he was assassinated. But Nobel Prizes are not awarded posthumously. However–possibly as a nod to Gandhi–the 1948 Peace Prize was not given out as "there was no suitable living candidate."

The list of Nobel Prize laureates in Literature contains such luminaries as Rudyard Kipling, William Yeats, Pearl S. Buck, George Bernard Shaw, Ernest Hemingway and John Steinbeck. But nowhere on that list is James Joyce. His 1922 book, *Ulysses*, is considered by many to be one of the greatest novels ever written. And *Finnegan's Wake*, released in 1939, two years before his death, has come to be regarded as a landmark work of speculative literature. Amazingly though, there would be no Nobel Prize for Literature for Joyce. But the snub keeps him in good company though: Arthur Miller, Virginia Woolf, Leo Tolstoy, Gertrude Stein, Anton Chekhov, Robert Frost, W.H. Auden and Mark Twain never won either.

If you ever studied chemistry–hey, even if you *didn't*–you've probably heard of the Periodic Table of Elements. Less known, however, is the name of the man who invented it–Dmitri Mendeleev. The entire organization of modern chemistry is based on Mendeleev's table, a true work of genius. So in 1906 when Mendeleev was originally selected by the prize committee to win the Nobel, the honor was overturned by the Royal Swedish Academy of Sciences. It seems that Mendeleev had dissed a scientific theory supported by Svante Arrhenius, an influential Swedish scientist considered a founder of physical chemistry. Arrhenius, a Noble laureate himself, had great influence with the Nobel committee and given a chance to get back at Mendeleev, he pounced.

TRIVIA: Alfred Nobel, inventor of dynamite, was fluent in six languages.

IT HERTZ TO BE SECOND

"It went against the notion you had to brag."

For 50 years, Avis tried harder.

In 1962, Avis Rent a Car rolled out one of the longest-lasting and most successful slogans in advertising history—"We Try Harder." The tagline was penned by women's advertising pioneer Paula Green, who got the idea when her boss asked an employee why anyone would rent a car from them, and not the leading competition. The answer of course was, "we try harder." So rather than hide from the fact they were #2 behind Hertz, Avis decided to play *up* that fact. The full text of their original tagline was, "When you're only #2, you try harder. Or else." Avis would use it for half a century. "It went against the notion you had to brag," Green said. And it worked.

The slogan turned around Avis's fortunes dramatically. They went from losing $3.2 million to turning a profit of $1.2 million—the first time out of the red in 13 years.

With its market share dropping, Hertz fought back. In 1966 they began an ad campaign that played off Avis's. "For years, Avis has been telling you Hertz is #1. Now we're going to tell you why." It worked—Hertz's market share improved and Avis never did catch them for top spot. But Avis's fortunes certainly changed for the better—and they had Paula Green to thank for that.

Avis wasn't the only company to exploit #2 branding. In January 1967, Toronto radio station CKFH launched its new Top 40 format with the tagline, "1430 CKFH—Number 2 Radio—we must be because everyone else is #1." When its number-two branding ended in 1968, CKFH had climbed behind CHUM as the #2 rock station in the market.

 TRIVIA: Avis was the first car rental company located in an airport.

PLATE FATES

"Mass. Automobile Register."

The first state-issued license plates were not the first automobile tags in the U.S.

Massachusetts issued its first plate on September 1, 1903 and a man named Frederick Tudor got the first one, appropriately numbered "1" (it's still actively registered to one of his descendants). These plates were sturdy affairs, made of iron and covered with porcelain enamel. The lettering was white set against a cobalt blue background. They cost two dollars. The only wording on it was "Mass. Automobile Register."

Two years earlier New York became the first state to insist that car owners have an identifying tag. However, these first plates were not state-issued. Instead it was up to New York car owners to manufacture their own plates which clearly displayed their initials should they run afoul of the law. New York cancelled that practice in mid-1903 when officials realized that many car owners were displaying fictitious initials–or weren't registering these plates and thus avoiding the one-dollar fee.

 TRIVIA: The second Canadian jurisdiction to require car owners to have licence plates was British Columbia in 1904; Ontario was first in 1903.

ROTTEN APPLE

"I had no business sense."

Steve Jobs and Steve Wozniak.

The two gained fame and fortune as co-founders of Apple Computers. But there was a third now-forgotten man at the beginning when the visionary software company was founded in the mid-'70s.

His name was Ronald Wayne, dubbed by some "The Unluckiest Man in the World." On April Fool's Day 1976, the 42-year-old native of Cleveland co-founded Apple along with fellow Atari workmates Jobs and Wozniak. Wayne designed the first logo for the Apple Computer Company (picturing Isaac Newton sitting under an apple tree), and penned the partnership agreement for the three men. The manual for the Apple 1 computer is also his handiwork. But the partnership didn't last long—Wayne was gone just 12 days later, selling his 10% share in the fledgling company for just $800. Today, those stocks would be worth $35 billion.

Why did he leave? *Slot machines.* "My passion was not in computers, but slot machines," Wayne said. "It was a handicap that I didn't realize I had no business sense."

Wayne stayed with Atari until 1978 when he joined a nuclear and science research facility in Livermore, California. He owned a stamp store in the late '70s but closed it after a couple of break-ins. Further bad luck came for Wayne when thieves stole his life savings of 145 ounces of gold and numerous collector coins, none of it insured. He began work as a chief designer at Thor Electronics in 1982, retiring 17 years later.

"If I had stayed with Apple and accepted the limitations on my philosophy of life, I could have well ended up the richest man in the cemetery," adds Wayne, who lives quietly in a small town about an hour out of Las Vegas, selling coins and stamps and living off his Social Security cheques.

Wayne, who never owned an Apple product until someone gave him an iPad 2 in 2011, shrugs off the fact he was left out of the 2013 *Jobs* biopic starring Ashton Kutcher. "Typical. I am, after all, the unknown founder. But it is not unreasonable."

 TRIVIA: The original Apple 1 computer sold for $666.66.

WHEN CHESS WAS KING

"Chess is war on a board."

He's the most famous runner-up in chess history, but Boris Spassky is hardly a loser.

In 1972, Spassky defended his world chess championship against American challenger Bobby Fischer in the most ballyhooed chess match of modern times. Set against the backdrop of the Cold War, this was the perfect match-up for the era—the quiet, unflappable Soviet champion pitted against the eccentric, emotionally charged American challenger. It was billed as "The Match of the Century"—and for weeks everyone was talking about, yes, the Sport of Kings, chess.

Spassky learned to play chess at age five while escaping the Nazis on a train heading out of his hometown of Leningrad. He was a quick study: stunning the Soviet champion at age 10 during an exhibition; becoming the youngest grandmaster in history to that time at age 18; and competing in a Candidates Tournament for the World Championship at age 19. Gaining a reputation as a strong all-around player, he became the 10th world chess champion when he defeated fellow Soviet Tiger Petrosian in 1969.

Before "The Match of the Century," Fischer participated in the "Game of the Century," the infamous 1956 match between future U.S. Chess Hall of Famer Donald Byrne and Fischer, who at 13 was the youngest U.S. junior chess champion in history. Fischer won the match and the following year he became, at 14, the youngest U.S. grandmaster to that point and the youngest U.S. Open champion. But Fischer was just getting started: he went on to win all eight U.S. championships he played in between 1958 and 1967. By 1971, he was ready to go for the biggest title in chess.

The 1972 World Chess Championship was part competition, part media circus. OK, a *big* media circus. The odds weighed heavily against Fischer, who had never beaten Spassky in five previous matches. As well, the Soviets had won every world chess championship since 1948. The outspoken Fischer set the tone, snarling that the match was, "the free world against the lying, cheating hypocritical Russians." Upset about what he felt was a piddling amount of prize money, he threatened to boycott the match in Reykjavik, Iceland. Finally appeased, he flew into Iceland a couple of days late then proceeded to complain about the lighting, the temperature of the room, the size of the chess board and the size of the table it sat on.

"Chess is war on a board. The object is to crush the other player's mind," Fischer once said. He proceeded to lose the first game after an early blunder, then dropped the second game by default when he refused to play because he claimed the TV cameras were too close. Spassky agreed to move to a room away from the cameras and Fischer pounced, winning the third game. Fischer then took control of the match, winning games 5, 6, 8 and 10. Fischer won by 12 $^1/_2$ points to 8 $^1/_2$ when his Soviet opponent resigned after the 21st game. Fischer became the first American world chess champion since Wilhelm "William" Steinitz in the late 19th century.

While he wasn't exactly sent to the Gulag, Spassky was roundly criticized by the Soviets not just for losing but for being so darned nice about it. Undaunted, Spassky won the Soviet championship the next year. He moved to France in 1976 and while he maintained a Top 10 ranking into the 1980s, he never won the World Championship again. Spassky lost to Fischer in a 1992 rematch.

"For some, he was a genius. For others, he was a crazy man," French chess commentator Jerome Maufras once said of Fischer.

In 1975, Fischer was stripped of his world title over a disagreement with the World Chess Federation. He vanished from the chess scene, lived at various times in Asia and Europe, resurfacing briefly in his winning rematch with Spassky. He was jailed for a few months in Japan in 2004-05 after the U.S. revoked his passport. After his release, Fischer moved to chess-crazy Iceland where he died in 2008, aged 64.

 TRIVIA: BELLE became the first computer to be named a U.S. Chess Master in 1983.

LIGHT YEARS

"A lot of personality ..."

They call it "The Eternal Light," and for more than a century it's lived up to its name.

On September 21, 1908–the year Henry Ford introduced the Model T–an electrician named Barry Burke installed a light bulb above the backstage door at the Byers Opera House in Livermore, Texas. The opera house became a theater later that same year, and a movie theater in 1920. Still the little light burned on ... through the Great Depression ... the Second World War ... and beyond. The bulb continued to blaze uninterrupted until 1970 when–in a truly shocking development–someone switched it off! Finally, a light bulb went off over the owner's head and soon signs were posted telling staff not to fiddle with the now famous light.

The old opera house (now the Palace Theater) was torn down in 1977 but that didn't mean the end of the little bulb. The hardy light was transferred to the Stockyards Museum in Fort Worth, placed into a display case and plugged in. Since then, it has been turned off only once (again by accident). It is now run on its own special circuit so it can longer be turned off by accident, teenage boys, or environmental activists.

Despite its incredible longevity, The Eternal Light will be eternally in second place as long as "The Centennial Light" keeps burning in Livermore, California. The Centennial Light began its working life in the summer of 1901 at a local fire department, according to the daughter of the man who donated it to the fire hall. The bulb has been subsequently housed in four different locations over the last 100 years–and since 1976 it has been burning night and day at Livermore Fire Station #6.

The Centennial Light was first recognized as the "The Most Durable Light" by *The Guinness Book of World Records* in 1972, replacing The Eternal Light which had previously been credited as #1. In fact, it was The Eternal Light's listing in *Guinness* that inspired the Livermore people to research the longevity of their own bulb.

And what of Barry Burke, who installed the The Eternal Light in the first place? For years, the electrician worried he would die when the light burned out. He needn't have concerned himself. Burke passed away in 1963, and ... The Eternal Light kept glowing. And it's still going, well into its second century–and still in second place.

Speaking of second place, Sarah Biles–administrator of the museum that houses the Fort Worth bulb–is undaunted by the fact that their bulb is in the bridesmaid spot for longevity. "We think that ours has a lot of personality, so it doesn't really bother us that there's one a little older," says Biles. "We win the personality contest."

 TRIVIA: Incandescent bulbs typically last from 1,000 to 2,000 hours.

MONEY FOR NOTHING

"It's one of those accidents of history."

At the time it didn't seem like a big deal.

In 1976, the NBA agreed to take in four of the six surviving franchises from the rival American Basketball Association in an historic merger. Cut out of the deal were the Kentucky Colonels and the Spirits of St. Louis. The Colonels took a $3 million buyout, but Spirits owners Ozzie and Daniel Silna had other ideas on how to turn this lemon into lemonade.

The Silnas agreed to drop out for $2.2 million, plus a one-seventh share in the four new NBA teams' television revenue–in *perpetuity*. No one thought twice about it–back then network TV interest in pro basketball was scant. (Imagine, NBA playoff games were shown on tape delay at 11:30 p.m. up until the '80s). But TV interest in the NBA has since exploded–and that's been great for the Silnas'—by 2012 the *New York Times* estimated that their one-seventh haul was $255 million and counting.

In 1982, the NBA offered the Silna brothers $5 million for their share. The brothers didn't take it. In 2014 the NBA finally settled, giving the Silnas $500 million.

"This issue has been a nuisance as long as I've been associated with the league," Ed Desser, former president of NBA Television told the *New York Times*. "It was never enough to be a serious distraction. It's one of those accidents of history." An expensive one at that.

 TRIVIA: The NBA had a team in St. Louis called the Hawks from 1956 to 1968.

CLOSE ON CANNABIS

"The end of marijuana prohibition is at hand."

J ust hours after Colorado became the first state to legalize marijuana, Washington became the second.

On November 6, 2012, voters in Washington voted 56 per cent in favor of Initiative 502, which legalized cannabis. The vote came on the heels of Colorado's Amendment 64, which OK'd "personal use and regulation of marijuana" for adults 21 and over in the Centennial State.

"It is costly, harmful and dangerously misguided to continue arresting adults for using something that is safer than alcohol, particularly the seriously ill who could benefit from using marijuana," said Ethan Nadelmann, executive director of the Drug Policy Initiative. "They (Colorado and Washington) should be congratulated for taking the first step toward sensible laws. The end of marijuana prohibition is at hand."

The hazy excitement in Washington was tempered somewhat by a controversial DUI clause. Under the new law, a limit of five nanograms per millilitre of active THC is considered evidence of DUI guilt. However, the low limit means nearly all daily cannabis users would be in danger of testing "DUI marijuana," as they would rarely test below 5 ng/ml at any time.

A time traveller from the mid-19th century might be surprised today about the fuss over pot. Recreational marijuana was listed as a "fashionable narcotic" as early as 1853, and hashish parlors were all the rage in the latter half of the 19th century. But in 1906 the District of Columbia became the first U.S. jurisdiction to restrict the sale of cannabis, and other states soon jumped on the bandwagon. In Canada, marijuana was criminalized with the Opium and Drug Act of 1923, but in 2018 was made legal for both medical and recreational use.

All states had some form of cannabis regulation by the mid-'30s and the door against cannabis was further slammed shut by the Marijuana Tax Act of 1937 which made possession or transfer of cannabis illegal in the U.S. At one time simple possession of marijuana would get you two to ten years in jail with a fine up to $20,000. However, the U.S. Congress repealed those mandatory sentences in 1970, a year after the Supreme Court ruled the Marijuana Tax Act to be unconstitutional.

 TRIVIA: Marijuana is the most commonly used illicit drug in the U.S.

NO ISSUE WITH SECOND

"Things and attitudes ..."

They are the most iconic of magazine covers, the first issues of the world's most famous publications.

But what of the forgotten second issues?

With television interest exploding after the Second World War, it was just a matter of time before a national magazine with TV listings emerged. *TV Guide,* which amalgamated several regional publications, launched April 3, 1953 and was a success right off the bat. A decade later it became the most circulated magazine in the U.S. *TV Guide's* first cover features Ricky and Lucy Ricardo's newborn son Desi Arnaz, Jr., under the headline "Lucy's $50,000,000 Baby." A small photo of Lucy appeared in the top corner. The second cover pictures Dragnet star Jack Webb.

H ugh Hefner thought *Stag Party* would be a good name for a new men's magazine he was planning to launch in 1953. But an adventure magazine called Stag threatened to sue if he used that name. So on the suggestion of a friend, Hefner picked *Playboy*–and it worked out pretty well for him. *Playboy* has become one of the world's most recognized brands–who doesn't know the *Playboy* bunny logo—which made Hefner a millionaire many times over. The first issue published in December 1953 doesn't have a date on it as Hefner was uncertain whether there'd be a second. Nevertheless, it was a huge hit with Marilyn Monroe featured on that first issue. The second issue is dated January 1954 and features two Playboy bunnies bookending a cartoon drawing of a rather jaunty looking male bunny.

S *ports Illustrated* was a magazine ahead of its time. There were plenty of naysayers when the prolific Henry Luce mused aloud about the idea of a national, general-interest sports magazine. But he ignored them all and on August 16, 1954, *Sports Illustrated* published its first issue. The inaugural cover featured Milwaukee Braves first baseman Eddie Mathews and New York Giants catcher Wes Westrum. The second issue that month showed a row of golf bags on the cover. After failing to turn a profit for its first 12 years, *Sports Illustrated* is now a multi-media success with over 3.5 million subscribers.

C ounter-culture journalism found a good home in 1967 with the founding of *Rolling Stone.* Co-founder Jann Wenner wrote in the first issue dated November 9, 1967 that *Rolling Stone* "is not just about the music, but about the things and attitudes that music embraces." The debut cover features a picture of John Lennon and an article about the Monterey Pop Festival. The cover of the second issue that month shows rising star Tina Turner along with an article about Bob Dylan.

*P*eople grew from the ashes of *Life*, which stopped weekly publication in 1972. Many former *Life* managers, editors, writers and photo-graphers went to *People*, including managing editor Richard Stolley who promoted a focus "on people, not issues." *People's* debut on March 4, 1974 features Mia Farrow on the cover (the only color photo in the entire magazine). The cover of issue #2, dated March 25, 1974, features Raquel Welch, who at age 33, was described as an aging (!) sex symbol.

TRIVIA: *Scientific American,* which debuted in 1845, is the oldest continuously published monthly magazine in the U.S.

HEAD OF THE CHURCH

"A woman should have a sign of authority on her head."

The second Pope has a very odd legacy.

Women's head coverings.

Only one instruction from St. Linus has survived and it's recorded in *Liber Pontificalis* (The Book of Popes): women should keep their heads covered during religious ceremonies "in conformity with the ordinance of St. Peter." The original instruction no longer exists, but it is referenced in St. Paul's first letter to the Corinthians.

> *... any woman who prays or prophesies with her head unveiled brings shame upon her head ... A man, on the other hand, should not cover his head, because he is the image and glory of God, but woman is the glory of man.*

For man did not come from woman, but woman from man;
nor was man created for woman, but woman for man; for
this reason a woman should have a sign of authority on
her head, because of the angels ... - 1 Corinthians 11:3-10

Times were tough for Christians in those days. When Rome burned in 64CE, Roman Emperor Nero blamed the Christians—then a brand-new sect—and doled out some pretty severe punishment. Some Christians were fed to the lions, others were crucified, and still others were clothed in animal hides and hunted down by wild dogs. Others were used as human torches for illumination at Nero's garden parties. Nothing survives as to how Linus guided his people during that difficult period, but we do know what he thought of women's head coverings at religious ceremonies.

And while the second Pope might be mostly forgotten, his head covering instruction lives on. In 1917, Catholic leaders confirmed in an updated Code of Canon Law that women should cover their heads when they assisted at Mass. To this day, women are expected to cover their heads while assisting with an Extraordinary Form Mass but going without is no longer considered a sin. However, with regards to the Mass of the Ordinary Form, it's positively a free-for-all as women don't need any head coverings whatsoever.

 TRIVIA: The day of Linus's death, September 23, is still celebrated as a feast day.

TALL TALES

"Sulphur dioxide and other unpleasant pollutants."

The second-tallest free-standing structure in Canada isn't exactly a household game.

The Inco Superstack in Sudbury, Ontario, went into operation in 1972 and was Canada's tallest free-standing structure until the 553-meter-tall CN Tower claimed top spot three years later. The Inco Superstack, which disperses sulphur dioxide and other unpleasant pollutants, remains the second-highest free-standing structure in Canada and in fact, the entire Western Hemisphere, but its days may be numbered. Should the 380-meter-high stack be demolished as planned in 2020, then First Canada Place in Toronto—at 298 meters—will take over the #2 spot.

The CN Tower has dropped to #3 among the tallest free-standing structures in the world, a ranking that will inevitably fall as more super structures are built. It's still considered "one of the Seven Wonders of the Modern World," on a list that includes the Panama Canal, the Chunnel, the Golden Gate Bridge and the Empire State Building.

TRIVIA: Originally referred to as Canadian National Tower, the CN Tower is now known as Canada's National Tower.

CHAPTER 15

NOT CLOSE AND DEFINITELY NO CIGAR

"You know what makes a good loser? Practice."
– Ernest Hemingway

WEB OF DEFEAT

"The sorriest shell of a team ..."

Stripped of their talent, cast off by their owners, disowned by their fans, the 1899 Cleveland Indians were the worst Major League Baseball team ever.

How bad were the Spiders?

The 1962 New York Mets–widely considered to be the worst team of modern times–won twice as many games.

The 1899 Spiders had everything going against them, including their owner. After Spiders proprietor Frank Robison bought the St. Louis Browns at a sheriff's auction, he decided that a good team would get better crowds in St. Louis, so he sent all of the big Spiders stars west. Moving from Cleveland to St. Louis were Cy Young and Jesse Burkett which left the Spiders with a motley crew of minor-leaguers and semi-pro players. The results were disastrous, though predictable.

The Spiders posted a 20-134 record in 1899. They lost 24 in a row at one point and only once won two in a row. Six times they lost at least 11 straight. They finished 84 games out of first and a stunning 35 games out of *11th* place. Charlie Knepper, the "ace" of their staff, had a 4-22 record. Former Spider Bobby Wallace hit 12 home runs that season for St. Louis–as many round-trippers as the entire Cleveland team that year.

Fans stayed away in droves. And things got worse. Spiders brass said that because of poor attendance fans didn't deserve a winner, and would be "punished" by having some of their home games moved to other cities. The team would then be run as a "sideshow." Total attendance for home games in 1899 was 6,088–an average of 145 individuals a game. They wound up with 101 road losses against 11 wins–a record that will never be broken as teams today only play 81 road games a season.

The Spiders staggered to the finish line losing 40 of their last 41 games, capped by a 19-3 humiliation by the Cincinnati Reds to close the season.

Eddie Kolb, a 19-year-old cigar store clerk and local amateur player, started the finale after talking the manager into it–his first and only major league appearance. After the game the Spiders are said to have presented their travelling secretary with a diamond locket because he "had the misfortune" to have witnessed every one of their games.

The Spiders, who baseball historian Lee Allen calls "the sorriest shell of a team ever seen in the major leagues," were dropped from the National League after that disastrous 1899 campaign. Their sad-sack performance did have one positive result, however–it led to the banning of syndicate ownership that created the mess in the first place.

 TRIVIA: The Cleveland Spiders won the Temple Cup–a forerunner of the World Series–in 1895.

NO ZIP TO CHIPPY

"The losingest horse in history."

He never won, sometimes placed, and occasionally showed.

But Zippy Chippy always lost.

Dubbed "the losingest horse in history," the hapless gelding ran in 100 races between 1991 and 2004 without once winning. Trainer Felix Monserrate traded an old Ford van for the 0-for-20 horse in 1995 to save him from the glue factory, but Zippy Chippy kept on losing. He was banned from racing at a New York track in 1998 after failing to leave the starting gate ... for the third time. In fact, Zippy Chippy even had trouble against humans. In 2000, he lost a 40-yard sprint to Rochester Red Wings center-fielder Jose Herrera.

By the time he finally retired in 2004–after finishing dead last in his final race–the Zippster had posted a record of eight second-place finishes and 12 thirds in 100 races with a total of $30,834 to show for it. In other words, Zippy Chippy made a little bit more than $2,000 a year–gross.

Zippy Chippy only won one race against a thoroughbred–in an exhibition contest against a horse named Paddy's Lady in 2001. Zippy finally triumphed, by a neck, after given a 20-length head start. The closest Zippy Chippy came to winning an actual race was in 2000 when, after leading from start to finish, he lost by a head at the now-defunct Northampton Fair track.

Showing that the meek really can inherit the Earth, Zippy Chippy started getting fan mail in the late 1990s. He was one of *People's* most interesting personalities of 2000. Thousands have visited Zippy Chippy at his home at Cabin Creek Farm near Saratoga Springs, New York. It goes without saying that folks just love a loser, and few have lost as much as Zippy Chippy.

"I think more people can identify with a horse that loses all the time than a horse that wins all the time," Michael Blowen, who purchased Zippy Chippy in 2010, told the *New York Times*. "I think that's part of the fun of it. Because there are more losers in the world than winners."

 TRIVIA: The all-time winless record for a thoroughbred is 105, set by Thrust in the 1950s.

NO FUN IN THE SUN

"A bunch of misfits."

For a time it appeared that the Tampa Bay Buccaneers might never win a game.

For the first season of their existence–and most of the second–the expansion Bucs did an O-fer, losing 26 games in a row before finally finding the win column. It remains the longest losing streak in NFL history.

The Buccaneers came into the NFL in 1976 and right from the start the mood was ugly. Dallas defensive end Pat Toomay, picked up by Tampa in the expansion draft, said going to the Bucs was like going from "football's penthouse to the outhouse." Asked for his prediction on the season, Toomay replied, *0-14.* "It was a joke," he said years later. "But not really."

Long-time USC coach John McKay, making his NFL debut, didn't win any friends when he scheduled twice-a-day workouts in the blistering Tampa heat. Decked out in gaudy tangerine uniforms that made grown men look like giant creamsicles, Tampa Bay didn't even score one touchdown until Week Four. The rout was on. The team that defensive back Mark Cotney described as "a bunch of misfits" fulfilled Toomay's prediction–they were the first post-war team to go winless over an entire season.

It wasn't pretty for the Bucs. They lost by an average of 20 points a game that first season. Tampa's exhausted defence at times played 90 snaps a game. Some of the losses were especially brutal but the low point may have come in Week 12 when the Oakland Raiders shellacked the team some were calling the Yuckaneers, 49-16. The dispirited Bucs endured a seven-hour flight back home only to be greeted at the airport at four in the morning by three drunk and unruly fans sarcastically chanting, "What have we got? Bucs! Fever! What have we got? Bucs! Fever!"

Season two wasn't much better. Tampa started with 12 straight losses and appeared to be headed for a second straight winless season. But the Bucs got their backs up in week 13 when New Orleans quarterback Archie Manning said that losing to Tampa would be a "disgrace." The Bucs went out and crushed the Saints 33-14, in New Orleans no doubt, for the first win in franchise history. "It was like we had won the Super Bowl," defensive back Mark Cotney said after thousands of fans in cars surrounded the team's bus on its way from the airport. For good measure the Bucs won their next game to finish the season 2-12.

One thing that made the Bucs losing run bearable was head coach John McKay. After his team was clobbered 42-0 by the Pittsburgh Steelers, McKay observed, "We didn't block real good, but we made up for it by not tackling." Addressing comments by NBC analyst John Brodie that quarterback Steve Spurrier's passes were too close to the ground, the coach quipped, "That's OK, we'll just get shorter receivers." And asked about his team's execution, McKay replied, "I'm in favor of it."

TRIVIA: The Buccaneers didn't return a kick-off for a touchdown until their 32nd season.

HOPELESS HOOPSTERS

"We never try to lose. It just works out that we do."

Millions of people all over the world have seen the Harlem Globetrotters. Their basketball wizardry has enthralled several generations of fans.

But who are those other guys on the court?

The Washington Generals are sport's biggest losers. Since their founding in 1952, the Generals have lost more than 13,000 games (and counting) to the Globetrotters. They've lost in all 50 states and over 100 countries, at venues as varied as leper colonies to bullrings, in front of popes, queens, princes and presidents. For the most part a foil to the incredible Globetrotters, they do their best to play "serious" basketball. "We play to win," one-time team captain Anthony Smith told the *Hartford Courant* in 2010. "We're a competitive team."

The Generals were founded by Red Klotz, who got the attention of Globetrotters head honcho Abe Saperstein when his team beat the Trotters on consecutive nights in 1949. An impressed Saperstein then invited Klotz's team to join the Globetrotters as their touring opponent.

For a time in the early '70s, the Generals performed under a series of nom-de-plumes, such as the Boston Shamrocks and the Atlantic City Seagulls, to create the impression that the Globetrotters were playing more than one team. They were the New York Nationals from 1995 to 2006, after which the Washington Generals moniker returned for good.

Now and then, the Generals actually beat the Globetrotters. On November 2, 1957, in St. Joseph, Michigan, a scoreboard malfunction showed that the

Globetrotters were winning late in the game when they were in fact losing. The Globetrotters started clowning around and after the game it was discovered they had been outscored 66-63. The Globetrotters, however, do not officially acknowledge this loss–which actually ended a 2,495-game winning streak. They do, however, recognize a 100-99 setback on January 5, 1971 in Martin, Tennessee. On that night, the Generals–who were the New Jersey Reds that night–took a 12-point lead with two minutes to go. The Globetrotters got serious and staged a furious comeback. But that fell short when the inimitable Meadowlark Lemon missed a hook shot with only seconds to go.

"We start every game thinking we're going to win," said Klotz, whose number 3 is the only number ever retired by the Generals. "We play our best and keep it as close as we can. We never try to lose. It just works out that we do."

 TRIVIA: The Washington Generals are named after General Dwight D. Eisenhower, the 34th president.

DEEP SIXED

"An ugly season."

Every now and then, some team threatens it.

The Dallas Mavericks came close once, as did the Denver Nuggets. The Charlotte Bobcats can lay claim to it, albeit with a big asterisk due to a shortened season.

But the Philadelphia '76ers record-setting NBA worst season has stood the test of time. No team in NBA history won as few games and lost as many in a full season as the 1972-73 Sixers.

Even before their record-setting season began, the Sixers were doomed. Leading scorer Billy Cunningham was gone, having defected to the rival American Basketball Association. The only other player remaining from

Philadelphia's great 1967 championship team, Hal Greer, was at the tail end of his career. Coach Jack Ramsay had also departed. His replacement, Long Island University coach Roy Rubin, had never coached in the NBA, or even in the top college ranks for that matter.

The Sixers season from hell began with 15 straight losses and didn't get much better. Coach Rubin was soon fired from what one Philadelphia newspaper called the Seventy-Sickers. The team was 4-47. He learned of his dismissal on television. "I'm not in the greatest mental shape," he said afterward. Nor was he in much better physical shape, since he had lost 45 pounds in the 105 days since the season began. He went on to become a stockbroker, ran a pancake restaurant and never coached another basketball game again.

Kevin Loughery took over coaching duties promptly turning a nine-game losing streak into an NBA record 20 gamer. Along the way they traded one of their best players, forward-center John Block, who made his only all-star appearance that season. A season-best stretch of five wins in seven games boosted the Sixers record to 9-60, but then the team completed what long-time Philadelphia sports commentator Sonny Hill called "an ugly season" with a 13-game losing streak. It added up to a never-equalled, never-surpassed, 9-73 campaign.

Gene Shue took over as coach the following season and soon all that losing became a distant memory. George McGinnis and Julius Erving helped get Philly to the NBA finals in 1977. The Sixers finally put it all together in 1983 when, behind an all-star cast that included Erving, Moses Malone, Maurice Cheeks, Andrew Toney and Bobby Jones, they won the franchise's third NBA title and first in 16 years. It came exactly 10 years after the Sixers posted the NBA's worst-ever record.

"We were the league's universal health spa," Fred Carter, a Sixers guard told *Sports Illustrated* in 1998. "If teams had any ills, they got healthy when they played us."

 TRIVIA: The Syracuse Nationals, the Philadelphia '76ers predecessor, were the last medium-size city to host an NBA team. They moved to Philly in 1963.

BRAINIAC BASKETBALL

"They were euphoric."

T he Caltech Beavers have plenty of brainpower.
Brawn? Not so much.
In a decade-long run of futility, the Beavers set a U.S. college basketball record by losing 207 consecutive games in NCAA Division III, the longest winless skein by a NCAA basketball team at any level.

"It was a combination sense of relief and happiness for the kids," Caltech coach Roy Dow said after the streak ended in January 2007 with a victory over Bard College. "They were euphoric." It was Caltech's first win against an NCAA opponent since 1996, but the misery had not ended.

At that time, Caltech had an even longer losing streak: 245 consecutive losses in conference play dating back 22 years. Even the best basketball minds from a school where 31 Nobel Prize winners had taught or studied (including Albert Einstein and Linus Pauling), just couldn't figure out a way to get this team a conference win. And they just kept losing. Finally–on February 22, 2011–the Beavers got their long-awaited victory: they edged out fearsome Occidental to finally snap a *310-game* losing skid in conference play.

How long had it been since Caltech beat a conference opponent? Ronald Reagan was in the White House, the Berlin Wall stood, and people still smoked on airplanes. Mobile phones were about the size of a brick, a tweet was a sound a bird made and a 23-year-old Barack Obama was working as a community organizer. Tiger Woods was nine years old.

It was a great moment for Caltech, which doesn't give out athletic scholarships (they're there for book learning, imagine!), and has an athletic budget barely above $1 million. But the losing stigma isn't going away easily. "When you play against Caltech, it's not about whether you are going to win or not," the father of Whittier guard Marcus Gibson noted. "It's about … having a point margin that's respectable."

Caltech's struggles in sports aren't limited to basketball. In February

2013, the Beaver's baseball team ended a 228-game losing streak with a 9-7 victory over Pacifica, its first win in nearly 10 years. Luckily (or not) for Caltech, the school broke an NCAA rule stating that student-athletes had to take full course loads. Which some weren't. So they were penalized: 112 of their games (all loses) were scrubbed from the records. So imagine: Caltech broke a rule, still lost profusely, and then had all those negatives cleared from the record books.

 TRIVIA: Caltech has not had a winning basketball season since 1954.

NO VICTORIES FOR VINCE

"Everything wasn't clicking."

It got so bad they started calling him the "Charlie Brown of Tennis."

For eight months—from August 1999 to June 2000—Vince Spadea suffered through the longest losing streak in tennis history.

Spadea seemed like an unlikely prospect to set a record for tennis futility. The Floridian had just completed one of his best seasons, with a career-best 9-4 record in the Grand Slams, highlighted by a quarter-final appearance in the Australian Open and a fourth-round showing in the U.S. Open. He also became one of four players to beat Roger Federer 6-0 in a set.

Then the losing started.

Spadea's streak started inauspiciously enough with a semi-final loss to Australia's Lleyton Hewitt in Lyon, France. He finished 1999 on a four-game losing streak. Loss #10-in-a-row was to Yevgeny Kafelnikov at Indian Wells, California, in March 2000. He made it 15 losses in a row in May when Rainer Schuettler of Germany beat him at Hamburg. When Justin Gimelstob beat him at Queen's Club in June the streak reached 20.

Not many people gave Spadea a chance as he prepared to play Greg

Rusedski at Wimbledon. Even Spadea's parents, who followed him around the globe, figured he didn't have a chance and flew home two days before the match.

But Spadea fooled them all. With fans screaming "C'mon, Greg" on nearly every point, the 25-year-old upset the 14 seed in a six-hour thriller. As the winning point fell in the gathering dusk, Spadea raised his arms, looked at the crowd and smiled skyward. His 21-game losing streak was over, and tennis superstar-turned-commentator John McEnroe gave him a huge hug in the dressing room.

"It was worth the wait, huh, people?" Spadea told the crowd after the match. "It doesn't ever come until the time when you're not ready for it. Then, all of a sudden, you're just, like, 'Oh, my gosh, what's happened to me?'"

Spadea won his only pro event in 2004 at Scottsdale, Arizona, and achieved his career high world ranking of #18 a year later. His combined career earnings in singles and doubles were just over $5 million. Tendonitis plagued him in 2009 and he played his last pro event the following year.

"It's been a rough patch in my life in tennis," Spadea said of his streak. "It didn't really faze me so much. I was trying to enjoy my life a little more, trying to improve my tennis game. Everything wasn't clicking."

 TRIVIA: The woman's record for longest losing streak is 17, shared by American Sandy Collins and Arantxa Rus of Holland.

THE YOUNG AND THE WINLESS

"An unusual record that may never be broken."

There was no hint of what was to come for Andrew Young when the 1992 season began.

On April 9, the New York Mets right-hander pitched a complete-game 7-1 win over the St. Louis Cardinals. He got another win April 19 with three-and-a-third innings of relief against Montreal.

Then the roof fell in.

Splitting time between the starting rotation and relief, Young lost his next 14 decisions over the rest of the season. He started the 1993 campaign in the bullpen, losing five more decisions to bring the streak to 19. Fans started sending in four-leaf clovers, horseshoes, anything to give him luck, but nothing worked. Young was put back into the starting rotation in June, and proceeded to lose seven more in a row for 26 consecutives notches in the loss column. He was again sent to the pen where he quickly earned his 27th L. (Loss #24, by the way, broke the major league record set by Cliff Curtis of the Boston Doves (later the Braves) in 1910 and 1911.)

Young would finally taste victory–but it wouldn't be easy. On July 24, 1993, after giving up a tie-breaking unearned run in the top of the ninth, Young watched as the Mets rallied for a pair of runs off Florida closer Bryan Harvey for a 5-4 victory. "That wasn't a monkey off my back," Young said of his breakthrough victory in relief. "That was a zoo."

Young appeared on the *Tonight Show* a few weeks later, just before his Fifteen Minutes of Fame expired (hmm ... that reminds me of another book I wrote and, ahem, highly recommend). Leno had razzed Young during his well-publicized streak, and offered the pitcher a chance at comic retribution. "You can make fun of my chin if you want to," the *Tonight Show* host jested.

"I got a bad rap on that," Young told Anthony McCarron of the *New York Daily News* in 2009. "I always said I didn't feel that I pitched all that badly." Surprisingly, the statistics back him up. Young had a somewhat respectable 4.36 ERA during the streak, which also saw him successfully convert 12 consecutive save appearances and post a scoreless streak of 23.2 innings.

Young retired from baseball in 1996, and began coaching kids. Still, Young doesn't mind when his young charges tease him about his famous losing streak: "I'm just happy to be able to make a difference in a young ballplayer's life."

TRIVIA: The longest losing streak by a team in major league history? Twenty-six, by the 1889 Louisville Colonels.

CHAPTER 16

BONUS ARTICLE

A HEARTBEAT AWAY?
NOT JUST FOR VEEPS

"In case of the Removal of the President from office, or of his Death, Resignation, or Inability to discharge the Powers and Duties of the said Office, the Same shall devolve on the Vice President and the Congress may by Law provide for the Case of Removal, Death, Resignation or Inability, both of the President and Vice President, declaring what Officer shall then act as President, and such Officer shall act accordingly, until the Disability be removed, or a President shall be elected."–Article II, Section I, Clause 6 of the United States Constitution, 1787

The term "just a heartbeat away from the presidency" usually applies only to the vice-president. But not always, and this is a forgotten part of American history.

On 17 separate occasions in U.S. history, the man constitutionally second in-line to the presidency has been first in-line because there was no vice-president at the time.

The U.S. Constitution, enacted in 1787, did not provide for presidential succession beyond that of the vice-president. So in 1792, the Succession Act was introduced which stated that the president *pro tempore* of the Senate would be first in-line to the presidency after the vice-president. The Speaker of the House of Representatives was next in-line. No further provision for presidential succession was made.

The Act was changed in 1886 to make the Secretary of State–as head of the oldest executive branch–first in-line behind the vice-president. State was followed by Treasury, War, Attorney-General, Postmaster-General, Navy and Interior, all ranked in order of their establishment. New cabinet posts added after 1886 were to be added to the bottom of the list.

The idea of the 1886 revisions was to ensure that if the office of president or vice-president were vacant, having a cabinet member next in-line would almost certainly ensure that a member of the same party would succeed to the presidency. Neither the president *pro tempore* of the Senate or the Speaker of the House were included in the new line of succession, just cabinet members.

Effective July 18, 1947, the Act was changed again. It made the Speaker of the House first in-line after the vice-president, followed by the president *pro tempore* of the Senate (flipping the original arrangement). Next in-line were the executive departments in order of establishment, starting with State and followed by Treasury, Defence, Attorney-General, Postmaster-General, Interior, Agriculture, Commerce, Labor, Health and Human Resources, Housing and Human Development, Transportation, Energy and Education.

Minor changes have been made to the succession list since, such as in 1971 when the Postmaster-General was removed when that position ceased to be a cabinet post. The Secretary of Homeland Security was added in 2006 as 18th and last on the succession list. The current succession is (1) Vice President (2) Speaker of the House of Representatives (3) President *Pro Tempore* of the Senate (4) Secretary of State (5) Secretary of the Treasury (6) Secretary of Defence (7) Attorney General (8) Secretary of the Interior (9) Secretary of Agriculture (10) Secretary of Commerce (11) Secretary of Labor (12) Secretary of Health and Human Services (13) Secretary of Housing and Human Development (14) Secretary of Transportation (15) Secretary of Energy (16) Secretary of Education (17) Secretary of Veterans Affairs and (18) Secretary of Homeland Security.

Never has the person second in-line to the presidency made it to the White House. But there have been some close calls.

In 1868, President Andrew Johnson came within one vote of an impeachment conviction in the Senate. Had Johnson been removed from office, then Benjamin Franklin Wade, as president *pro tempore* of the Senate, would have risen to the presidency since Johnson had not appointed a vice-president.

In 1844, President John Tyler narrowly escaped death when he was aboard a ship on the Potomac that suffered an explosion. Six men died, including the father of Tyler's future wife, but the president was under decks at the time and survived. As Tyler had no vice-president, had he died, the presidency would have conferred on the president *pro tempore* of the Senate at the time, William P. Magnum. Tyler himself had risen to the presidency on the death of President William Henry Harrison in 1841. There then followed a three-year, 11-month stretch without a vice-president, the longest such gap in U.S. history.

Some historians mistakenly believe David Rice Atchison, president *pro tempore* of the Senate, was president for one day in 1849. It so happened that March 4, 1849–the day Zachary Taylor was scheduled to be sworn in as president–was a Sunday, so Taylor had the swearing-in delayed to Monday. Since the terms of outgoing President John Polk and Vice President George Dallas expired at noon March 3 and Taylor's hadn't started, some argue that Atchison had claim to the presidency for the one day: March 4. However, Atchison's old term as president *pro tempore* expired March 3 and he was not sworn in for his new term until March 5. Since the office of Speaker of the House was also vacant, then technically, no one was president of the U.S. on March 4, 1849.

Secretary of State John Hay spent about five years first in-line to the presidency, longer than many vice-presidents. Hay first moved to within a heartbeat of the presidency under William McKinley for one-and-a-half years beginning in 1899 when vice-president Garrett Hobart died. Hay again moved into the first-in-line spot when McKinley was assassinated in September 1901 and vice-president Theodore Roosevelt became president. Hay remained first in-line for the presidency for the remaining three-and-a-half years of Roosevelt's first term.

The most recent non-vice president to become first in-line to the presidency was House Speaker Carl Albert. Albert assumed the role in 1973 during the two-month period between when Vice President Spiro Agnew resigned and Gerard Ford succeeded him. Albert was first in-line again for four months in 1974 after president Richard Nixon resigned and Nelson Rockefeller became Ford's vice-president.

In the hectic months after John F. Kennedy was assassinated on November 22, 1963, there were fears that president Lyndon Johnson might be targeted as well. That in mind, House Speaker John McCormack–next in-line for the presidency–was offered Secret Service protection. He refused it but remained first in-line to the presidency until Hubert Humphrey became vice-president in January 1965.

Four different non vice-presidents took turns being first in-line to the presidency after President Roosevelt died in 1945 and was succeeded by Harry Truman. Since Truman had no vice-president, Secretary of State E.R. Stettinius, Jr., was first in-line to succeed him. Stettinius was replaced in 1945 by James Byrnes, who in turn was replaced in 1947 by George Marshall. In July 1947, the law was changed to make the House Speaker first in-line to the presidency, so the line of succession was now headed by Joseph R. Martin. Things returned to normal in January 1949 when Alben Barkley became vice-president as Truman began his second term.

There have been two other occasions when the Secretary of State was first in-line to the presidency. The first was in 1923, after Warren Harding died and was succeeded by Calvin Coolidge. Since Coolidge had no vice-president, the man first in-line for the presidency was Secretary of State Charles Hughes.

Thomas Bayard moved to within a heartbeat of the presidency in 1886 after the Succession Act was changed to make the Secretary of State second in-line to the presidency. Since there was no vice-president (Thomas Hendricks had died the year before) then Bayard became first in-line.

Just a year earlier, there was a nearly two-week period when no one was in-line for the presidency. VP Hendricks died November 25, and it was another 12 days before John Sherman was sworn in as president *pro tempore* of the Senate (the House Speaker's position was also vacant). President Cleveland did not travel to Hendricks' funeral for fear something might happen to him and throw the country into a constitutional crisis. A similar problem occurred September 19, 1881 when President Garfield died and Chester Arthur succeeded him. Arthur did not have a back-up until Thomas Bayard was sworn in as president *pro tempore* of the Senate on October 10.

Here is a list of the occasions in U.S. history when a person other than the vice-president has been first in-line for the presidency.

President First-in-line

1812-1813 James Madison • William H. Crawford

1814-1817 James Madison • John Gaillard

1832-1833 Andrew Jackson • Hugh Lawson White

1841-1842 John Tyler • Samuel L. Southard

1842-1845 John Tyler • Willie P. Magnum

1850-1852 Millard Fillmore • William R. King

1852-1853 Millard Fillmore • David Atchison

1853-1854 Franklin Pierce • David Atchison

1854 Franklin Pierce • Lewis Cass

1854-1856 Franklin Pierce • Jesse D. Bright

1856 Franklin Pierce • Charles E. Stuart

1856-1857 Franklin Pierce • Jesse D. Bright

1857 Franklin Pierce • James M. Mason

1865-1867 Andrew Johnson • Lafayette S. Foster

1867-1869 Andrew Johnson • Benjamin Franklin Wade

1875-1877 Ulysses Grant • Thomas W. Ferry

1881 Chester Arthur • Thomas F. Bayard

1881-1883 Chester Arthur • David Davis

1883-1885 Chester Arthur • George F. Edmunds

1885-1886 Grover Cleveland • John Sherman

1886-1889 Grover Cleveland • Thomas F. Bayard

1899-1901 William McKinley • John Hay

1901-1905 Theodore Roosevelt • John Hay

1923-1925 Calvin Coolidge • Charles Hughes

1945 Harry Truman • E.R. Stettinius, Jr.

1945-1947 Harry Truman • James Byrnes

1947 Harry Truman • George Marshall

1947-1949 Harry Truman • Joseph W. Martin, Jr.

1963-1965 Lyndon Johnson • John McCormack

1973 Richard Nixon • Carl Albert

1974 Gerard Ford • Carl Albert

A FEW WORDS OF THANKS

It has long been my dream to write a book about the runner-ups, nearly-weres and the other forgotten people and events of history. I would like to thank the good people at Fitzhenry & Whiteside and Red Deer Press for giving me the opportunity. First a note of great appreciation to Richard Dionne for his guidance and editing magic. Kudos also to Lois Abraham, John McGrath and Dr. Carlos Yu for their suggestions. But most of all, thanks to my wife Sherree for her unwavering support during my long process of researching and writing *Close, But No Cigar*. I hope you enjoy it.

SOURCES

BOOKS

Barnette, Martha. *The Bill Schroeder Story*. Morrow, 1987

Boller, Paul. *Presidential Campaigns*. Oxford, 2004.

Bronson, Fred. *The Billboard Book of Number One Hits*. Billboard, 1985.

Brooks, Tim & Marsh, Earle. *The Complete Directory to Prime-Time Network and Cable TV Shows* (1946-present). Ballantine Books, 1995.

Bruns, Roger. *Almost History*. Hyperion, 2000.

Buckingham, William, Ross, Sir George Villam. *The Hon. Alexander Mackenzie: His Life and Times*. Haskell House, 1892.

Byer, Rick. *The Greatest Stories Never Told*. MJF Books, 2003.

Cray, Ed, Kotler, Jonathan, Beller, Miles. *American Deadlines*. Facts on File, 1990.

Denault, Todd. *The Greatest Game*. McClelland & Stewart. 2010.

Edwards, Gavin. *Is Tiny Dancer Really Elton's Little John? Music's Most Enduring Mysteries, Myths and Rumors Revealed,* Three Rivers Press, 2006.

Farris, Scott. *Almost President. The Men Who Lost the Race But Changed The Nation*. Lyons Press, 2010.

Gambacchini, Paul. Rice, Tim, Rice. Jonathan. *British Hit Singles*. Guinness, 1993.

Halberstam, David. *The Fifties*. Ballantine, 1993.

Harris, Cecil. *Breaking the Ice: The Black Experience in Professional Hockey*. Insomniac Press, January 2004.

Harrison, Ian. *The Book of Firsts*. Cassell Illustrated. 2006.

Hyatt, Wesley. *The Billboard Book of Number One Adult Contemporary Hits*. Billboard Books, 1999.

Hyatt, Wesley. *The Encyclopedia of Daytime Television*. Billboard, 1997.

Jancik, Wayne. *The Billboard Book of One-Hit Wonders*. Billboard, 1999.

Kane, Joseph, Nathan. *Presidential Fact Book*. Random House, 1999, 1998

Kennedy, Ted. *Charts Canada*. Canadian Chart Research, 1989.

Kenworthy, John. *The Hand Behind the Mouse*. Disney Editions, 2001.

Kirchner, Paul. *Forgotten Fads and Fabulous Flops*. General Publishing Group, 1995.

MacCambridge, Michael. *America's Game*. Knopf Doubleday Publishing, 2005.

Nemec, David. *Beer & Whiskey League*. The Lyons Press, 2004.

Pearson, Will, Hattikudur, Mangesh, Hunt, Elizabeth. *Mental Floss Presents Forbidden Knowledge*. Harper, 2005.

Pilon, Mary. *The Monopolists*. Bloomsbury, 2015.

Purdy, Dennis. *Kiss 'Em Goodbye: An ESPN Treasury of Failed, Forgotten and Departed Teams*. Ballantine Books, 2010.

Ribowsky, Mark. *The Supremes*. Da Capo Press, 2009.

Ross, Irwin. *The Loneliest Campaign: The Truman Victory of 1948*. Signet, 1968.

Sampson, Curt. *The Lost Masters: Grace and Disgrace in '68*. Atria Books, 2005.

Sandler, Martin W. *Lost to Time*. Sterling, 2010.

Smith, Daniel. *Forgotten Firsts*. Metro Publishing, 2010.

Southwick, Leslie H. *Presidential Also-Rans and Running Mates*. McFarland, 1984.

Uncle John's Bathroom Reader Extraordinary Book of Facts and Bizarre Information. The Bathroom Reader's Institute. Portable Press, 2006.

Uncle John's Monumental Bathroom Reader. The Bathroom Reader's Institute, 2007.

Wallace, Amy, Wallechinsky, David, Wallace, Irving. *The Book of Lists*. Bantam Books, 1977

Wallace, Amy, Wallechinsky, David, Wallace, Irving. *The Book of Lists #2*. Bantam Books, 1980

Wallace, Amy, Wallechinsky, David, Wallace, Irving. *The Book of Lists #3*. Bantam Books, 1983

Wallace, Irving and Wallechinsky, David. *The People's Almanac*. Bantam Books, 1975.

Wallace, Irving and Wallechinsky, David. *The People's Almanac 2*. Bantam Books, 1978.

Wallace, Irving and Wallechinsky, David. *The People's Almanac 3*. Bantam Books, 1991.

Wallechinsky, David, Wallace, Amy, Basen, Ira, Farrow, Jane. *The Book of Lists. The Canadian Edition*. Knopf Canada, 2005.

Ward, David. *The Lost 10 Point Night: Searching for a Hockey Hero*. ECW Press, 2014.

Whymper, Edward. *Scrambles Amongst the Alps: In the Years 1860-'69*. J.P. Lippincott & Co., 1872.

Whitburn, Joel. *Joel's Whitburn's Top Pop Singles 1955-1990*. Record Research, 1991.

Whitburn, Joel. *Top Pop Singles 1890-1954*. Record Research, 1986.

ARTICLES

Adler, Margot. Before Rosa Parks, "There Was Claudette Colvin." *npr.org*, March 15, 2009.

Aldridge, David. "The Lakers Plane Crash That Wasn't." *espn.com*, January 24, 2010.

Anderson, Dave. "Sports of The Times: The Mismanaged Career of David Clyde." *New York Times*, June 22, 2003.

Auter, Philip J. & Boyd, Douglas A. "DuMont: The Original Fourth Television Network." *Journal of Popular Culture*, 1995.

Aykroyd, Lucas. "The Greatest Tie Ever: Montreal versus Red Army in 1975." *hockeyadventure.com*, August 11, 2007.

Bastable, Alan. "Scott Hoch Reflects on the Missed Putt That Cost Him the 1989 Masters." *golf.com*, March 31, 2014.

Bechtel, Michael. "Broom At The Top." *Sports Illustrated*, January 19, 2004.

Beck, Howard. "Nets Seem Unlikely Threat to 1972-73 Sixers Loss Record." *New York Times*, January 17, 2010.

Bennett, Kathy. "Pete Best: The Man Replaced by Ringo." *AARP Bulletin*, August 16, 2010.

Billington, Michael. "Top of the Class." *The Guardian*, May 29, 2004.

Bishop, Greg. "When the Bucs Went O For The Season." *New York Times*, December 2, 2007.

Branch, John. "Sky-High SATs, But The Team's at Rock Bottom." *New York Times*, December 15, 2010.

Brodersen, Marnie. "Where in the World is Former American Idol Host Brian Dunkleman?" *wetpaint.com*, January 20, 2014.

"Brooklyn Dodgers." *www.sportsecyclopedia.com*.

Callahan, Tom. "Left in Shambles: Everyone Remembers Secretariat's Great 1973, But What About That Horse He Kept Beating?" *Washington Post*, May 2, 1993

Carter, Bob. "Stokes' Life a Tale of Tragedy and Friendship." *espn.com*.

Clarence Chamberlain. "The Race to Cross the Atlantic." *iowapathways*.com.

Clyde Pangborn and Hugh Herndon, Jr.. "First to Fly Non-Stop Across the Pacific." *historynet.com*, June 12, 2006.

Connolly, Ray. "Pete Best: The Happiest Beatle of Them All." *Daily Mail*, April 7, 2007.

Crisp, Simon. "The 'Eternal Second': Getting Into The History Books Without Being a Winner." *sicycle. wordpress.com*, November 5, 2012.

Crowe, Jerry. "In 1960, the Lakers Had Their Worst Trip Ever." *Los Angeles Times*, April 11, 2010.

Curtis, Bryan. "The Stokes Game." *grantland.com*, August 16, 2013.

Daubs, Katie. "Danforth byelection: John Turmel Has Lost 74 Elections, And is Ready to Lose Another on Monday." *Toronto Star*, March 16, 2012.

Dawes, Richard. "Whirlwind White Still Holding Out Hope He Can Someday Win That Elusive World Title." *Daily Mail*, November 25, 2013.

Delear, Frank. "First Licensed U.S. Woman Pilot." *historynet.com*, June 12, 2006.

Desborough, James. "The Unluckiest Man in The World." *Daily Mail*, August 10, 2013.

DiAmato, Gary. "Taking a Swing Back in Time." *Milwaukee Journal-Sentinel*, August 4, 2009.

"Different Era: St. James More Readily Accepted Than Guthrie." *Associated Press*, May 24, 1992.

Dixon, Robyn. "Gherman S. Titov; Cosmonaut Was Second Man to Orbit Earth." *Los Angeles Times*, September 22, 2000.

Donaghy, Jim. "1961 Phillies: They Made Their Mark in Baseball History With 23 Consecutive Losses." *Associated Press*, May 1, 1988.

Ebner, David. "August 7, 1954: The Miracle in Vancouver." *Globe and Mail*, August 13, 2014.

Elliott, Steve. "Washington Becomes The Second State in One Day to Legalize Marijuana." *tokeofthetown. com*, November 6, 2012.

Evans, Ben. "'A Bad Call': The Accident Which Almost Cost Project Gemini." *americaspace.com*, 2012.

Fang, Marina. "Congressional Republicans Rail Against Legalization of Marijuana." *Huffington Post*, July 31, 2014.

Feinstein, John. "Family Tragedy Puts Q-School in Perspective." *golfchannel.com*, November 30, 2012.

Fleitz, David. "The 1899 Cleveland Spiders: Baseball's Worst Team." http://www.wcnet.org/~dlfleitz/cleve.htm.

Folkart, Burt. "Jerry Lester; Comedian, Host of First Late-Night TV Show." *Los Angeles Times*, March 25, 1995.

Folsom, Brad. "He Could Not Rise Unless The President Fell." h*istorybanter.com*, November 21, 2013.

Folsom, Jim. "The Ultimate Sports Curse: The City of Cleveland." *bleacherreport.com*, May 15, 2010

Fox, Margalit. "Izola Ware Curry, Who Stabbed King in 1958, Dies at 98." *New York Times*, March 21, 2015.

Fusilli, Jim. "Woodstock's Forgotten Man." *The Wall Street Journal*, August 6, 2009.

Greene, Andy. "Exclusive Q&A: Original Beach Boy David Marks on The Band's Anniversary Tour." *Rolling Stone*, March 16, 2012.

Hammond, Pete. "Peter O'Toole's Long and Frustrating Half-Century Dance With Oscar." *deadline.com*, December 15, 2013.

Hattikudar, Mangesh. "7 Geniuses and One Entire Science That Never Won The Nobel." *mentalfloss.com*, November 23, 2007.

Helgason, Gudjon, Church, Brian. "Fischer's 1972 Match Was Cold War Battle." *USA Today*, January 19, 2008.

Henderson, Bruce. "Who Discovered the North Pole?" *Smithsonian Magazine*, April 2009.

Hernandez, Greg. "Mary Wilson Dishes About Motown, Dreamgirls, Diana Ross And The Long-Lost Fourth Original Supreme..." *Out in Hollywood*, January 14, 2009.

Hewitt, Bill. "Out of Luck." *People*, April 19, 1999.

Hollandsworth, Skip. "The Killing of Alydar." *Texas Monthly*, June, 2001.

Ingram, Clark. "DuMont Television Network Historical Web Site," www.dumontnetwork.com.

James, Chelsea. "Harvard Beats Yale 29-29." *Washington Post*, November 20, 2014.

John Jaremey. "Inducted as a Swimmer in 2004." *soloswims.com*

Kent, David. "Norman Reveals Why He 'Choked" to Allow Faldo to Win 1996 Masters ... And it Was All Due to a Bad Back." *Daily Mail*, September 10, 2013.

Keown, Tim. "1994: What Could Have Been." *espn.com*, August 12, 2014.

Keyser, Tom. "Lovable Loser Zippy Chippy Still a Fan Favorite." *Albany Times-Union*, September 10, 2010.

King, Susan. "They Snubbed Oscar." *Los Angeles Times*, February 26, 2012.

Klein, Christopher. "The Midnight Ride of William Dawes." *history.com*, April 18, 2012.

Koncius, Jura. "Inside the Vice-President's Residence." *Washington Post*, November 27, 2008.

Krebs, Albin. "Harold Stassen, Who Sought G.O.P. Nomination for President Nine Times, Dies at 93." *New York Times*, March 5, 2001.

Lennartz, Karl. "The 2nd International Olympic Games in 1906." *Journal of Olympic History*, Volume 10, December 2001/January 2002.

Leonard, Kevin. "Why Does Charles Darwin Eclipse Alfred Russel Wallace?" *BBC News*, February 26, 2013.

Lester, John. "Recognizing First U.S. Women's Golf Champion is a Step in the Right Direction." *womengolfersmuseum.com*, July 9, 1996.

Liebling, Abbott J. "Second City." *New Yorker*, January 12, 1952.

"Light Bulb Methuselahs," *roadsideamerica.com*.

Litsky, Frank. "Jug McSpaden, 87, a Top Golfer Known For Finishing in Second" *New York Times*, April 26, 1996.

Logan, Joe. "Missed Putt Changed His Life Doug Sanders Visits British Open Again." *Philadelphia Inquirer*, July 13, 2005.

"Los Angeles Replaces Chicago as Second City." *Associated Press*, April 8, 1984.

Martinez, Michael. "A Perfect Night For Stieb is Ruined by Kelly." *New York Times*, August 5, 1989.

Maki, Alan. "Expansion Capitals Learned Valuable Life Lessons During Record Losing Season." *Globe and Mail*, April 15, 2013.

Mastropolo, Frank. "The History of Rock Around the Clock: How a "B" Side Became a Rock Classic." *ultimateclassicrock.com*. May 28, 2014.

Maugh II, Thomas H. "Adrian Kantrowitz Dies at 90; Surgeon Performed First U.S. Heart Transplant." *Los Angeles Times*, November 20, 2008.

McCarron, Anthony. "Where Are They Now? Former Met Anthony Young Emerges a Real Winner." *New York Daily News*, January 3, 2009.

McGee, Ryan. "Janet Guthrie Outraced Insults to Make History." *espn.com*, February 20, 2013.

McGill, Douglas C. "Ex-Rep. William Miller, 69, Dies; Goldwater's 1964 Running Mate." *New York Times*, June 25, 1983.

McKenzie, Sheena. "Jockey Who Refused to Stay in The Kitchen." *cnn.com*, October 2, 2012.

McNamara, Melissa. "Oscar's Biggest Loser" *www.cbsnews.com*, February 11, 2009.

Min, Janis. "The Lost Beach Boy." *People*, December 6, 1993.

Mell, Randall. "Kim Returns to Kraft One Year After Missed Putt." *golf.com*, March 31, 2013.

Mickey, Lisa D. "Laura Baugh: From LPGA's Golden Girl to Stay-at-Home Mom." *lpga.com*, 2010

Mitra, Prithvijit, Ganguly, Arnab. "Beautiful Mind: The Story of Dr. Subhas Mukherjee, Creator of India's First Test-Tube Baby." *Times of India*. June 13, 2009

Montague, James. "The Third Man: The Forgotten Black Power Hero." *cnn.com*, April 25, 2012.

Morrison, Jim. "Seven Famous People Who Missed the Titanic." *smithsonian.com*, March 1, 2012.

Mueller, Rich. "Where is Original NFL Championship Trophy?" *sportscollectorsdaily.com*, March 14, 2007.

Murphy, Richard. "Canadian Inventions: The Light Bulb." *dww.com*, October 5, 2011.

Neville, Anne. "Daredevils of Niagara Falls: Bobby Leach." *imaxniagara.com*, August 8, 2011.

Nightengale, Bob. "Tie in '02 All-Star Game Mattered." *USA Today*, August 11, 2007.

"Patricia Cooksey Ends Her Riding Career." *bloodhorse.com*, June 25, 2004.

Pearce, Al. "Where Are They Now: NASCAR driver Harry Gant." *Autoweek*, August 6, 2013.

Peneny, D.K. "Bob Horn." *www.history-of-rock.com*

"People and Events: Elisha Gray". *www.pbs.org*

Pilon, Mary. "Monopoly's Inventor: The Progressive Who Didn't Pass Go." *New York Times*, February 13, 2015.

Plummer, William. "Haunted by Her Past." *people.com,* August 6, 1984.

"Prairie View A&M Ends 80-Game Streak." *Los Angeles Times*, September 27, 1998

Price, Mark J. "Local history: Searching For Lost Trophy." A*kron Beacon Journal*, April 25, 2011.

Rasmussen, Frederick N. "'Last First Olympian' Was Baltimore Scion." *Baltimore Sun*, August 14, 2004.

Relph, Sam. "Acker Bilk Dead: Jazz Legend Passes Away at 85 After Battle With Cancer." *Mirror*, November 2, 2014.

"Robert Falcon Scott (1868-1912), The Terra-Nova Expedition (1910-13)." *www.south-pole.com*

Roose, Ed. "Wings' First Outdoor Game Was in Prison." *detroitredwings.com*, February 2, 2009.

"Samuel Tilden." *spartacus-educational.com*.

Sandimor, Richard. "Little Consolation in Third-Place Game." *New York Times*, February 5, 2011.

Sandimor, Richard. "No Team, No Ticket Sales, But Plenty of Cash." *New York Times*, September 6, 2012.

Saracino, Frank. "Classic 1972 USA vs. USSR Basketball Game." *espn.com*, August 6, 2004.

Scanlan, Kevin. "Judy LaMarsh: Gentle And Loyal 'Not at All What People Thought'." *Toronto Star*, October 28, 1980.

Schwartz, John. "Astronaut Teaches in Space, And Lesson is Bittersweet." *New York Times*, August 15, 2007.

Schlogol, Marc. "Singer Doesn't Miss Miss America." *Baltimore Sun*, February 15, 2002.

"Scott Norwood Honoured By Bills." *Associated Press*, November 6, 2011.

Shinabery, Michael. "MISS: America's First Military Goal of a Moon Landing." *beforeitsnews.com*, June 23, 2013.

Simmons, Lee. "Action Heroes Owe Everything to Stunt Pioneer Yakima Canute." *wired.com*, May 10, 2012.

Smith, Maurice. "The Father of Modern Science and an Unsung Hero ... Robert Hooke." *Micscape Magazine*, March 13, 2000.

Snowden, Paul. "Why Ken Rosewall Was Wimbledon's Greatest Ever Loser." *Liverpool Echo*, July 4, 2009.

Snyder, III, Gib, "Buffalo: A City Cursed With Bad Luck." *Observer Today*, January 16, 2012.

Sobel, Jason. "Forty years Later, De Vicenzo's Gaffe Remains Unbelievable." *espn.com*, April 5, 2008.

"Spadea Ends Longest Losing Streak in Tennis History." *The Associated Press*, June 27, 2000.

Stevenson, Seth. "We're No. 2! We're No. 2!" *Slate*, August 12, 2013.

Stengle, Jamie. "29 Times a Bridesmaid, Finally a Bride." *Deseret News*, July 5, 2010.

Stromberg, Jean. "When The Olympics Gave Out Medals For Art." *smithsonian.com*, July 25, 2012.

Sullivan, Ronald. "Jerry Lester, Early TV Host And Comedian, is Dead at 85." *New York Times*, March 26, 1995.

"The Channel Swim, Burgess Successful in His 14th Attempt." *Otago Daily Times*, September 8, 1911.

"The Missing Piece for Mickelson is The U.S. Open." *The Associated Press*, June 6, 2014.

"The First of Many: Masanori Murakami, The First Japanese Player in the Big Leagues." *baseballhall.org*.

Thomas, Jr., Robert McG. "Kasey Cisyk, Singer, Dies at 44; Made Mark in Commercials." *New York Times*, April 13, 1998.

Timmons, Grady. "Return to Winged Foot." *Hana Hou!*, October/November 2012.

Tonnesson. Oyvind. "Mahatma Gandhi. The Missing Laureate." *nobelprize.org*, December 1, 1999.

Trow, Paul. "The Major That Never Was." *Kingdom Magazine*, Issue 25.

Upton, Michael A. "They Love Lucci." *People*, June 7, 2009.

Wainwright, Oliver. "The Dogs That Conquered Space." *The Guardian*, September 2, 2014.

Weinreb, Michael. "The Tie Will Be Unbroken." *Grantland*, June 18, 2013.

Weir, William. "The Washington Generals: A Life Losing to The Harlem Globetrotters." *Hartford Courant*, March 19, 2010.

White, Mary C. "Detailed Biographies of Apollo 1 Crew." *history.nasa.gov*, August 4, 2006.

"William Schroeder And The Artificial Heart." *Indianapolis Star*, January 10, 2013.

Yaqobov, Shakir. "Mr. Fair Play." *www.visions.az/sport,94*, Summer 2006

ABOUT THE AUTHOR

*C*lose But No Cigar, Runnerups, Nearly-Weres and Also Rans, is Dale Patterson's third book. His first was *What Time of Day Was That? History by The Minute* in 2001, pinpointing the time of day events took place in history. That was followed in 2013 by *Fifteen Minutes of Fame: History's One-Hit Wonders*, a look at those who were very famous for a very short time. Both can be purchased at www.fitzhenry.ca.

Patterson worked for 35 years as a reporter and editor for The Canadian Press news agency in Toronto. Since 1996, he has published the website *Rock Radio Scrapbook*, focusing on the history of Top 40 radio in Canada and the U.S. Check it out at www.rockradioscrapbook.ca.

Dale lives in the Toronto area with his family.

"Close doesn't count in baseball.
Close only counts in horseshoes and grenades."
–Frank Robinson